Believe Me

Carly

*For you &
with so much
love. I believe
in you!!*

Andrea

ANDREA POWELL

WORLDCHANGERS
MEDIA

DISCLAIMER: This work is a memoir based on true events. It reflects the author's present recollections of experiences over time. Some names and characteristics have been changed, some events have been compressed, and some dialogue has been recreated. Some names and identifying characteristics have been changed or omitted to protect the identity of survivors, and for safety and confidentiality reasons Any resulting resemblance to persons either living or dead is entirely coincidental.

The publisher and the Author make no representations or warranties of any kind with respect to this book or its contents, and assume no responsibility for errors, inaccuracies, omissions, or any other inconsistencies herein. This book is not intended as a resource for individuals suffering from the legal, physical, mental, or emotional results of sex crimes or trafficking. The contents of this book does not constitute legal advice. Nor is it a substitute for a consultation with a licensed physician or mental health professional. The use of this book implies your acceptance of this disclaimer.

At the time of publication, the URLs displayed in this book refer to existing websites owned by Andrea Powell and/or the authors' affiliates. WorldChangers Media is not responsible for, nor should be deemed to endorse or recommend, these websites; nor is it responsible for any website content other than its own, or any content available on the internet not created by WorldChangers Media.

Hardcover ISBN: 9781955811613
Paperback ISBN: 9781955811620
E-book ISBN: 9781955811606
LCCN: 2024904978

First hardcover edition: July 2024

Cover design: Bryna Haynes
Cover artwork: Noel Keserwany
Author photography: Mark Story
Layout and typesetting: Paul Baillie-Lane
Editors: Maggie Mills, Audra Figgins, and Paul Baillie-Lane

Published by WorldChangers Media
PO Box 83, Foster, RI 02825
www.WorldChangers.Media

Praise

"Andrea Powell's book is more than a book about justice; it's also about infusing social change with love and a fierce commitment to compassion. A must-read."

Justin Baldoni, author, actor, filmmaker, and podcast host

"*Believe Me* is the extraordinary story of two women: Tiffany, a teenage victim of sex trafficking sentenced to jail for thirty years, and Andrea, a passionate advocate fighting for Tiffany's freedom. I have had the honor of witnessing their ten-year journey together. A journey of trauma and healing, courage, and ultimately, Revolutionary Love. Read this book for these women to inspire you, as they have me."

Valarie Kaur, bestselling author of *See No Stranger* and founder of The Revolutionary Love Project

"*Believe Me* is an honest accounting of what trafficking looks like today. Not the sensationalized stories you hear in the news but the real stories and real voices of this issue. I met Andrea over a decade ago when I was first beginning my own journey into the anti-trafficking world. I learned much from her. She is a fierce advocate, fighter, and expert in this world. I am honored to know her and support her work and her story on behalf of women and children everywhere."

Marisol Nichols, actor

"Andrea Powell's book is urgent and vital. No one should be incarcerated because of crimes committed against them. This book is a story of fierce love leading to justice for so many survivors. It's a call to action and proof that when women come together, change happens."

Carmen Perez-Jordan, CEO and President of the
Gathering for Justice Foundation

"As a former prosecutor, I have worked alongside advocates like Andrea to ensure that survivors are protected, not incarcerated, as a result of their own trafficking. *Believe Me* is the true story of a courageous survivor and her tenacious advocate's enduring fight for justice. Andrea is the real deal, and this book is a must-read for anyone wanting to make the justice system more just."

Maggy Krell, author of *Taking Down Backpage*

"I have known Andrea for fifteen years, and her passion to ensure that no survivor of trafficking is left alone to suffer has always moved me. I hope everyone reads her words and feels their calling to support survivors. I truly am excited to see the impact Andrea's book will make for survivors and, honestly, anyone who has felt unheard, disbelieved, and simply discredited because of their past. This is a must-read and a true story of love overcoming fear."

Geena Roceri, model, writer, producer,
transgender advocate, and public speaker

Contents

Introduction: Breaking the Cycle   1

PART ONE: REACHING OUT

1. What Inspires You?   23
2. Shine Bright Like a Diamond   35
3. Well, I'm Here to Stay Now   57
4. Meeting Tiffany   71
5. Where She Belongs   87
6. How to Be a Mom   97
7. Damaged Goods   111

PART TWO: CEMENT BOXES

8. A Safe Place to Live   127
9. Bills, Bills, Bills   141
10. Girls Aren't for Sale, but They Are on Backpage   153
11. New Hope, Old Pains   161
12. Survivors Alone in the Lone Star State   175

PART THREE: AN OCEAN OF LOVE

13. Lack of Love   199
14. Tiffany Takes the Stand   209
15. I Think They Finally Believe Me   221

16. The Waiting Game   231
17. We Have All the Minutes Remaining   247

Afterword   263
Where Are They Now?   265
How to Help   271
About the Author   275
About the Publisher   277

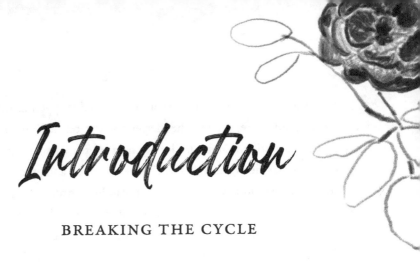

Introduction

BREAKING THE CYCLE

After dinner, I curl up on the sofa to read the letter again. It's one page inside a crumpled envelope. It came from someone I've never heard of: "Tiffany Simpson, Inmate 100142344, Pulaski State Prison." She sent it two weeks ago, but I've only just received it. Her handwriting is big, loopy, and perfectly formed.

> *Dear Andrea,*
>
> *My name is Tiffany Simpson. I am 18 and when I was 17, I was arrested for sex trafficking and I'm doing 20 of 30 years in prison down here in Georgia.*
>
> *My pimp said I was not making enough and he used my phone to convince this other girl to come with us. He sold us both to these guys in a trailer by a construction site.*
>
> *He said he was going to burn down my grandmother's house and stab our baby out of me if I didn't do it.*
>
> *Now, I can't see my son and my pimp's mom is trying to get custody of him from my mom. I'm worried I'll lose him forever.*
>
> *I saw that girl Alyssa's story in that USA Today story you were in. My dad sent it to me from his prison.*
>
> *So, I wanted to know. Am I a victim of sex trafficking or a prostitute?*

After leaving my office earlier that evening, I'd stopped at the street corner. I stood there, reading her letter for the tenth time. The cool October breeze stilled, and I no longer noticed the cars speeding by in the rush-hour traffic or the lights waving between red and green and back to red again. I would never be able to unread her words. I could already feel my life was about to change, the world momentarily fading around me. How could a seventeen-year-old girl be in a Georgia prison for sex trafficking? How could she think she's a prostitute if she was being sold by a man twice her age?

I never expected to become an advocate for a teenage girl convicted of child sex trafficking. I'd always thought that once it was proven that a child was a victim of sex trafficking, they would get the help they needed; they wouldn't be arrested. Tiffany's letter defied my belief, and a cold chill filled me. How many more teenage girls like her were out there?

By the time Tiffany Simpson's letter was in my hands in 2012, I'd met hundreds of survivors across the United States and around the world in my ten years as a victim advocate. (Now, I've met over 2,000.) I've worked with girls trafficked blocks from the White House and even out of their own childhood homes in places from Alabama to Maryland. As I'd explain in TV interviews and the law enforcement trainings my team and I led each month, sex trafficking involves three groups of people: victims, traffickers, and those who benefit from the victim's exploitation, namely the sex buyers. Each represented one point of a triangle. But Tiffany's words made it clear that it wasn't always so simple. Tiffany's trafficker had forced her to lure another teen girl into sex trafficking by threatening to kill her unborn baby. *How can she be two points in the triangle?* I wondered.

More than a decade has passed since I stood on that busy street corner reading Tiffany's letter. I assumed that first letter wasn't telling me everything, but I sensed a sincere and lost person who hadn't given up on herself. I wrote back, and she replied. She opened up more and more as our letters continued. I got to know Tiffany, and the more I knew, the more I believed her. The story of her childhood and all the ways in which her trafficker exploited and abused her were so similar to the other girls and women I'd worked with over the years. I'm still learning about everything she's been through in her life, not least of which is trafficking.

It would be years before I understood how my own sexual assaults and exploitation played a role in the work I do. After bonding through hundreds of letters and emails, Tiffany was the first person I told about my own story. For many years, our bond existed in Times New Roman typeface alone.

* * *

When you think of "sex trafficking," what kinds of images come to mind? Sex trafficking in media and movies is often depicted as an intense, action-packed kidnapping scene: An innocent child is abducted on her way home from school and sold in a dark web auction where no one can find her. Or a young woman is drugged at a bar, dragged into a car, and tied up in a creepy basement dungeon. Though these situations may be based on some sensa-tionalized versions of the truth, that isn't the way it goes for most victims. The truth is often much more complex. Real sex trafficking often looks like a teenage girl standing next to a much older man at a motel as he books a room. Or a teen boy who suddenly has a new phone and clothes skipping school to hang out with a much older man. Or a teenage girl in a doctor's office being watched by a man who speaks for her about her injuries. Or that girl whose online friends are all older guys.

Tiffany wasn't locked inside a hotel room or hidden away in a trailer park. She wasn't kidnapped, and she didn't just stop showing up at school. Instead, Tiffany was disappeared by the system. Those who are meant to protect victims wanted to lock her up instead of untangling her compli-cated situation with compassion. It was as if they felt that labeling her a criminal meant they didn't have to help her, that she would just disappear. Tiffany could easily have faded away behind bars.

In time, I realized we had to make Tiffany *re*appear. We had to make Tiffany exist on the outside while she was still locked up on the inside. This was the only possible way to help her become free. The media follows big-name cases of sex trafficking like Jeffrey Epstein and R. Kelly, spraying every detail across the front pages, but there was only one tiny newspaper article about Tiffany Simpson and that disappeared long ago. It listed her as a seventeen-year-old sex trafficker, right alongside the thirty-four-year-old who stabbed, beat, and trafficked her.

I thought helping Tiffany toward freedom was my personal calling. Very quickly though, I found that I cared for her deeply as a person. I talked to my mom about her and incessantly asked friends to send support, bringing the people around me into Tiffany's world. I also came to care for Tiffany's father, even though he played a role in Tiffany's exploitation. Tiffany's dad committed a crime that led to a life sentence, leaving her vulnerable with a mom who struggled with alcohol abuse. He often blames himself for not being there, and over time, I learned his childhood was not so different from Tiffany's. Tiffany has taught me the meaning of unconditional love, and it's her father who taught me about unconditional forgiveness.

You should know up front that this isn't a fairytale. While on November 23, 2022, Tiffany was released from prison, her story isn't wrapped up with a neat little bow; it's ongoing, and it continues to be a struggle. But Tiffany's advocacy for herself and survivors like her, along with the help of lawyers, advocates, other survivors, and so many people who care, are changing the laws that almost let her disappear behind bars forever. Together, we want to make sure no more victims suffer the same injustice and fate.

* * *

It's March 2021. Nine years and five months after that first letter from Tiffany. I'm staring at my computer screen, waiting for Tiffany to dial into the video link from the jail service. She warned me it might not work. After eight years, this will be our first time seeing each other's faces. She's only allowed two people on her video list, and after years of trying, she was able to add me after dropping her mom, who doesn't have a computer or cell phone. It's 3:15 p.m., and she said she'd call me at 3:00. I'm not allowed to call her, so I have to wait.

"Just connect," I whisper to myself. I'm staring at my computer screen watching the clock tick. Finally, the screen flickers in and out, and then, there she is before me.

"Hey, Andrea? It's me, Tiffany," she says in her Georgian accent. Her voice is faded, as if she's speaking from a hollow room. The only visuals I've had all these years are her arrest photo and a photo of her taken months before she was arrested that still lingers as her Facebook profile. Seeing her for the first time, even on a computer screen, makes my hands shake a little. She somehow still looks seventeen, even though it's been nine years since she was sent to Pulaski State Prison in Hawkinsville, Georgia. She is smiling down into the screen, almost giggling.

I press my fingers into my headset to hear her better. "Tiffany! We're finally doing it!" I say, jumping up and almost knocking the green cafe chair over. I'm too excited to sit, and I lean in closer to see her face better. The video screen continues to flicker in and out, as if there aren't enough pixels for her to remain fully there.

Her bright smile seems out of place in the washed-out gray of the call area. "It's so bright out there. You look great!" she says.

I flip the screen on my computer around to show her the birds-of-paradise flowers and succulent plants around me. "I can't believe I'm looking at you. How much time do we have?"

"I guess about fourteen minutes now because we're only allowed fifteen. I can try to call back, though, for another fifteen, or you could try to set up another video."

That isn't enough time for everything we have to talk about, but it's better than before, which was zero minutes. I'm speed talking, loudly. The time limit presses down on my words and hers.

"Did you hear from Susan?" I ask. "She said she'd be in touch. I read there was a law passed last year about vacating criminal records for sex trafficking victims. So, when you get out, we can work on that, and you can get your son back." Susan Coppedge is Tiffany's new attorney after agreeing to help her in the fall of 2020. Her previous pro bono attorney, Stephen Reba, hadn't been in touch with Tiffany in months at that point. Susan is the best; she's spent countless hours prosecuting human traffickers. "So," I had explained to Tiffany when I first told her about Susan, "she really will know how to fight for you."

"Would I qualify?" Tiffany suddenly looks serious, leaning toward the screen and balancing the black handset of the phone on her shoulder. It's connected to the wall with a coiled cord that dangles below her shoulder and tangles in her long, wavy, mahogany hair.

"I don't know, but it's a law worth exploring. You were a victim of sex trafficking, and you were a child when you were charged, but there are some crimes they won't vacate."

Tiffany leans even closer, whispering so that other inmates can't hear. "Well, I guess we'll have to cross that bridge when we come to it. I know it's going to happen."

Yes, when, not if, I think, staring into eyes that are filled with deep conviction.

"They are lifting COVID restrictions here, so my new attorney could visit me. Maybe you can come with her."

I highly doubt that the prison warden will approve me visiting her, but I smile anyway. "I can't wait for that, Tiffany."

"You have one minute remaining," the recorded voice reminds us. The jail video system is ruthless.

Oh, no! "Tiffany, try to call back, but just in case you can't ..." I quickly say a few more things, and then the screen goes black.

Minutes pass and then, suddenly, the familiar vibration pulses in my hand.

"Do you accept these charges from an inmate in ..."

I quickly push "1" to accept.

"Tiffany!" I'm too loud again.

She laughs. "I said I'd call you back, girl."

Our conversation turns to the most recent release effort. We've gained support from a small grassroots network of advocates called Dressember to create a short film about Tiffany's life that we'll use to keep advocating for her release. Part of the goal for today's call is to finalize the script using Tiffany's words. We have a month to complete it before we launch our national campaign to free Tiffany.

While the film focuses on Tiffany's story, it isn't solely to garner support for her release. There are survivors like her all across the United States who are in jail due to their own trafficking. Some were convicted of sex trafficking, others for crimes as small as truancy. For years, Tiffany's release seemed impossible because she wasn't seen as a victim by the system. Instead, she was portrayed as a perpetrator.

But then in August 2019, a survivor named Cyntoia Brown was released from a Tennessee jail after sixteen years when the governor granted her clemency. She was convicted for shooting and killing the man who bought her and was about to rape her. Another survivor, Alexis Martin, who was convicted of killing her trafficker, had also been set free in 2020. Tiffany deserves her freedom too. I'm in regular touch with reporters from the *Washington Post* and *The New Yorker*, and I've written nationally about Tiffany and justice for survivors, but so far that hasn't been enough. We need to go bigger.

"It's time, Tiffany. I know it." She smiles, saying nothing as her fingers play with the black cord of the phone.

We have the draft script for the film, but it has been written purely from the emails Tiffany and I've exchanged over the years. We need to refine it, dig deeper. We haven't found the true root of how Tiffany fell into trafficking. It's never just one tragedy or misstep that leads someone into sex trafficking, and I know that something hasn't been said yet.

"Tiffany, I'm going to patch in our film director, Noel." Noel Keserwany is a world-renowned Lebanese filmmaker living in Paris. She is political, feminist, artistic, and passionate. She also knows almost nothing about sex trafficking.

Noel had asked me earlier that morning, when we were editing the script, what the chances were of Tiffany being released. I wish I knew. "The more noise we make, the closer we will get to Tiffany's case being taken seriously," I'd replied. I'd never really cared what others thought of the survivors I served, but getting the public passionate about Tiffany and showing the district attorney that she has people who are willing to fight for her could make the difference between another ten years in prison or freedom before age thirty. Working with Noel is part of our bigger strategy to free Tiffany.

Susan and I had explored a parole hearing, but Tiffany isn't eligible until 2025. We could reopen her case with something called a habeas petition, which is a civil action that questions if a person's detention is valid. But while there is a new judge, the risk is that the same prosecutor who worked on Tiffany's case could convince the judge that Tiffany deserves more years, not fewer. At this point, Tiffany has already served nearly a decade.

"That's the minimum sentence for sex trafficking in Georgia," I'd told Noel.

Releasing her isn't like they are letting her off easy. According to Susan, the prosecutor still believes he locked up a child trafficker and sex offender. That is why this film has to perfectly bring to light the real story of Tiffany Simpson and not what the media has said about her. For the past few weeks, Noel and I have talked constantly, waking each other at all hours, feeling the pressure of Tiffany's potential freedom.

Today is Noel's first time talking to Tiffany. "It's like I'm meeting a celebrity. I'm nervous," Noel had confessed earlier that morning. Now, here we are.

"Noel, can you hear us?" Noel's video appears on my screen. She can't see Tiffany, and Tiffany can barely hear her as I hold my phone to the computer speaker.

There isn't really time for banter. "Noel, we only have about fourteen minutes. Let's get started."

Tiffany is silent for a few moments.

"I'm kinda nervous. I don't know why. Maybe you can ask me questions to help," she suggests.

Noel assures her that nothing she says can be wrong or bad. I know Tiffany well enough to understand she's always worried that she'll say or do something wrong. That's how it is for most victims of abuse.

"Tiffany, just tell me more about you. Let's start there," says Noel.

"I like your French accent a lot," says Tiffany.

"I'm from Lebanon, actually. I live here in Paris for now, though."

Tiffany nods and says, "Ohhh." She has never heard of Lebanon. She takes a deep breath and begins. "I was seventeen when I was arrested with my pimp for sex trafficking another girl named Kassie, who was thirteen years old. She was messaging me that she was sick of being home with her grandmother. She asked me if she could come stay with us. My pimp saw the messages."

The first time Tiffany was sexually exploited, she was fourteen, just a year older than Kassie. Noel asked how Kassie knew where Tiffany was and how her pimp, Yarnell Donald, knew she and Kassie were messaging. Most people don't have every single text they write reviewed by their "boyfriend." But trafficking victims like Tiffany usually do. If they aren't texting about making money, they are often not allowed to text at all.

"Well, once Yarnell saw our messages, he said he wanted her too. I was pregnant and getting fat, so he decided she could replace me for a while. He used my phone and offered to help her run away, just like he had said he would help me, and I couldn't warn her because he was watching my every move," says Tiffany.

Pimps know how to make their victims feel like they're helping them. Tiffany really did need help when they met; she was homeless. From what Tiffany told me, the same seemed to be true for Kassie—she was just a young girl looking for a safe place to land. But in both cases, Yarnell was only trying to help himself.

Noel jumps in, almost as if to save Tiffany from having to share more of this pain with a total stranger. "Tiffany, to make this film, we have to create colors and be very visual. You don't have to tell me everything like facts. I want to know you really from the heart."

Tiffany doesn't understand. "I don't really know what is from my heart, I guess, ma'am."

"You don't have to call me, 'ma'am,'" Noel says, laughing.

I'm a Southern girl, too, and know there's no way Tiffany isn't going to call her "ma'am." We are taught from birth to say, "Yes, ma'am," "No, ma'am," "Thank you, ma'am," to any woman who's even slightly older than we are. Noel tries again.

"So, like this, Tiffany—I want to ask you about your relationship to colors. What would you say your life was like in colors before going to jail?

And what's life like now in jail? What colors describe it, and what do you think your life will be like in colors when you are free?"

Tiffany pauses while her image flickers in and out with the poor internet signal on her end.

"My life before jail was dark. Like total darkness. I think Yarnell could have killed me, and no one would have really noticed. It was kind of like I was invisible out there."

She's said that to me before, but I still almost cry. *You can cry later, Andrea, not now*, I think to myself.

"But here, I slowly started to see some gray, some lighter colors. I think it's because I feel like it's safer here in some ways. There are basic things like being able to sleep and feeling like I can do things like get my GED. But there isn't really color because they control you all the time, and the other women can be rough to deal with."

"That's really interesting," Noel says. "Most people would think it was the other way around in colors. You're surprising me."

Tiffany smiles, and so do I.

"I feel like now I have time to imagine my life in colors," she continues. "My future when I get out will be so bright. I keep a journal of all my dreams, like seeing California or Hawaii. Andrea sends me photos from everywhere she goes."

After a pause, Noel says, "I didn't see that answer coming. I didn't expect you to say such valuable things. Andrea and Tiffany, can we record this?"

Tiffany says yes. I push the record button on my phone. The audio will be weak and full of static and background noise, but it's the only way to do it. I have learned from Tiffany that jail is a place where you have to be innovative to have a life.

"Keep telling me what life was like before. What led you to jail? I'm sorry if I'm asking you too many questions."

I intervene. "Tiffany, we can always stop."

Tiffany shakes her head from side to side. "No, I want to do this. After Yarnell picked up Kassie, he took us to this trailer park where we were each forced to have sex with these men there. There were three men I had to have sex with, and one Kassie had to have sex with too. I felt so bad for her because I was in her shoes too."

"Maybe Yarnell thought he could make it so that Kassie thought he loved her and was just using Tiffany. She trusted Tiffany and he knew that too. So, he could use a blend of love, fear, and trusting another girl. All classic pimp tactics," I tell Noel.

"That's messed up, Andrea."

Tiffany keeps going, speed talking through the final minutes of our call.

"Kassie was scared. I kept thinking of my baby and how Yarnell said he would kill him if I tried to run. After the men were done with us, Yarnell took Kassie home, but she didn't stay quiet like me. She says he raped her too, and she told her grandmother, who called the police. They arrested me and helped Kassie. At the time, I kind of thought I deserved it, though. She was my friend. My grandmother and her mom were friends too." Tiffany looks down, clearly still anguished at the pain she'd caused someone she cared about.

"Tiffany, you know now that's not true," I remind her. "You said it before: Yarnell could have killed you." He might be locked up now, but I think he's still there in her head, gaslighting her even in her memories. I've been gaslighted by someone I wanted to love me too. That's something Tiffany and I have in common.

"We only have a couple more minutes, Noel," I add.

"Okay, okay. So, what is day-to-day life like for you now, Tiffany?"

Tiffany begins to answer, twirling the curly black phone cord in her fingers, her voice lifting up a bit to rise over a few inmates screaming in the background. "I'm focused on getting this group together with Andrea where we can talk to other women about trafficking and help them feel like they have support. I really want to help other girls."

I'm smiling like a proud big sister. "Noel, Tiffany is being really modest. She's always writing blogs, and we started a justice initiative for survivors. We're going to get a bill passed to ensure survivors are not jailed because of their own trafficking. She's doing all of this, and it won't even help her personally."

Tiffany smiles. If the video quality didn't turn everything gray, I'd think she might be blushing. "I love that work," she says. "For now, though, I just keep my head down and focus on getting out of here. COVID makes things, like, real tense here."

For the past few months, Tiffany has been trapped in her cell twenty-three hours a day. No sunshine. No fresh air. I don't think anyone who's not been locked in a box like that could understand.

"What do you want life to be like when you're free?"

"I need to get a job and find a way to go to school. I have to get my son back. I want to help girls like me... It's a lot." Tiffany is always talking about her son, Ayden.

"That's amazing, but what I mean is, like, what's the first thing you want to do for *you*, Tiffany?"

"Oh, I want to grab my bag and get on a plane to California. I want to run into the ocean and swim for the first time with my son by my side!"

"That's beautiful. Why the ocean? Tell me why the ocean?" Noel asks. "How do you know? You see, I'm asking because something is there. I feel it."

I already know. It's not just about a vacation or a sweet memory.

"I guess you could say that when I became a mother, I finally realized I'd been like a rose that never bloomed. Honestly, I'd never even seen love before that was unconditional. I didn't know how to open myself up and be free. There was no water."

I can relate to this. A few years ago, after I ended an abusive relationship, my therapist asked me what I thought unconditional love was like. I didn't have an answer either. I felt like unconditional love was an open invitation to be abused or controlled by someone else. That's what abuse teaches you—you have to minimize yourself to survive. Tiffany seems to have gotten that lesson in life too, and we've been unraveling this together.

"I was just in this ocean of a lack of love," Tiffany continues. "I realized after I had Ayden that I had to swim for him. It wasn't about me anymore. My little boy taught me what unconditional love was. I just never had that. I really didn't know what love looked like, and that's why I drowned in all the lies from Yarnell. The ocean, for me, is about finally being free. It's about love."

I'm nodding my head. Having my daughter also taught me what unconditional love truly is.

"You could say I was abandoned every day by my mom who drank, and my dad was locked up since I was six years old. So, I grew up without my parents. I didn't want that for my son. I want him to have a different life than I did."

"And this is very important, because this is what breaks the cycle. It's bigger than you or even him," Noel adds, intensely scribbling on her pad of paper.

The one-minute warning comes again, so we say our goodbyes and I close my computer.

I hadn't noticed the California sky darkening while Tiffany, Noel, and I were talking. All around me are blooming hibiscus flowers, hipsters drinking kombucha, and gigantic surfboards. The sunset is gliding into the Pacific Ocean. The beauty is not lost on me as my mind lingers inside that gray jail with Tiffany. *I'm surrounded by the colors Tiffany should be drenched in*, I think to myself. I feel like I'm emerging from another planet, heavy from yet again hearing Tiffany's story and, at the same time, full of light because I can see we're getting closer and closer to telling the world what really happened to Tiffany.

* * *

Meeting Tiffany has changed me profoundly as a person and as an advocate for survivors of sex trafficking. Seeing the gross atrocity of a child, a sex trafficking survivor, with a thirty-year sentence showed me that justice is a part of healing that cannot be ignored. Yet, it's so often denied for survivors like Tiffany, whose own victimization is part of what's being used to jail them.

I co-founded my first nonprofit, FAIR Girls, in 2004 in Washington, D.C. FAIR is an acronym standing for "Free, Aware, Inspired, Restored," and the purpose of FAIR Girls is to provide intervention and care to female survivors of human trafficking. In the beginning, I thought we'd work internationally because I believed most victims were from other countries. I was wrong. Most of our clients were American girls who grew up right in Washington, D.C. In fact, in the United States, most survivors of sex trafficking are young women and girls of color, but boys can be trafficked too. But I wasn't the only one with that misconception. In the early 2000s, aid and support for victims of human trafficking was largely focused on foreign national victims.

There are also a lot of misconceptions about what sex trafficking is and how a perpetrator is defined. It was not until 2000 that the United States passed a federal law, the Trafficking Victims Protection Act, that defined sex trafficking so that anyone under the age of eighteen was automatically considered a victim, not a prostitute. With this law, it doesn't matter if the child thought they were acting of their own free will—they are a victim.

But it would be a long time before states like Georgia, where Tiffany was arrested in 2011, would pass laws to protect children from arrest for prostitution. In 2021, only thirty states had such laws. State law trumps federal law when it comes to how a crime is prosecuted, and although federal law is often a standard model to follow, the Trafficking Victims Protection Act didn't help Tiffany—more than a decade after the act was passed! The judge, and even Tiffany's own attorney, didn't seem to believe she was a victim of child sex trafficking. This was despite, by their own admissions in court, she was a child "induced to commit a commercial sex act," which was the very definition of sex trafficking. Also, like most survivors, Tiffany didn't consider herself a victim.

As a child, I grew up in the Christian faith, where we are asked to believe that Jesus Christ is the son of God. We were told to believe this purely based on faith; there isn't any evidence that would hold up in court. This form of belief is a common feature of many faiths. Throughout my relationships with Tiffany and so many other survivors, I learned that the lack of belief plays a critical and dark role in what leads them to prison, or worse. No one around them believes in them, which leads them to not believe it themselves. Belief is powerful, but it's also demanding. It's all or nothing—either you fully believe that Jesus is the son of God, or you don't.

When I say we should believe survivors, I'm asking that we fully believe them—even without knowing all the facts. Even if the facts seem fuzzy or contradictory or outlandish. We have to believe them, support them, and have faith that the full truth of the story will come to light if we do. This will lead to more survivors receiving the care they so desperately need instead of years of unjust incarceration. For those who believe in a higher power, you'd think this openness to belief would be innate, but many are not so willing to make that leap for their fellow humans.

I still regularly meet people who have no idea that American girls and boys can be—and are—sold into sex trafficking. They are shocked to learn that there are victims in hotels, on street corners, and in apartments right up the street from where they live. The victims are often young people who have grown up in poverty in foster care or broken homes, experiencing sexual assaults, child abuse, and homelessness before they are trafficked.

There is so much I've learned along the way, and of all my clients it's Tiffany who's taught me the most about how wrong I was concerning the real nature of sex trafficking in America. My hope is that this book shines a much-needed spotlight on a difficult topic that has been shoved under the rug for far too long. Tiffany, along with other survivors, share their stories for all of us to understand how sex trafficking is really happening in our country, and how we got to the point that survivors are sentenced to prison—sometimes for life—for crimes that either happened to them or that they were forced to commit. The myths and misconceptions about sex trafficking are wrapped up in perceptions about who can be a victim, where trafficking happens, and even how our social welfare and justice system responds. We're going to unpack all of that in this book.

My life's work has been to promote the understanding that justice is a form of kindness that every single human being deserves. We have all survived so many things.

"Tiffany, trafficking is what happened to you. It's not who you are," I wrote back in response to her first letter.

The media loves a victim story, but what they really want is the "perfect" victim. So, don't be too loud; don't be promiscuous as a teen; and ideally, be blonde, white, and conventionally cute. Oh, and if you're a boy, it will be assumed you're gay if you were trafficked. Also, don't call your trafficker your "boyfriend" because then it's considered "just domestic violence"— which is a whole different can of worms. Don't be a runaway and don't do drugs because, if that's the case, then you were asking for it. Of course, you must come from a good nuclear family with a mom and dad and cute dog. Oh, and if you have any prior arrests or are a juvenile delinquent, forget it. You're a lost cause, not a victim worth saving. You should also get ready for endless questions about why you didn't just leave. And, if you fought back against your trafficker or the man who bought and raped you, why didn't you let the police handle it? Clearly, you're just a violent criminal.

Stereotypes about what makes someone a "perfect victim" are why the public, school systems, and courts do not see most people in trafficking situations as victims crying for help. In my time speaking to media outlets, I try to debunk these myths because they're a direct threat to victims. Many times, people who are in a situation to help are deliberately looking away from victims because they think they're not savable, just a waste of time, and a drain on societal resources.

Through Tiffany's story, I've learned what leads a survivor down a desperate path where they end up being sold for sex to hundreds or sometimes thousands of people. When the criminal punishment system finds them, they are arrested instead of helped.

Activist and author Ibram X. Kendi reframes the "criminal justice system" as the "criminal punishment system" to more accurately speak to the reality that "justice" is not necessarily the goal or outcome of this system and that, in the United States, punishment has never been enforced equally—or even accurately. This rings true for Tiffany and thousands of survivors of sex trafficking, some of whom you will meet as you read this book. I use Kendi's term to more accurately describe their experiences in court, jail, and other facets of what's traditionally called our "criminal justice system."

Trafficking is a pathway, sanctioned by our criminal punishment system, to being put in chains—and these aren't just figurative. In prison, Tiffany wore literal chains on her arms and legs. Her arms were chained to a heavy belt locked around her waist, leaving her unable to reach above her elbows for sometimes more than twenty-three hours a day. They were so heavy that she had back pain, making getting in and out of bed almost impossible some days.

Sex trafficking is not inevitable. To stop it, we must stop making excuses like "the system failed them." When Tiffany was six years old, her father was sentenced to life in prison for murder. By the time she was thirteen, her mother's descent into depression and alcohol abuse led the court to take Tiffany away and grant her grandmother custody. When Tiffany began missing school at fourteen, she was not offered counseling. No one asked her what was wrong or what kind of support she needed. She was considered a "bad kid" and, not surprisingly, soon stopped going to school altogether.

The system is made of people—teachers, social workers, police officers— who can and should see people like Tiffany as children in need. Increasing awareness of sex trafficking helps us recognize the potential threat to these children. It's not the system that fails, it's the people running the system whose failings begin when they don't believe victims.

When those who are supposed to help children ignore or push certain girls and boys out of society, traffickers step in to make their move. Children who are alienated, left to fend for themselves, and treated like criminals are vulnerable. But if traffickers can see these vulnerabilities, so can people who are in positions of power.

Child survivors like Tiffany are whole people worthy of our belief and support. They're just like you and me; they deserve love, opportunities, and community. We need to see the person under the victim or trafficker label, something that, once applied, seems to obscure their personhood. You can't "catch" sex trafficking, so there's no reason to run from anyone who's experienced it. And yet, there continues to be a frustrating lack of understanding about what sex trafficking is and how it works. This is coupled by sensational media stories and inflamed statistics that some in the movement to end sex trafficking use to solicit sympathy and, frankly, funding. Telling the true stories of all kinds of survivors is a part of the process to change that too. As you meet survivors like Ashley, Alyssa, Jordan, Jessica, Asia, and so many others in these pages, you'll see that no one is just their victim story.

Many victims of sex trafficking are never even identified. Children are instead arrested for crimes like running away, truancy, or even for not showing up to custody hearings when their parents have neglected them. In 2011, the year Tiffany was arrested, there were 1,769 children charged with running away in Georgia alone. These kinds of "offenses" often signal larger issues, but they're never looked into. No one is asking *why* these children are running away.

While Tiffany had also run away from home, no one reported her missing. This is common among trafficked and exploited children, so imagine the number of children who run away and are not part of that statistic. Traffickers target young people who are already considered "lost" or "too far gone." There was never a police report filed when Tiffany didn't come home. If no one is looking for a child who is all alone, that makes it easy for traffickers to control them. These kids are then sucked deeper into a world of abuse and exploitation that becomes harder and harder to escape. Yet, even if they're found, they're often not believed.

With *Believe Me*, I aim to illuminate how we can all take part in helping to stop sex trafficking, simply by believing survivors. The key is to take the collective past of those who have been trafficked, like Tiffany, and use it to create better futures for those who are vulnerable now.

When we believe survivors, we believe that every child has a right to live a life that's safe, loving, and nurturing. This leads to safe spaces, such as an after-school program where a child being abused at home can ask their mentor for help. Or a court program that connects juvenile offenders to therapy and services rather than detention and damaging criminal sheets that follow them for life. Or a place where a single mom running from abuse can find a safe bed and food rather than sleeping on the streets where traffickers can target her.

Sex trafficking is the world's second largest form of organized crime. It's also a crime that can be prevented when we truly know what we're looking for and reach vulnerable people before they fall prey to it. Survivors are judged by their families, their teachers, their friends, law enforcement, and the courts. They also judge themselves after years of abuse and conditioning by their traffickers. Judgment is the death of hope, and it leads many victims to stay victims. Hope is our weapon against victimhood. To have hope, you must have people who believe in you and your worth. That requires community.

I know this after supporting thousands of women and girls in their escape and healing from human trafficking. This includes building community and providing safe housing, support in their education, training in how to find employment, and true kindness in understanding and helping them recover from their trauma. Of the over 2,000 survivors I have met and served, almost every one suffers from post-traumatic stress disorder, depression, or many other debilitating conditions that either occurred because of their trafficking or was a root cause of their exploitation.

Their healing begins with someone believing in them.

If you've survived human trafficking, sexual exploitation, domestic violence, intimate partner violence, online sexual image abuse, homelessness, child abuse, or neglect, then I believe in you too, dear reader. Together we can come closer to each other in acts of fierce kindness, redefine survivorship, and create laws and support systems to end trafficking and further victimization of trafficking survivors once and for all.

Together we can break the cycle.

Part One

REACHING OUT

Chapter 1

WHAT INSPIRES YOU?

"What inspires you to do what you do? How can you hear these sad stories day in and day out?"

I hear these questions a lot when asked about my work as an advocate for victims of sex trafficking. I always think of a friend from many years ago, Aischa, who I knew was in a troubling situation. One day she disappeared, and her fate is still unknown to me. Even so many years later, in interviews with CNN, the BBC, and for documentaries, I often tell her story. I also think of how Tiffany has been so open about sharing her story, always in the hope that it might help another survivor avoid what she's gone through. It's been a difficult road, but I'm even becoming more willing to share the depth of my own survivorship.

But these are not just "stories." They're the truths that connect me to my community. They're the source of my willpower, hope, and belief. They're what get other people to care about survivors. Still, it's taken me years to understand how to answer the question, "What inspires you?"

I was seventeen when I knew advocacy would be my life's work, but the seed was planted in me much earlier. In grade school, I was drawn to the girl in my class who everyone else said was weird. Her name was Elizabeth, and she had Down syndrome. I knew she was different, but that made me curious about her and how she experienced the world. I just couldn't stand the unfairness and cruelty she endured because she wasn't who everyone else thought she should be.

Every day, Elizabeth sat next to me in Mrs. Schafer's class and would stare aimlessly out the window as we listened to instructions. I wondered about what she saw and what she thought about when she looked out the window. Why was she scared of our school swing set but wanted to play on the monkey bars for hours? Why did she like me but not my best friend, Jenny?

One day before recess ended, I came into class early and heard Mrs. Schafer talking to another teacher about moving Elizabeth to the "basic" class. I knew what that meant. The teachers thought she was stupid! She wasn't, but it sometimes took her longer to understand what was required. My insides stung with the injustice, so I started secretly doing her homework for her. Though misguided, it was my attempt to help Elizabeth out, since our teacher didn't take the time to make sure she understood. The required cursive writing was hard, so even I had trouble making my fingers create those small, rounded letters. Still, I filled her page, often forgetting to fill my own. I drew bunnies and hearts around her homework, just like I did mine. This turned out to be my demise. I was caught!

Mrs. Schafer called me to her desk, which was covered in little framed quotes like "You Can Do It!" and "Be All You Can Be." I felt my chest burn as she asked me why I'd been doing Elizabeth's work. I told her I only wanted Elizabeth to get a fair chance to stay in our class.

"How can Elizabeth be all she can be if you won't let her try?" I asked, pointing to the signs. Mrs. Schafer listened to me as I shared that all she had to do was slow down and listen to my friend. "She's really smart. You just have to talk to her so she can understand."

Two days later, a new teacher's aide joined our class. She sat next to Elizabeth and explained the assignments to her. (But she would not let us draw on our homework anymore!) I felt that sting in my chest fade. Running out to the playground, I felt almost giddy. This was my first true taste of activism. It may have been small, but it felt like being on top of the world.

In junior high, I decided that I would eventually become the next Jane Goodall, my hero, or take over the Environmental Protection Agency or Greenpeace. I thought I wanted to work for the environment and our planet on a large scale, but that's not what the universe had in mind for me. Instead, I kept discovering a kindness gap: the universe kept pointing me toward lost people in need of help, and showing me how I could assist by creating spaces where they could be found and healed.

For example, my friend Rachel and I were sitting alone at lunch one afternoon, the Texas sun streaming down on our lunch trays in the school courtyard and melting our squares of cheese pizza into a sort of pizza pudding. We had ten minutes before the bell and raced to the girls' bathroom. As we went in, two of the popular girls grabbed Rachel and wrote "SLUT" on her forehead with a permanent black marker. Rachel screamed but no teachers came. The other girls ran out. I sat on the floor of the bathroom trying to rub it out with soap and water, but it stayed. Right after the bell rang, the principal came into the bathroom and told us to get to class. She only smirked as I begged her to let Rachel go home.

"Everyone will make fun of me," Rachel whispered, the principal's fierce glare following us down the hallway. "Get to class or you'll get detention," is all she screamed.

And the girls did make fun of her. The taunts never stopped for the rest of the year. Rachel soon started skipping school and by high school, she had dropped out altogether. She had an older boyfriend who I would often see yelling at her in town. While I will never know if that horrible day in the girls' bathroom directly contributed to Rachel's fate, I was just as enraged by her abuse as I was by the fact that our principal refused to see her pain or believe us when we said this would break her. The sting of injustice was deep, and I carried it with me.

While in high school, I co-founded our school newspaper with the intent of exposing the sexism in the administration. I was determined to see the world beyond my small Texas town. Our local university, Texas State, allowed me to enroll early in college classes like political science, biology, and anthropology. I combined this with online courses and advanced placement classes with college credit and graduated high school with over forty credits of college courses. Next, I wanted to explore the world. My travel dreams came true when I was accepted in 1997 as the youngest student to travel on an international exchange program in Germany. My plan was to get from there to Paris, my dream city.

After I arrived in Hannover, Germany, I met a nineteen-year-old girl named Aischa in one of my classes. She immediately drew me in with her bubbling, quiet giggle, which she often suppressed with the scarf that was always wrapped around her head, neck, and shoulders. Her pale olive skin, hazel doe-eyes, and long shiny black hair reminded me of Jasmine from my favorite Disney film, *Aladdin*. When I told her this, she laughed, calling me her blonde surfer girl. Aischa secretly loved watching *Baywatch* and *90210*, but she couldn't tell anyone in her house about her guilty pleasures.

She was the youngest of four wives of a Syrian man who seemingly married her as part of an arrangement with her parents. Aischa cooked, cleaned, and served everyone in his family. She was even younger than his oldest daughter. When Aischa would laugh as we ran across the street to the local Turkish cafe, I often saw the bruises that were not at all funny.

"Aischa, what happened to your lip?" I would whisper in my broken German.

"I talked back to her," she whispered back. I wondered which wife she meant.

On another day, she came to class with a bruise on her wrist that was barely covered by the long shirt and gloves she would only remove so we could take notes.

"Aischa, did you fall on the ice?" I asked.

"I didn't iron his shirt correctly," she quietly answered. Aischa would never look me in the eyes when I questioned her injuries. Instead, she focused out the fogged, icy windows, gazing into what was turning out to be Europe's coldest winter on record. She squeezed my arm and said, "Don't worry, my little Anka," which was her nickname for me. Only, I did worry. I looked around at the teacher and other classmates. Didn't they see her bruises? No one ever said a word.

Despite (or perhaps because of) her circumstances, Aischa had a vast imagination, and we loved dreaming outside of our realities.

"What would you do if you could do anything ever?" I prompted one day as we skipped German class to meet in a local cafe.

"I would be a dental assistant and help kids smile better."

Whoa. I'd had braces I hated and never really considered the joy or advantages they gave me. She also wanted love and her own kids, which her husband didn't want.

The bruises continued, and still no one seemed to notice.

Over time and a lot of stilted German conversations, we developed a plan for her to escape. I was saving money from teaching English and Aischa had a little money too. We would take the train to Frankfurt together after class one day and buy two flights from the airport there to Austin, Texas, and explain at customs that Aischa was being abused by her husband. She could live with me and my parents until we were able to reunite her with her family in Bosnia. Though I had not shared this plan with my parents, I was sure they would say yes.

Then, Aischa disappeared. The first two days of class she missed, I just thought she might be sick. The next week, I asked the other women in class if they'd seen her. They would barely speak to me, looking out the window like they didn't hear me. Aischa had told me that they thought I was a bad influence on her because I was unmarried. Finally, on the fifth day, I couldn't stop staring at Aischa's favorite desk, now empty, and wonder if anyone else was worried too. That night, I asked my boyfriend what he thought.

"Andrea, you know this is just how it is. She likely just decided not to come, or her husband decided she didn't need to go."

It wasn't good enough for me to speculate. I wanted to know for sure. Did her husband find out we were planning to run away together? That could be disastrous for Aischa. Plus, I was the only one who'd noticed her bruises, I thought. The next morning, instead of class, I packed my dictionary and a note with all I knew about Aischa and headed to the police station.

Please don't be angry at me, Aischa. I promise I'm not telling the world your problems. I am just worried, and I miss my only friend here, I wrote in my journal before heading out into the snowy Hannover streets, slowly navigating the stairs and bridges that led to the police station. When I arrived, the station was quiet. I didn't understand the German-speaking station attendant.

"Do you have a form for me to fill out? I think my friend Aischa is missing."

"What makes you say this?" the young policeman asked.

"She hasn't been to our German class for over two weeks. She never misses."

"Perhaps she is ill, on vacation, or just missing class."

"Yes, sir, I agree these things are possible. Only, Aischa really is dedicated to learning German. We also never just not tell each other things. And her husband beats her. So do his other wives."

"Where is your friend from?"

"Her name is Aischa. She's nineteen. She's from Syria, but she was living in Bosnia before she came here. I don't know much more, to be honest."

"Do you know her street address?"

"No, I don't." My face flushed hot.

"How long have you known Aischa again?"

"I have known her three months. We met in class. She's my best friend here."

"Where are you from, miss?"

"I'm from around Austin, Texas. I'm studying here at the University of Hannover, and I met Aischa in German class."

"So, she's your best friend, and you don't know where her family is or even where she lives?"

The tears started coming down from the shame. *What kind of friend was I?* I thought.

"Come back if you can tell us her address."

"Wait, can't you just talk to the school? I had to put my address on my application, and they're sure to have hers as well."

"Miss, come back when you know more. You know she just could have left. These girls are like this." That was the second time I had heard "these girls," and I started to wonder if I was also "one of these girls."

I nodded. I could feel the anger moving up through my lungs, causing me to hold my breath. I was scared of being deported or getting in trouble.

Breathing out felt like defeat. On the train home, I started to write out everything I knew about Aischa. I knew she liked strawberry ice cream, that she loved kittens but not cats, that she dreamed of California and being a dental assistant. I felt like I knew nothing about my friend that was useful.

"She's a lost cause, Andrea," my boyfriend said again that night. But I couldn't give up. Months later, I used all my savings from waiting tables and teaching English classes and flew from Germany to Sarajevo, Bosnia, to look for her. It was a secret mission.

The smell of tobacco on the old Ottoman Turkish streets was almost sweet, curling around me like an almond delight. Patterned glass lamps glittered their light across the sea of scarves and onto the cobblestone streets. Sarajevo was more colorful than I'd expected, considering that the Balkan War had only ended a few years earlier. It seemed that no one could have more than a five-minute conversation without insisting on Turkish coffee with a side of war story. The stories were told as if they were recounting the day's weather, the rain casually falling between the cafe umbrellas, ashtrays, and limitless sugar packs. Everyone ate ice cream. Grown men, little girls, police, and United Nations soldiers. Everyone. All day long. And then, there were the girls dressed provocatively, desperate to attract any expat man who might be their ticket out of a country where jobs were scarce.

Through a German friend, I met a woman named Zora who helped me translate as I talked to women's groups, judges who I found online, and youth organizers, all with the desperate hope of finding Aischa.

I began to hear shocking and awful stories about sisters watching each other being raped by militants, girls being exchanged for food for a starving family, girls disappearing and never coming home. Each one offered different details, names, and descriptions, but similar themes. The stories were endless, and rather than sucking out my hope, they fueled my desire to keep going. My eyes were truly open.

"This is bigger than Aischa," I said to Zora after our third day.

I left Sarajevo devastated, without any leads about where Aischa could be. But I did learn that girls like Aischa were disappearing all over Bosnia,

Serbia, and the Balkans. I saw brothels where girls were traded to men amid coffee and beer as the police walked by, doing nothing. The women activists I met asked me to come back to help call attention to the horrible conditions so many Bosnian girls were facing there. Leaving Bosnia, I felt smaller than I ever had—and more alive too. I felt I'd found my purpose.

Aischa, you broke my world open. I'm not going to fail you, I wrote in my journal on my way back to Germany. Shortly thereafter, I returned to Texas, and it would be another five years before I found my way back to honoring Aischa.

* * *

The year is now 2003, and Aischa's fate still haunts me. I will never know what happened to her. Statistics vary, saying there are between 50,000 and more than 27 million victims of human trafficking all over the world. That's a pretty big discrepancy, and to me, all it says is that no one really knows. I know only the truth that survivors have told me. They're not only being disappeared by traffickers, but also by cops, lawyers, and social workers who don't believe them. I know Aischa wasn't part of that count because no one believed me that she was in trouble. It's painful to know I failed to find Aischa all those years ago. I don't even have a photo of her. But I see Aischa in the eyes of every girl I meet, whether she is from South Boston or Bosnia.

All I know is that I want to help as many girls as possible escape abuse and troubling circumstances. I co-found FAIR Girls with Caroline, a woman I met on a Harvard women's rights forum. Our goal in starting the organization is to provide interventions and eventually safe housing for victims of trafficking. Friends and other advocates I meet suggest I do an internship, go back to school, or just volunteer instead of jumping directly into launching a nonprofit, but Caroline bolsters my confidence. She's a few years older than me and has traveled all over the Balkans. She's just as comfortable sitting in an Albanian woman's one-room home as she is in a Parisian cafe with her family, and she was moved by my experience in Bosnia. We quickly bond over our shared rebellion, even though her Newport, Rhode Island, life feels a world away from my country woods Texas childhood.

When we file the paperwork to begin FAIR Girls, I don't think about how hard it will be to raise the $20,000 we need to go back to Bosnia. Even though Caroline's family has money, we want to do as much as we can on our own.

How am I going to pull my weight? I write in my journal. My day job is managing a six-university program on global women's studies, and my office is in the basement of a building at Harvard University. *I just want to make FAIR Girls fly. Everyone thinks it's prestigious that I work at Harvard while Will* [my fiancé] *is in Harvard Law School, but my heart belongs to FAIR Girls.*

When Caroline and I get the letter from the IRS approving our non-profit status, we go out into Harvard Square to celebrate with Thai food. After eighteen months, we can finally begin raising the money we need, and I have an idea.

"Caroline, you have friends and family with money who you can tap for donations. I don't. But I found lists of women donors in Texas who gave to Planned Parenthood. I'm from Texas. Trust me, they're mad that they're stuck there where women's rights are so far behind. I'll write them each a handwritten note—Texas girl to Texas girl!"

Cate thinks I'm crazy, but I'm determined. Night after night, I come home from work, find addresses to go with the names, and enter the data into a spreadsheet. Then I begin handwriting letters to each of the 200 women on my spreadsheet. My homemade stationery piles up on our green, thrifted kitchen table. As I work my way through the list, Will studies law in our living room.

> *Dear Mrs. Martin,*
> *My name is Andrea Powell. I'm a young woman from San Marcos, Texas. I graduated high school with almost two years of college under my belt. At seventeen, I traveled to Hannover, Germany, as an exchange student from Texas State University in*

their geography and planning program. You see, my dream was to be an environmental activist, but life had other plans for me. While there, I signed up for German classes and met a friend named Aischa who I believe was a modern-day slave because she was forced to work without pay and was treated like she was a slave. When Aischa disappeared from our classes, I went to the police, but no one would help me. I think she was punished for trying to run away, but I'll never know.

So, I started FAIR Girls after graduate school to help prevent what I think happened to Aischa from happening to girls here in the United States and around the world. I still can't believe girls my age can be basically treated like slaves.

You are from Texas, like me. I know we both believe in women's rights, and we know what it is like to be treated like our rights don't matter. I learned that you are a big supporter of Planned Parenthood. We have that in common! We agree that women should have the ability to determine their bodily rights. Well, human trafficking is all about controlling another person's life and body. It's happening to girls all over America, too.

Mrs. Martin, I know you have a lot you care about. I also know I'm young and FAIR Girls is new. I am hoping you might trust me a little to take your contributions to help stop human trafficking. I can't do it alone. I will do all I can to honor your gift. I've enclosed an envelope and I'll keep you updated if you choose to join us. I seek to raise $20,000 to go back to Bosnia to help prevent the trafficking of girls like my friend Aischa, and to reach American girls. Join us and I think we can do a lot together!

With gratitude,
Andrea Christine Powell
Co-founder, FAIR Girls

Each letter is handwritten on light cream letterhead with our FAIR Girls logo. I soon think my hand will fall off from writing all those letters!

After signing the last one, I load them into my backpack, and Will and I walk them to the post box in Harvard Square. He heads off to class and I go to my basement office at Harvard University.

That night is the monthly board meeting for the Harvard Graduate Consortium of Women's Studies, and I work as their program manager. I manage the program while ten women professors sit around talking about feminist theory courses, barely eating the Italian food I order each month. I take notes, clean, and write down our action items. My favorite part of the meeting nights is later, when I take the leftovers to my friend Niels, a tall, Black, homeless man I met at Harvard Square. After cleaning up, I text him, like usual, to meet at the train station and begin trudging through the frigid December night.

"Hey, beautiful girl. You got some fine food tonight!" he says as I hand him the three trays of lasagna and salad, plus two bags of soda.

"Niels, you know the deal. You gotta find like fifteen friends to eat all this!" My arms ache from carrying all that food, but seeing his smile lifts my spirit. He laughs his deep chuckle, which is often riddled with a rough winter cough. I never know if he sleeps outside or in a shelter.

"You drive a hard bargain, blondie. I'll share with the guys."

Niels looks like the kind of guy who played piano at a jazz club, and I love jazz. He once told me he couldn't even think about college after coming back from a tour in Iraq. He was lost in paperwork and anger. There are days he doesn't seem to recognize me as I walk past. We often sit on the gray, commuter-worn stairs to the red line train station as he talks about growing up with his single mom and wanting to make her proud of her only son. I told him my dream of finally working on FAIR Girls full-time. That night, I tell him about the letters and how much I hope someone replied.

"Girl, you are so close."

I want to believe him. I say I have to get home to Will.

"You tell your man he's a lucky one," he says. I blush, like always, and start the fifteen-minute walk home through the below-zero Cambridge night.

A few days later, Will is grinning ear to ear when I come home from work. On our table are three small envelopes with my name on them. I tear them open. "We have $1,700 in donations," I shout, jumping up and kissing him. One of the return letters is from Mrs. Martin!

"You're really doing this, Andrea."

That night, I whisper to the Aischa I can visit only in my mind, *I told you I wouldn't forget you.*

This is eight years before I meet Tiffany, but there are many other girls in need who I'm going to find along the way.

Chapter 2

SHINE BRIGHT LIKE A DIAMOND

After Will graduates Harvard Law School in 2004, we get married in the open air overlooking the Austin skyline. We move from Boston to Washington, D.C., to follow his first legal job. I pack up box after box of FAIR Girls work and throw it in the moving van that we drive eight hours to our new two-bedroom row house apartment. It has a tiny back room with its own entrance door, and I use it as the world's smallest office. I'm still working twenty hours a week at the Graduate Consortium of Women's Studies, which has just moved to the Massachusetts Institute of Technology.

By 2007 though, FAIR Girls is getting bigger, and Will says he can't handle my interns being all over our apartment and eating all of our food anymore. Besides just wanting to get the nonprofit out of our personal life, FAIR Girls needs more space. We need a real office. Luckily, our elderly German landlord agrees to rent us a 500-square-foot space in the basement of the row house for $1,250 a month. At night, I sit alone in the office after our interns and the teen girls in our small support group leave. Will often joins me as I write to donors and apply for grants, and our landlord rarely complains when we are inevitably late with rent. Every month, making rent is a tiny terror for me, and Will is starting to ask when I think FAIR Girls can finally offer me a salary. I have no idea. Most people still don't even know what human trafficking is.

"Who's going to donate to us? Look at all these women leading multi-million-dollar organizations. They have book deals and all this media and are twice my age," I whine to Will.

"Andrea, you have something they don't. You actually understand what human trafficking is because you know real victims," Will says. He's referring to Aischa. Will always knows how to calm me down. Sometimes the topic of getting a day job comes up, but the thought of giving up leaves me feeling like I would fail the girls who need us.

The outreach we do is not just searching for donors, it's also to raise awareness. I line up speaking engagements wherever I can, and on a bus ride coming back from a talk at a private Quaker school in Providence, I meet Steven. He's an executive at Yahoo and cannot believe that sex trafficking is happening to kids in America. As we get off the bus, he invites me to apply for a Yahoo grant, which could be used to stop child sex trafficking. Within six months, we have $40,000 to educate teens in D.C. on how to stay safe from human trafficking. I can finally hire my first employee, Makiko, who interned for us months before.

Makiko is a newly graduated student from Japan, and she tirelessly commits to our crusade. Sometimes I pretend I'm going upstairs to my apartment so Makiko will stop working and go home. I say goodnight, turn off the lights, and we both leave. Then, I sneak back down fifteen minutes later—only to soon hear a knock on the door. It's Makiko, who's figured out I was going to keep working. We stay up until midnight writing, talking, and planning. Six months later though, Makiko's visa lottery application is denied, and she has to return home. We sit together on our dirty, donated sofa and cry.

But still, I'm building a little momentum and am lucky to keep finding passionate people who want to help create change. I hire Samantha, a recent college graduate who wants to help at-risk girls. Soon, she's sitting next to Amelia, our part-time fundraising director. A few months later, nineteen-year-old college student Eve joins us. I joke that you could literally put the four of us in the closet and no one would ever hear of FAIR

Girls again, but in the back of my mind, I know that we can make real change happen—this is the start of something big.

In 2007, FAIR Girls receives another grant, this one from the University of Massachusetts Lowell, to interview runaway and homeless teens in D.C. and Boston. A criminal justice professor I met while working at Harvard University partners with us, and we aim to learn why some teens on the streets fall into commercial sexual exploitation and trafficking while some don't. Samantha and I stay up until 3 a.m., sitting with kids in train stations, shelters, and foster homes. Samantha looks so young that the teen girls think she's in high school like them.

"I didn't run away. I just left home, and no one came to find me," says a fourteen-year-old girl who was trading sex for money so she could stay with a man in his fifties. He said she could live with him rather than going back to her father, who would rape her while her mother was asleep. She felt safer with this man than her own family and didn't see that what he was doing was wrong. But eventually the man got bored with her. "So, now I'm back out there, you know. It is what it is," is all she says.

That night, I walk her to a youth shelter, and soon she's coming to our drop-in center and office after school. Each day, the girls in our program come to our office to do homework, make art, eat everything in our kitchen, and bond. This gives them a safe space to spend time rather than being out on the streets or in an unpredictable home. Soon, our office is filled with books, art, plush pillows, and donated clothing. The 500 square feet feel more and more like a shoe box.

That fourteen-year-old is one of 135 teens we interview this year. The man who sexually abused her is never arrested, though. "He was nice to me. I don't want to get him in trouble," she says over and over. The police tell us she is a repeat runaway with charges for missing school and stealing. They don't believe she's a victim of anything. But we do.

I want to shine a light on the trafficking that's happening right here in America, but I haven't forgotten about what I'd seen abroad. I look for ways to engage in the fight internationally too. Most of the leaders in the emerging anti–human trafficking movement ignore me because I'm barely out of graduate school. Then, I meet Alison Boak, another younger leader who lives in Brooklyn but has spent years working in Eastern Europe. Like me, Alison was drawn to preventing human trafficking after learning about it during her time as a Peace Corp volunteer in Estonia. Years earlier, while searching for Aischa, I found women's groups all over the former Yugoslavia. One woman who was even younger than me was opening the first youth drop-in in Belgrade.

Alison invites me to join her in presenting to a donor an idea to reach dozens of street-involved and orphaned youths in Serbia and Bosnia with a program to prevent their trafficking. From his Brooklyn high-rise office, the German donor listens, and then gives FAIR Girls $20,000! Alison and I partner with our Serbian youth colleagues at their drop-in center to create twelve classes on how to find a job, find an apartment, report a sexual assault, and decide if you should travel to another country for work. We create games and make lists of community groups that could help. We train students at the school of social work in Belgrade and, within a year, we have educated sixty-five teen girls who are leaving orphan care across Belgrade.

"I'm creating the program I wish Aischa could have had, even though she wasn't an orphan," I say to my new Serbian co-worker, Tanja. While visiting Serbia for three weeks during the program, I learn from our students that there are four sisters living with their trafficker in an abandoned house in Belgrade. They ran away from the orphanage located miles out of the city. One of the sisters is Vida, a fourteen-year-old girl who Tanja had heard about months earlier.

I saw teenage kids on the streets of Belgrade every time I was there, and most of the teens I saw at night were ethnically Romani. "It's like being Black in Mississippi in the 1940s," I say to my D.C. interns as I try to explain what being Roma is like in Serbia. These kids, I think, need to be a part of our program so they can get connected to help. Tanja agrees.

Our local youth outreach partners know of a house where the orphaned sisters and other girls might be trapped in sex trafficking. One night while walking through Belgrade with the volunteers close to midnight, we find the sisters in the abandoned house. It's where their trafficker arranges for men to come and have sex with them. There are people, mostly young teens, coming in and out of the house, navigating the icy concrete stairs that lost their railings long ago. The window frames have remnants of broken glass from a time when the three-story house could keep people warm from the harsh Balkan winters. Now, it's just a shell, like so many buildings that were bombed during the Yugoslav wars.

Outside, a young man in a ripped black leather bomber jacket stands smoking and checking his phone as he surveils the people going in and out. He doesn't ask me who I am as I negotiate the ice on the stairs and pull myself up to the landing. My backpack, heavy with juices, snacks, and other fun treats, makes my passage all the more difficult. He laughs as I try to find my balance before walking into the decaying house.

"He's the one selling the girls," one of the youth volunteers whispers.

"Why is he letting us come in here and give the girls food," I whisper back. Wouldn't he think we would get the girls to leave?

"He doesn't care if outreach workers come in here. He can always get a new girl."

Immediately, I see Vida sitting on a suspiciously red-stained mattress. She looks up smiling, showing her missing front tooth. I walk over and hand her a sandwich and orange juice box. She drinks the juice so fast that I give her the other five from my backpack. She taps her heart and says, "*Hvala*," which I'd learned means "Thanks," as she downs the other juice boxes. She doesn't speak English, and I only know a few phrases in Serbian, but we have an immediate kinship.

It's twenty-five degrees outside, and the snow has turned to slick ice along the sidewalks. Vida's feet are calloused and bare. After sitting with her for a few minutes, I hear raised male voices speaking in Serbian outside. I see police talking to the trafficker and two girls I think might be Vida's sisters. The men enter the room, wearing uniforms that look more military than local police. I link my arm with Vida's as I whisper, "It'll be okay. My name is Andrea." She smiles as if the police are not standing two feet in front of us. I'm not so calm, though. I think I see a gun in one of their hands, and I put my head down, my heart pounding.

Then, as quickly as they came, the police leave. I slowly stop clinging to Vida and unravel my arm from hers. Her trafficker walks into the room and asks in English, "You okay?" I'm fine but confused. So, the trafficker is concerned about us?

Vida looks closely into my eyes, smiling her toothless smile, and touches the purple amethyst necklace I'm wearing. It's a necklace I made—I enjoy the soothing, repetitive nature of beading and jewelry making, and I'm often wearing my own creations. I take off the necklace and place it around Vida's neck. "This is my favorite lucky crystal necklace. You need the luck more than me. Do you want to learn to make jewelry with me, Vida?"

Her trafficker translates. She smiles and nods. Her sisters have wandered back into the room where we're sitting on the floor, and they nod too. "It's a deal, Vida. I'll see you soon." As I hug her goodbye, she pulls a faded, baby-pink glitter ring off her finger and pushes it into my palm. I clutch it like it's gold. That night, back in the room I'm sharing with Tanja, I string it on a chain my grandmother had given me.

The next day, Tanja and I plot how we can get Vida and her sisters away from their trafficker if they come to make jewelry with us. Vida needs medical care. They all do.

Not long after that, I have to return home. On my flight from Belgrade to Washington, D.C., I think only of Vida and going back. Three weeks in Serbia felt like a lifetime to me. I email Tanja every day about Vida. *Can you tell me if you saw Vida? Is Vida okay?* I know she isn't. She's fourteen and on the streets being trafficked in plain sight of the cops.

"Andrea, Vida isn't Aischa," Will says as we lay in bed talking about the girls in Serbia.

"I know." I'm fixating because I don't want to lose Vida like I did Aischa. I play back that night with the cops, Vida, and the pink glitter ring over and over in my head as Will gently tickles my back until I fall asleep.

The week after I return home, Samantha and I write to a local jewelry store in Dupont Circle and ask the owner if they would donate beads to help trafficked girls in Serbia learn how to earn an income and get emotional and medical help. They donate over $10,000 of beads! My Aunt Charlene sends boxes of supplies from Texas too. By the time summer comes around, JewelGirls is born. My suitcases are filled with beads, wire cutters, and donated clothes for Vida and fifteen more girls who want to be our first members of JewelGirls as I take off for Belgrade again.

"I'm a bead mule," I joke to Tanja, unpacking bags that all together weigh more than me. We stay up late that night in the tiny hotel room and fill plastic boxes with beads, wire-cutting supplies, and small booklets on how to make jewelry. The next day, we sit in the sweltering un-air-conditioned drop-in center, waiting for the young women to come. Girl after girl shows up, eating the snacks we'd brought, which may be their only meal that day. If they're able to stay for a while, we set them up with the beading kits and soon the room is filled with lively chatter as they craft jewelry.

Vida and her sister walk in, panting from the sweltering temperatures. They must have had to walk miles in the August heat. She smiles, recognizing me and the pink ring that still dangles from my neck.

Beads are everywhere by the end of the day, including, somehow, in my hair. The girls and young women put their creations in their bags and agree to come back the next day. Afterward, one young woman comes up to Tanja and me, cautiously sharing that she has a sexually transmitted disease and needs help because she has no money. During the next class, another teen girl asks us for help finding a place to stay.

"It's working, Tanja. We are getting them to start trusting us," I say as we walk back with all our bags of beads to the hotel. By the time I'm back on a plane home two weeks later, the participants have created over 200 pieces of jewelry and forty girls are interested in continuing to be a part of JewelGirls.

I'm so immersed in the lives of these girls that I sometimes find it difficult to live my own life. On a Saturday afternoon two months after

I left Belgrade, Will drives me to a friend's baby shower at her Victorian brownstone in Georgetown. The caterers carefully display trays of tea cakes, sandwiches, fruit punch, and pink cupcakes. The presents pile up. The room looks like a display from *Parenting* magazine. Everyone is smiling and hugging my friend, who's so excited about her first child.

After leaving a white stuffed bunny in the mix of gifts, I pull back into the corner, an uncomfortable feeling gnawing at my stomach. When I see the trays of mimosas, I think of Vida drinking all six orange juice boxes in a matter of minutes, as if she'd not had juice in months. I wonder if Vida has eaten today. I silently watch as my friend begins opening the gifts. The Elmo Sesame Street playhouse alone costs $300—enough money for Vida to eat for three months. I move into the kitchen to cry while the catering staff continue to carry out trays laden with food.

"Will, can you come get me?" I text. He replies that he's ten minutes away. I hug my happy pregnant friend goodbye and run out of the house. The tears explode as I get into the car with Will.

"Vida has nothing. None of those girls do. It's not fair, Will." He pulls over on a side street to hug me.

"Andrea, you have to retrain your brain to not always think about those girls. You can't burn yourself to the ground like this." I know he's right, and I also know that I'm not going to stop. After Will falls asleep that night, I get out of bed and stay up until 3 a.m. making jewelry and thinking of new things I can teach Vida and the other girls. That makes me smile again.

The next morning, an idea hits me. Tanja has been sending me photo after photo of all the jewelry that Vida and the other girls are creating. I call Tanja. "What if we sell the jewelry at a big event to launch the start of them making an income and finally having a way to start supporting themselves?"

I call Caroline, a donor who's become my "D.C. grandmother," to see what she thinks of the idea. Caroline is a fierce women's rights advocate who funds small programs like FAIR Girls. I met her a year earlier at a women's rights gathering in D.C., and I relished her stories of meeting Audrey Hepburn and writing letters to senators demanding equal pay and access to healthcare for women. Sitting at Caroline's favorite elite downtown D.C. restaurant, Equinox, where the owners always ensure Caroline has a place amid the regular lobbyists and political strategists, I show Caroline photos of Vida and pitch her the idea of hosting an event in D.C. to help the girls.

Caroline immediately starts making a list of names and people who have to be involved. The next week, I meet with the director of a small historic house where we could hold the event. Tanja organizes sending over all the jewelry along with information about the girl who made each piece. I write to all of our local women donors and ask them to join us in finding food, drinks, and other auction items. Will plays drums with a local jazz band and they agree to be the evening's entertainment. A whirl-wind two months later, on a rainy November night, over 150 people come to support our girls, and it's a huge success. After, I tally how much jewelry has been sold, and it comes to $18,500.

"I knew you'd find a way to help Vida and the girls learn how to make an income. It's way better than just constantly trying to find ways to send money," Will says as we pack up what's left of the jewelry and walk home. As soon as we get in the door, I write Tanja about how amazing it went. I forgot to eat at the event, and as I finish my third bowl of Lucky Charms, I close my laptop and get ready for bed. Hanging on my wrist is the small white pearl bracelet Will bought me—it's the first piece of jewelry that Vida ever made.

* * *

A year after our first JewelGirls event, the number of women and girls in our Serbian JewelGirls program is still growing. Tanja is also now a bead mule, dragging bags of supplies among the three orphanages, the drop-in center, and a small but truly kind safe-home program called Atina. Meanwhile, our D.C. drop-in center is so full that we take the pillows off the sofa and turn them into floor cushions to make more space for seats. We are inundated with requests for help with counseling, re-enrolling in school, and finding safe houses. Mostly, the teen girls we serve want a place where they feel like they're part of a community. Our tiny basement is overflowing, and I love the sound of their music and the constant trail of glitter from the therapeutic art projects.

So many of our young teen clients are living at a local youth shelter that we decide we should offer the shelter staff training on what human trafficking really looks like in D.C. Maybe then they would understand that the girls we send them are not just runaways but victims of a crime. With our bright indigo and coral logo, and drawings from the girls in our program, we create sixty-seven training slides on how to look for red flags indicating a teen may be a victim, and a lot of examples of trafficking based on the American kids who had been part of our study. Almost every single victim was a Black girl between the ages of fourteen and twenty-one.

I'm overjoyed when Makiko gets a new visa after being away for over a year. The day her visa is approved, she books a flight and is in the office that next Monday. I'd greatly missed her, and she brings a new burst of energy to the work.

"What if we created workshops for teens in schools?" I ask Makiko one day. "Sort of like how we created workshops for the teens in orphan care in Serbia?" Soon, our nights are filled with ideas on what would make teenagers want to listen to a group of women talking about human trafficking.

We call it Tell Your Friends and use the $40,000 from Yahoo's grant program to start it up. Soon our office is full of markers, glitter, poster paper, and tiny note cards.

Three months later, we have an agreement with the director of a small foster group home for teen girls to pilot our Tell Your Friends program. The girls in her program have been sent there by the court or social services either because they can't go home or because they have been arrested and the foster home is a sort of stepping-stone after juvenile jail before going back home. We tell her that our four workshops will unpack what human trafficking looks like in America and how it can happen to a teenager in Washington, D.C.

The only time that all the girls are home is after 6 p.m. So, loaded with boxes of pizza and our art supplies, one evening we drive in Makiko's car to the group home nestled next to other family homes in southeast D.C. The older African American woman who runs the program in the evenings opens the door with a huge smile and a hug for us both. Her flowing purple dress and gold bangles look more fitting for a classy concert rather than a foster group home, but that's just the kind of bright, fun energy she brings to the place.

The narrow, brown-carpeted staircase spirals down into a basement covered in handcrafted posters sharing photos of famous Black women, art, makeup, jewelry, and fancy homes. Each poster has a name in glitter on it—Tiara, Amie, Jasmine, and Liana. We set up pizza, apple juice, fruit cups, and the art supplies on foldable tables. The girls come bouncing down the stairs and begin asking questions as they load their plates with the food.

"What's in your bags?"

"You from that church downtown?"

"Who are you?"

"Why are you here?" shouts a girl with tightly cropped hair as she dives into her pizza slice. I look at Makiko and smile as if to say, *Let's do this!*

"Have you ever heard of something called sex trafficking?" I ask. A few girls giggle and some are playing with their phones.

"Like, prostitutes," says one girl with braces.

"Well, sex trafficking is when someone is forced into a situation of something called commercial sex—where they're paid money to have sex—and they don't want to do it. Then, someone else takes the money and controls them." I try to explain it simply, so they understand.

"Oh, like pimps and hoes," calls out another girl.

"Can a girl under eighteen be a prostitute?" Makiko asks.

"I guess. If that's how she wants to get her money," answers the same girl with braces.

I'd learned while working with the girls in Serbia that kids have a variety of learning styles, and so doing something visual and artistic seems like a good way to get the girls interested. "Let's take a moment and draw what we think sex trafficking looks like in D.C.," I prompt the group.

The girls gather around the card tables and use paper and markers to draw what they think sex trafficking looks like. The word "hoe" is written on most of the pictures. Many of the girls are laughing as we tape the drawings onto the wall. "Please go up to the drawings and tell me what things you see that they have in common."

The girls keep giggling, but one by one, they start to call out. "The girls look sad," or "She's making him his money."

"Why is it *his* money?" I ask.

"Because that's how it works. Pimps up and hoes down."

The girls know more about sex trafficking than they realize, but the vernacular is just different. Words like "pimps and hoes" are what they were used to hearing and saying.

"Is it fair that the pimp takes the money, and she gets beat if she doesn't give it to him?" I ask.

Silence.

"No. But she chose that life, so it's on her," says another girl who'd refused to walk up to the drawings. I notice she's drawn a girl with a gun next to her head, but I don't want to ask her about it in front of the other girls.

Next, we use my laptop to show a five-minute video about a twelve-year-old girl who's been sex trafficked by a man who's convinced her that he loves her. Our goal is to show how it looks like the pimp is going to take care of this girl, but in the end, he only uses and exploits her for his own gain. The girls gather around my computer in a circle as we cut the lights.

"Whoa," I hear a girl whisper as the video ends and we turn up the lights.

"That's really messed up. She didn't deserve that, for real," says another girl.

"Why did she run away?" Makiko asks.

"Because her stepfather beat on her."

"What did she need?"

"She needed love."

"What did the pimp offer her?"

"He offered her love."

I can almost hear the bells ringing in their minds as they continue to talk.

"He shouldn't have done that to her if he really loved her."

"Did he really love her?" I ask.

"No," says the girl with braces.

"Maybe he loved her, but he needed the money too," says the girl who made the gun drawing. She looks away, but I think I see tears through the long braids hiding her face.

She's the last girl to leave the group. As we walk upstairs, she says, "A lot of girls out here just don't want to admit they did it too."

"How old are you?" I ask.

"Seventeen," she says, and tells me her name is Macy.

I hand her my FAIR Girls business card with my cell phone number written on the back. She takes it and shoves it in her jeans pocket.

"I'll call you," Macy says as she runs up the stairs. Makiko and I pack up our supplies and drive back across town. I'm too tired to even take my clothes off, so I just drag myself into bed and fall asleep next to Will.

At 2 a.m., my phone rings.

"Let it ring," Will grumbles, half asleep.

"It could be Macy," I say, crawling out of bed.

"Who?" I hear him mumble into his pillow as he rolls over.

I fumble with my phone before answering. "Hello?" It is indeed Macy.

"Miss Andrea, I need your help. They sending me back to my mom tomorrow, and I don't know if I should go."

Macy doesn't know what to do. She's torn between going back to her adoptive mother, who beats her, or going with a guy she'd met who seemed cool, but she wondered if he was a pimp. Living in a foster group home meant curfews, strict rules, and often fights and stealing among the girls. Staff are often overworked and underpaid, and the girls are left to fend for themselves on top of dealing with the trauma of being taken from their families and placed in a group home.

"Macy, does the woman at the foster home know why you're there in the group home?"

"Yeah, cuz I ran away."

Right, like it's her fault. Why would the police arrest a girl who ran away from home?

"Macy, what if I come get you tomorrow and you come to our office so we can talk? I want to know what makes you think this guy could be a pimp because women's instincts are often right." I'm thinking about the times I trusted guys who, it turned out, only wanted to hurt me. When Macy hangs up, I lay back down on the sofa and close my eyes. Then, I quickly open them again. I can't think about my past with my eyes open because I don't want to see it.

My first kiss wasn't given or sweet, it was taken and harsh. Like a surprising sting when you don't realize the wasp is sitting on the blanket next to you at a picnic.

He was twenty-two or twenty-three, a college student who was volunteering at a church camp. He'd convinced me to come pray with him by the lake at 10 p.m., after camp curfew. Instead, he kissed me hard on the mouth as my hands grasped at the wet dirt we sat on. I said nothing as he continued to lead us in a prayer I remember nothing about now. Later, I crawled back into the lower bunk of my church camp dorm room. I told one friend that night, who told me she'd heard he'd done the same to other girls. I was twelve, almost thirteen. So, *I'm not special*, I thought. I was just the next girl on his list.

The next morning, I remembered it like a vaguely confusing dream. I spent what felt like an hour using my toothbrush to pick the dirt from my fingernails. My friend and I walked to breakfast, and he waved hello. I waved back, pretending everything was normal and I was fine. I shoved the memory of the night before away into the pockets of my pre-teen mind.

When I was fourteen, I really wanted more than just to be an average girl with average grades and average looks. The hallways of my high school were like a maze: one wrong turn and you would find yourself in a strange alcove or confusing stairwell, not knowing how to find your way back. There were so many things to do, though. I loved theatre after school and debate class, and I wished I was good enough to join the dance team. But considering I often tripped over my own long, skinny legs, I decided not to try. By November, I had a boyfriend, David, who I thought was the smartest and cutest guy at school. He was also the best debater on our team, according to me. We watched Dead Poets Society on my parents' sofa for our first date and he kissed me under the stars by his car. I was a teenage girl in love. It was the kind of love where I felt like I was skipping as I navigated to my English, history, and algebra classes. I believe in soulmates, people who come into your life to teach your soul about the universe and yourself. David was my first soulmate and true love. He taught me how to read horoscopes and name constellations.

In the winter of my freshman year, some of the older girls invited me to a party one Friday night. One friend's boyfriend, who'd already graduated high school, was having it at his house where he lived with roommates. I was excited because I would be among the older kids, the worldly kids. That night, I got dropped off at a friend's house who was old enough to already have her driver's license. I'd never been to a party before that didn't involve birthday cake and somebody's parents hanging around in the background. I'd heard that some of the foreign exchange students who were in our high school would be there too.

When we walked in, I saw the beer and other bottles of stuff that looked like alcohol. I got some pizza and water and started talking to a friend, but a few hours in, I was tired and had a splitting headache from the cigarette smoke around me. I could feel the familiar flush of fever and a sore throat too. I went to lay down in a room down the hall and told my friend to get me when she was ready to go back to her house.

I don't know how long I was in there sleeping on the bed when the door opened. I recognized the person opening the door as a guy from my high school who I knew had been saying gross stuff to a friend of mine. I knew something was about to happen and my body seized up in terror. Prey always knows when they're being hunted. I just knew something bad was happening.

My heart was beating so strongly that I'm sure he could hear it. As he came toward me, he grabbed my leg, hard. He pushed me down on the bed and held me by my neck. I didn't move. I couldn't move. I didn't even move when two more guys I didn't know came in. They took turns. One after the other. The sheets were suddenly wet, but I didn't know why. They laughed as I tried to bite one of them. As my head was laying backward off the side of the bed, I could see out the window. I thought I saw a friend watching, but she later denied seeing me there. When they were done, they whispered no one would believe a slut like me. As they got up, I saw the other two guys hand the older student I knew money. How much? I didn't know. At the time, I didn't think it was important. I didn't think at all.

I just didn't want to be anymore.

They left the room, and I curled up in a ball with my clothes back on. When my friend came to get me, it was 4 a.m. I didn't say a word. I didn't say a word the next morning either. When my mom came to get me, I didn't say a word. I didn't want to be a slut. I didn't want the police to talk to me. I didn't want to get in trouble or hurt my parents. I didn't want David to break up with me. I didn't want anyone seeing me like that in their minds, judging me.

My nightmare wasn't over, and there's more to this story. This is, however, as much as I want to share. I'm not looking for my own justice. I'm not looking to expose anyone. My silence in the face of my own exploitation and assault are my choice. And, as I got to know survivors like Tiffany, Asia, Alyssa, Ashley, Lisa, Tutu, Phoebe, and so many others, I realized my silence was a strange, dark kind of privilege that many who go through sex trafficking do not get to have. Instead, the criminal punishment system exposes them as perpetrators, not victims. They have to fight to be believed in court and, in some cases, the public eye. All their secrets, shames, and struggles laid bare for everyone to judge and form their own opinions about.

You could say that realizing I was sold to those two boys is why I do this work. But it's not that easy. My life's work is not merely a reaction to what those boys—actually young men at the time—did to me. I do this work because I want more justice and kindness in this world, and my experiences give me insight into what that could be for survivors. I want a better world for girls who're coming up behind me.

That starts with believing survivors when they speak their truth. I do this work so that other survivors are believed. I fall asleep thinking of the girls, grants, and people to call. It's easier to shove the memories back into the corners of my mind where they've been silently dwelling since I was fourteen.

* * *

That next day at our office, Macy and I sit on our tiny, used-to-be white sofa. She cries as she tells me about her years of being abused by her adoptive mother and feeling like she has no one else in her life.

"I don't trust that guy, but I like it when he says he loves me. I need that."

We don't have a counselor or a social worker. It's just me, Makiko, and Samantha. I feel out of my depth.

"Please come to our drop-in tomorrow. I know we can figure this out," I say, though I'm not sure I have the know-how or resources to really help her. Macy never comes to the drop-in the next day, and she runs away a few days later.

"She'll turn up," says the woman who runs the foster home.

Maybe, I think. A few days later, the police arrest her for prostitution on New York Avenue, and she's sent to detention. The pimp is never found. When the foster group home director calls me to say Macy is back, I go straight to the home. She's back at home with her adopted mother within a week, though, and I imagine the stress all that yo-yoing around is adding to her life. Two nights before Thanksgiving, which is three days before her eighteenth birthday, Macy calls me again at 2 a.m. Her words are falling between tears and gasps for air.

"Macy, please take a breath. I'm going to help. Just slow down so I can understand you." Her voice starts to come back after a minute of silent crying.

"My mom threw me out. I only have on my t-shirt and underwear because I was going to take a shower. She just threw me out again, and she's threatening to call the cops because we got in a fight."

"Macy, I should call 911 and get them to come get you. It's really too cold for you out there and I don't have a car," I reply as calmly as I can.

I call 911, but they say it's a non-emergency unless she was physically harmed. I keep her on the phone while I try to reach her social worker. No response. I call a youth division detective I know who has over fifteen years of experience working with kids. He doesn't pick up.

At 4 a.m., I hail a cab to her block and pick her up at the bus stop where she's hiding from the sleet falling to the ground. I'd stuffed some of my smaller jeans and a sweater into my bag, and she puts them on as the cab navigates back to my office. She passes out asleep while I look for better clothes for her in our donation boxes. At 7 a.m., we go to a cheap corner cafe and order bagels and fruit. She eats two bagels before we jump in another taxi to drive to Child and Family Services.

We drive past the National Mall, a gray dawn lighting the brown November grass. I point out the Lincoln Memorial, and Macy says she's never seen it before. I insist our taxi driver stop. We get out and walk up the steps, watching our breath create a mist of cold morning fog. We have to see this together.

"Macy, Abraham Lincoln was our president when slavery was abolished in the United States. That was in December 1865, but we still have a long way to go today. Human trafficking is modern-day slavery."

Macy nods. She's too tired and falls asleep again on my shoulder as we drive away.

This starts a tradition of taking FAIR Girls' survivors to the Lincoln Memorial on their first day of freedom. We look up at Lincoln, not saying a word as a few early-bird tourists flutter around in sweaters and coats. It always feels like a profound moment of looking back to see how far we've come while keeping our eye on what we have to do next.

I've never been to Child and Family Services before. After the security guards run every single thing we have through their machines, we sit with our little pull-out number card and wait. Two hours later, her social worker comes out and pulls me to the corner of the waiting room.

"Look honey, that girl is a lost cause. She's grown anyway."

"You can't place her for a few nights until she's eighteen? I just need time to figure out what to do."

"She's gotta learn there are consequences if you want to run the streets," is the last thing she says as she takes a cookie from the holiday tray at reception and walks back inside, sucking her Starbucks coffee down.

I grab Macy's hand, and we stomp out. I've no idea where to go with her, so we take the metro back to the office. As soon as we get to my basement office, Macy wants to sleep. I get the number for her adoptive mother and decide I'd better call her and let her know Macy is with me.

"She isn't going to care, Andrea. I'm a $638 check to her, and as soon as I'm eighteen that business is over."

I dial her number and the theme song for Toys R Us starts to play. Her adoptive mother works at Toys R Us? I introduce myself as soon as the manager gets her on the phone. "Hi, I'm Andrea, and I'm Macy's mentor. I picked her up at four this morning, and she's currently asleep on my sofa." Her adoptive mother begins yelling that I better bring Macy back or she'll call the police.

"Macy reported to me that you kicked her out, and she only had a t-shirt on when I came to get her. Do you really plan to let her stay with you once she turns eighteen?"

She says no with more than one expletive to emphasize her decision. I hang up.

Macy is hungry again when she wakes up, so I go out for pizza. As she eats, I ask her if she has any friends or family we can call. She doesn't, but she remembers a woman named Denise who works at a Sun Trust Bank somewhere in D.C. She met her in church and thought she seemed nice. Denise had joined the youth group on a few outings and always sat next to Macy. That's all I have. Denise. At a Sun Trust Bank. Somewhere in D.C.

As Macy tries on the clothes I found for her, I print out a list of Sun Trusts in D.C, Maryland, and Virginia. I call seven banks looking for a

Denise. It's 4:20 p.m. as I call the eighth bank. Forty minutes before closing time on Thanksgiving Eve, a woman answers and I ask for Denise. "In loans?" she asks.

"Yes, I think so," I say hesitantly. She transfers me.

"How can I help you?" the voice on the other end of the line asks.

My heart pounds. "My name is Andrea. I'm the founder of a nonprofit called FAIR Girls, and a girl named Macy I'm helping says she knows you. Do you know a girl named Macy who you met in church as part of a youth outreach program?"

She says yes. My heart starts racing as I tell her everything I know. I've barely finished when Denise says, "Be here at five o'clock. She's welcome to stay with me as long she needs."

I wake Macy up. "I found Denise! Let's go!"

Macy jumps up and hugs me. "OMG. For real? I can stay with her? Yes!" she screams.

We run to a taxi and make it to the bank. Denise's black 1990s Blazer is rusty but perfectly warm and ready. Macy crawls in with her tiny bag of all she owns. I give Denise my number and tell her I'll be ready twenty-four hours a day to help. Life looks better for Macy, at least for the moment.

* * *

In the next month, we hold six more workshops with girls in foster homes and shelters. The youth workers at the shelters call our office, asking if we can talk to girls who they think might be targets for traffickers. One afternoon, Macy and another teen girl who's been coming to our tiny office ask why the bathtub is filled with boxes of beads and jewelry supplies. I explain that we use the bathroom as storage. "We teach girls in another part of the world how to make and sell jewelry. We call it JewelGirls."

"Well, teach me too," Macy says as she sits down at the wooden kitchen table that lives in the middle of our office. Makiko gives me the side eye as I pull out wire cutters, pliers, and beads, and teach her to make a tiny pearl-and-glass bead bracelet.

"Can I make one for my little sister?" another girl asks.

"Sure, let's do it," I reply. Two more girls come over to join in.

"This is cool. Can we do this tomorrow?" Macy asks.

"Ok, why not?" I say.

Three hours later, we have six bracelets and the beginning of a local JewelGirls program.

Weeks later, there are twelve Black teen girls coming in to make jewelry. Local stores donate snacks, and along the way we develop workshops focused on healing from trauma, talking about feelings, and finding ways to advocate for yourself. Each girl has a plastic box with her name on it that she fills with beads and her creations. We're not trying to build a tiny army of jewelry designers but rather create a safe space for girls to grow their confidence. They often tell us they feel unworthy of belonging, but here they can shine like each bead they string on their creations. Macy says it feels like being brighter than a diamond.

Chapter 3

WELL, I'M HERE TO STAY NOW

*S*oon, we have so many D.C. teen girls in our JewelGirls program that we're looking for a larger space to house the project. One of our partners offers us space at Covenant House, a youth shelter, at no charge on Tuesday and Thursday evenings for three hours. We fill the large room with yoga supplies, donated clothes, toiletries, and over twenty boxes of beads and jewelry-making supplies. In addition to making the jewelry, the girls fill out inventory lists, help order supplies, and price and package their jewelry for customers.

The week before Christmas, we invite all the girls to our office for a homemade meal. I get up at 5 a.m. to begin cooking the potato rolls, sweet jam, pumpkin pies, sweet potato casserole, green bean salad, and pasta. A volunteer is bringing the turkey because as a vegan, I've no idea how to cook one.

One fourteen-year-old girl who I've grown to really care for comes early. As she helps me cut fruit, she picks up a blueberry.

"What's this?" she asks, examining it.

"It's a blueberry. They are the best!"

"It's so big."

It isn't.

"I've only seen blueberries in a can," she adds.

"Here, have a few," I say, turning back to cutting the potatoes.

When I look back moments later, the entire bowl of blueberries is gone. I text Will, "We need more blueberries, can you grab some? We have a blueberry bandit."

Blueberries are expensive, but I've never thought about them as a luxury food. Many of the teen girls who come to dinner that day live in foster care or are in homeless youth shelters. Some of the girls want to go back to school, many have nowhere to go, and shelters are often full. The girls need counseling along with basic things like food and a sense of safety. About half of them need legal help. They come to the drop-in center to meet with our therapists and case managers—a new development that we've been working to add in since my small team isn't trained to help in every capacity. They also come to spend time with other survivors like themselves.

One thing most of them have in common is being sold online, no different than a bicycle or used clothing. It's 2009 and Craigslist has long been a household name to find roommates, bikes, used furniture, and more. I've always liked the community hippie vibe, but until recently, I had no idea their business model included selling online sex ads masked in the "erotic" and later "adult" sections. And that inside that world of consenting adults are also women and children being sold into sex trafficking.

An eighteen-year-old survivor named Asia often shudders when we walk past hotels. She's four foot nine inches and so small that, if she stands behind my five foot seven inches frame, you can't see her. Her short, cropped hair and studious face makes her seem serious even though she's often the one who makes me laugh the hardest. When I see her visceral reaction to the hotels, I wonder how so many men knew where to find her. Was her pimp just wandering around downtown D.C. walking up to random men? That's when Asia shows me Craigslist and Backpage.

"It's so obvious that it's funny, Andrea," she tells me as we sit together in the office. Her pimps had sold her across the country on websites.

While some women are advertising there willingly, among the thousands and thousands of sex ads posted each day on these websites are victims of trafficking. Many of them are victims of economic and social circumstances who've been forced into hotel rooms and photographed for these ads by their traffickers. I scroll through the pages, shocked.

How do people not see this for what it is? I wonder to myself. There are pictures of practically naked women and some of them do not look eighteen, or even fourteen. *Doesn't someone at Craigslist look at these ads? Why would you let abuse go on if you saw it?* Scrolling through the pages and pages of ads, I feel daunted though. Even if it was a priority, law enforcement can't keep up with the hundreds of ads posted every day—and that's just in D.C. alone.

"If you were going to figure out if an ad was a sex trafficking victim and not someone who was selling themselves without a pimp, what would you look for, Asia?" So begins my crash course on how sex trafficking victims are sold online. She rolls a chair over to my desk from the table she was using to apply for jobs.

"So, if the ad says 'no pimps,' that's because there's likely a pimp. And if the ad says 'no black men,' that's also likely a pimp who thinks a Black man is more likely to be another pimp. It's so twisted, Andrea."

"Even on the streets, this is how pimps can maximize profits," Asia says, remembering how her trafficker advertised her: "New to town. Teenage dream. Anything you want. 120 Roses. Two Girl Special. No Pimps. No Cops."

"New to town"? This was true. Asia had no idea what city she was in on any given night. Each week, her trafficker would force her onto a bus or a flight across the country. Asia was first sold in an old, decaying Motel Six in Wisconsin, but soon traveled to Chicago, Dallas, Baltimore, and finally D.C.

"Teenage Dream"? Asia was just eighteen. Only this wasn't her dream. She'd always wanted to be a nurse, not a sex slave. This was a nightmare.

"Anything you want." That meant they didn't have to use condoms. No protection. Asia was at their mercy.

"120 Roses." Who would give 120 roses to a date? Everyone knew this was a transaction, each rose representing $1 in cash. Asia was the product. Sex was the service.

"Two Girl Special." This means two girls were for sale by the same pimp. The other girl was there to control Asia for her trafficker. She was both a victim and victimizing Asia at the same time. Asia said the other girl was older and looked sick.

"No Pimps. No Cops." These are the words Asia said were surefire ways to know that this ad was written by a pimp. The words were signals to other pimps.

Asia explains to me that the ads would end with a coded number like this: 1-Five5Five.Eight28.4Two5Nine, which is the traffickers' attempt to hide actual phone numbers from the cops searching for possible victims or pimps. Most of the time, though, no cops are looking.

Many of the girls who come to FAIR Girls are scared of law enforcement after being arrested or seeing family members shot. I hear countless stories of girls who had to have sex with cops to get out of being arrested. They often were arrested anyway (afterward), and speaking up meant being harassed more once back on the streets.

"Men would line up around the hotel. You had the late-night creeps, the party guys, the married men on their way to work. Some would pay to bring me to their house while their wives and kids were sleeping upstairs. That's called an in-call," she says.

"Didn't someone at the front desk or another hotel worker wonder what was going on with a group of men coming in and out of a hotel room all night?" I ask.

"They didn't care. They just thought I was a hoe, and they were getting their money. I wasn't usually the only girl stuck in a room like that in the same hotel," she answers. Asia had to have sex with five to ten men a night.

One night, she tells me, a man shows up at Asia's hotel room with ropes and a knife. She still has the carpet burns on her knees from where she knelt, begging for her life. After raping her, her attacker leaves and her pimp is nowhere to be found, so she tries to run. It was early in the year, ice glistening on D.C.'s power center, K Street: a lobbyist bullpen by day and a trafficker's playground by night. The cherry blossoms are still more than a month away. A few blocks away, the White House glows in the security lights. Asia is wearing heels and a black dress suited to a summer block party, but the temperature is barely above freezing that night. Asia fears what the trafficker will do if he finds her, so after wandering the streets for half an hour in the frigid cold with no idea what to do or where to go, she goes back to the room. He's waiting for her.

"My pimp decided I needed to be punished for trying to run away, so he put me out on the streets. I was terrified," she says.

Asia had always been told by her trafficker that it was more dangerous to work on the streets, so she was lucky to have him setting her up in hotels. Now, he demands, "You will stay on the track until you make me my money, bitch." Being on "the track" was punishment for trying to run away. It meant she had to walk the streets until someone drove by and wanted to buy her.

That night, instead of getting into a black sedan with a man motioning her to get inside, Asia runs as fast as her four-foot-nine body can go in high heels. Six blocks away, she runs through the doors of a Holiday Inn and waits in the lobby until the guests are gone. Finally, she walks up to the desk manager. Barely containing tears, she says, "I'm out here on my own. I'm eighteen. My pimp is putting me on the streets. I want out."

The manager walks around the counter and offers Asia some tea and fruit while he thinks about what to do. "Do you want me to call the police?" he asks. Asia nods, sinking into the worn, mustard-yellow lobby sofa with exhaustion. She exhales a "yes" and falls asleep.

When the police show up, Asia isn't sure if they're there to save her or arrest her. A week earlier, two local police officers in Prince George's County, Maryland, had set up a sting operation using online ads to find possible sex workers. They went to Asia's hotel room and one of the police officers pretended to be there to buy her for sex. As soon as she agreed to the amount of money he offered her, his partner came in and they arrested her for prostitution.

Asia had been too scared to tell them about her pimp. The officers didn't ask Asia if she needed help. They didn't ask her where she was from or how long she'd been in that hotel room. She spent the night in central booking with a dozen other women who were mostly there for drugs or theft. At 5 a.m., when Asia was released, she was told she would have to go to court in three months to plead guilty or not guilty.

"When I was walking out the door, I heard the female arrest officer say that it must be Christmas because they let the hoe, hoe, hoe go. I ran into the parking lot and he [her trafficker] was there, waiting to take me to D.C."

But the night the Holiday Inn manager calls the police, they take her to a women's shelter. Unfortunately, there are no beds or food available. She thinks of going back to her trafficker. She thinks of trying to go home to Wisconsin, but she has no family to go back to there either. Asia walks out of the shelter, the rain coming down hard. That's when she sees the huge illuminated cross on top of the church in the distance and begins walking toward it.

She's met at the door by Pastor Jeffries, who I'd recently led a training with. Pastor Jeffries calls me early the next afternoon while I'm with my team getting the girls in our drop-in center ready to go back to their group homes or foster families. A new shipment of donated clothing has distracted them from our therapy group, and they are bundling into their new coats and stuffing more clothes in their new backpacks. We call days like that "random Christmas day." Pastor Jeffries asks me to bring clothes and to find Asia a place to stay, then passes the phone to Asia.

"Hi, I'm Andrea. I hear you might need some help," I start.

"I really do," she whispers into the phone.

"Do you feel safe where you are right now?" I ask.

"No. I mean, he wants the money he thinks I owe him," she responds, referring to her trafficker.

"Do you mind if I call a detective to see if he can meet with us to talk about how to make sure you're safe?"

"I guess it's okay," is all she says.

At the same time in a small town in southern Georgia, Tiffany is fifteen years old and already being sold to boys across town in exchange for drugs. She's no longer attending school. Her father has been in jail nine years and her mother is in and out of rehabilitation centers. Like Asia, she feels alone. She's heading down a path that started a lot like Asia's.

Though Tiffany wasn't sold online, she's one of the thousands who are never found by the police or advocates. She was only found by the countless men who bought her because her trafficker had connections in her small Georgia town. The streets and the online world have something in common, though: pimps sell their victims with impunity.

I get connected with Detective Schwalm through another detective who's too busy to take on Asia's case, and he's at my office in ten minutes. I run out into the icy rain and jump in his car with my pink duffle bag of clothing. "Going on spring break?" he quips. I'm used to a little hazing from the detectives, who don't usually trust advocates like me.

We drive through the row houses, onto K Street, and then the highway. We're driving toward a part of town known for historic houses, where a lot of victims are lured by their pimps. Pimps go to the side of town where there are vulnerable girls like Asia, and then take them to places where men want to buy sex, like K Street. The large Baptist church where Asia is waiting for me is at the nexus of it all.

D.C. traffic moves in stilted jolts in-between intersections, so it takes a while to make our way to the church. I wonder if Asia thinks I'm not coming after all.

"Don't worry, she isn't going anywhere," mumbles Schwalm as he looks straight ahead.

"What makes you think you know that?" I reply, not looking at him either.

"Well, you said she has nowhere to go."

That was true.

Back to radio silence.

Ten minutes later, I ask, "How long have you been the lead detective on the human trafficking unit?" I'd just learned of the existence of the unit a few hours earlier. He only offers curt, one- or two-word answers.

But then he asks, "How did this girl get your number anyway?"

"I have a reputation around town."

"Like what, the prostitute whisperer?"

"Okay, now you're just trying to provoke me."

He laughs. "Well, is it working, Rescue Barbie?"

"Hardly, and that's not even close to appropriate," I say back.

He laughs again.

"So, what does that make you? Some disgruntled cop from season one of *Law and Order*?"

"That's my favorite show, thank you."

Back to silence.

Detective Schwalm has that hard look of someone who's seen the worst and expects it to happen every day. His red hair is closely shaven and his blue eyes are circled by worry lines. His skin looks sunburned, but it's just his Irish temper flaring up at the traffic.

"You're so white that you must just blind the pimps before you arrest them," I quip. I'm used to cops throwing shade at me, so I decide to throw some back.

He laughs. "Well, my badge has a really special way of getting people to open up to me."

This time, I laugh too.

"So, I'm going to talk to her first and get her statement," he tells me.

"Really?" I say, looking directly at him this time. "She won't tell you anything. She doesn't know you."

"Well, she doesn't know you either."

"True, but I'm the one with the bag full of food, clothes, and stuff."

"Exactly."

"What?"

"You have stuff she wants. I'll tell her you're ready to give it to her if she's honest with me and helps me with my case."

"Oh, so this is a case now?"

"Well, yeah. I mean, you called me. I didn't come here to be your taxi service."

"Okay, but she just ran away from a pimp. She's terrified of him. She's scared of being arrested. She's not going to talk to you."

"Really? Because people have a very hard time saying no to me." He flashes his badge like a cop in a bad movie.

"Just let me give her some clothes and food to help her feel safe," I say.

"If you give her everything, she won't have any incentive to talk to me or give up her pimp."

"Circle back. She already ran from him. Keep up."

"Well, she needs some motivation."

This is ridiculous, I think to myself.

"Don't roll your eyes at me," he says.

"I didn't."

"You did it in your mind."

"She wants help. She literally ran from him."

"True."

So, I arrive with a surly but possibly effective detective, hoping Asia will trust me and maybe him. The situation is not perfect. Even though we find Asia a place to stay, it's just a hotel for two nights. Finally, an older retired couple who are church friends of one of FAIR Girls' board members invite Asia to stay in their guest room. Their home is two miles from the nearest metro station. When we arrive, dinner is cooking, and Asia immediately starts helping shell the green beans. *This could work*, I think. Three weeks later, a local youth shelter calls me to say that they finally have a bed for Asia in a room with three other young women. She moves in the next day.

Asia has nightmares, a gaping hole in her resume, and fear and anger toward pretty much every man she sees. She also has a prostitution charge with a court date coming up. Character letters from people in the community could help the judge see that Asia is not a criminal but a victim who's doing her best to become a good community member. So, we gather letters from her cafe employer, me, her counselor, a former U.S. Ambassador, and even the great grandson of Frederick Douglass.

On the day, we're up at 6 a.m. to get to court on time. You never know if there will be a train delay, and being late would mean jail. Asia's makeup and hair are impeccable. She looks like a court intern, not a teenage girl charged with prostitution. But I can see her shaking in the extra-small blazer that's still three sizes too large on her tiny frame.

"What if that arresting cop is there?" she asks me. It would be normal for Asia to be scared or even angry at this cop for arresting her. I know I am. But the real reason she's shaking is because the cop took her number and texted her several times, asking her to meet up with him. He referred to her as "baby girl."

"That's the same exact thing my pimp called me when we met," Asia tells me as we walk from the train to the courthouse.

Asia grew up without her mother and father around. Her mother struggled with schizophrenia and left her when she was a baby; the illness Asia most feared she would also have. Her grandmother adopted her, but she struggled to feel accepted at home. By the time Asia met her trafficker, she was walking down the street with her belongings in a trash bag—nowhere to go and no one to call. Her trafficker offered her help and love. She believed him.

I really think that her charges will be dismissed in court. We have proof she's a victim of trafficking. I want to see the prosecutor look like the jerk he is for going after her. We make our case and present our letters. In response, the prosecutor says under his breath as he walks back to his chair and piles of folders, "I'm sick of little Black hoes up in my courtroom." He says it just loud enough for us to hear him, but the judge doesn't appear to notice. I'm too scared to speak up—*what if the judge takes it out on Asia?* I wonder.

The sting of his words makes my eyes water as Asia looks down. Her public defender suggests a deal of community service and a fine. Asia agrees. The only saving grace is that the court clerk misspells Asia's name as "Asias." So, a simple search of her name in public records will not pull these charges up.

"This is the best typo ever," I tell her.

"I guess I just have to hope no one searches my name. I'm one letter away from being unemployable even by McDonalds," she says. Prostitution is a sex crime. Being convicted of a sex crime means not being able to work in most places where a child might be, including a swimming pool or library. Asia also can't apply for jobs in her field of cosmetology because her conviction precludes her from working in industries that involve touching customers. The legal system literally says Asia is not allowed to touch people because of her past arrest. Even two years later, Asia will still be feeling the weight of the arrest as she tries to enroll in cosmetology school, only to be turned down over and over.

After court that day, I ask my husband if it's legal to call a defendant a "little Black hoe." He says we can file a complaint, but Asia doesn't want to. She doesn't want to pursue a complaint against the sexual harassment from the cop who arrested her either.

"They didn't catch my pimp, they charged me, they called me a hoe. I'm just sick of it all. The system is trying to break me."

But the people who make up "the system" don't break her. They make her more determined to rebuild her life and fight back.

One year later, Asia speaks at our second annual FAIR Girls gala at the Austrian Embassy and shares her story with 200 attendees. We work on her story for weeks to make it impactful without sharing too many of her personal details. When Asia begins speaking, the room falls completely silent, and it stays that way throughout her tale. That moment is like a match being struck.

A few weeks later, a woman named Malika Saada Saar, who runs a girls' rights nonprofit, Rebecca's Project, calls to ask if Asia is open to becoming a national survivor voice to speak out against companies like Craigslist.

We set up a meeting at a small cafe a mile from the FAIR Girls office. Malika tells me that a national campaign to fight online sex trafficking is mounting against Craigslist. She thinks that having survivors who have been sold by their traffickers on Craigslist would be powerful and capture the attention of reporters and the CEO of Craigslist, Craig Newmark. She asks me if Asia and I will join them to speak publicly to the media and testify on Capitol Hill. I've never been to Capitol Hill. I've never testified before Congress. I certainly have never spoken to national media alongside a survivor like Asia. But I listen to Malika and take notes to share with Asia.

Asia says yes almost immediately, but we decide she'll remain anonymous for the national media. Her trafficker is still out there, and so is the rapist who almost killed her that night in a Maryland hotel.

Asia pushes herself hard. She goes to counseling and studies for the SATs to apply for college. She's in a housing program and making friends. Her life is moving forward, yet the memory of that horrible night is still with her. She frequently thinks she sees the rapist, even though at this point it's been over a year since the attack. He's still never been found, and neither has her pimp. She was the only one arrested.

I'm not sure if the advocacy will give her purpose or make her feel like she's reliving her past, never truly moving forward. But she wants to help, so a hearing is set for Asia, with advocates, and actress and activist Demi Moore, to speak before congressional members.

The morning arrives, and Asia and I stop to grab coffee and bagels before jumping on the metro. As we stand in line, Asia thinks she sees her rapist. We hail a taxi so she can calm her nerves in private.

"It's okay, Asia. It's going to take time," I say as she twists her bangle bracelets around and around her wrist nervously. "Are you sure you want to do this? You know you don't have to," I tell her as we walk into the Russell Senate Office Building.

"No, I want to. That man bought me off Craigslist. Him and hundreds more," she says. Asia can barely see over the microphone when she joins the panel, so I hunt down a FedEx box for her to sit on.

"Classy, Andrea," she says, laughing.

"Should I have brought a booster seat?" I joke.

"You think you're so funny." She shoves the box on her seat and steadies herself. I go to sit among the congressional staffers and other advocates, watching Asia's face intently. I mouth, "You okay?" Asia rolls her eyes and smiles.

The room falls silent as Congresswoman Maloney begins to speak. "When I learned sex trafficking was happening right here in America, I was shocked. There are hundreds of thousands of children being sold across the country. It's time we do something about it!" After the congresswoman from New York introduces the panel and makes remarks, Asia begins.

"I was walking in the dark. The rain was making the trash bag with my clothes heavy as I walked to the next shelter after my dad kicked me out again. When this cute guy rolled up and said he and his sister could give me a ride, I got in."

Asia stops and stares at the people in the room. They sit frozen in their standard-issue Capitol Hill suits, rows of alternating black, gray, and navy. I can hear my heart beating like a drum against the quiet pause in her testimony. The senators all look transfixed. *Just wait*, I think. I know Asia is going to kill that speech.

"Men would be lining up around the hotel door. My pimp would be around in the parking lot making sure I didn't run, but he didn't care what happened to me in that room as long as he got the money. I had to make $1,000 a night or no food. I had to ask permission to eat." She stops again and looks around the room. I hear the wall clock ticking. Demi Moore looks close to crying. Asia rests both hands around the base of the microphone, her feet dangling from the chair.

"My pimp made money. The men who bought me got what they paid for. Night after night. The men who were letting my pimp sell me on their website made money. Everyone profited but me. My body was the new cocaine. I was the only one who was arrested and spent a night in jail. I can't even do the job I want to do because of that arrest. Girls like me are the drug you can sell over and over again. And there are thousands of us."

She starts in on the owner of Craigslist.

"He's America's biggest pimp. He's just not on the street. He's behind a computer screen. Craig Newmark—do you think girls like me should be for sale on your website? It's well past time you pay for what you're letting happen to girls like me."

While other advocates and survivors go to meet President Obama, Asia is not allowed due to her arrest. I stay behind with her to meet congressional staffers. Asia says she's fine with it, but I can feel the sting.

Four months later, Craig Newmark shuts down the adult section of the Craigslist website. Within weeks of that though, the advertisements are migrating by the thousands to Backpage.

"We have a long way to go, Asia."

"Well, I'm here to stay," she replies.

Chapter 4

MEETING TIFFANY

*S*oon, I'm leading a virtual "street" outreach with my team. I teach our small, growing staff what Asia taught me about how to recognize online sex ads that are veiling trafficking. We search on Backpage and send the ads we're really concerned about to the D.C. Metropolitan Police Department's Human Trafficking Unit. At this time, the unit is mainly just Detective Schwalm, the same detective who helped Asia over a year before. If he isn't available, Officers Melvin and Wilkes answer our calls and texts. So that means there are three police detectives to monitor between 400 and 1,000 ads a night.

When we find ads that we think could be a child or even an adult victim of sex trafficking, we google the phone number. That's how we stumble on websites where men talk about the women they purchase for sex. They're not on the dark web or hidden. In minutes, you can find information about girls who are currently listed on Craigslist or Backpage. Like Asia said in her congressional briefing, pimps like online ads because they're easy for men to use. But that means they're also easy for us to use.

Erotic Review, USA Guide, and Too Sluts are sites where I find the most reviews. Most rate the sex or a girl's body, but some complain that girls are crying, dirty, or try to refuse to have sex. Or they complain that the pimp gave them a hard time for more money. Other times, the Human Trafficking Unit, Youth Services Division, or the FBI call us to help with both adult and child victims of sex trafficking who they find in raids. It feels like a never-ending battle to find victims and then locate a safe place for them to live because most are homeless.

By winter of 2012, we have the media's attention. Still, Backpage's CEOs refuse to change how they manage their website, and the sex ads are growing in number. A survivor who used the name Alyssa recently shared her story with Congress and wants to do more. After meeting her, I offer her a job at FAIR Girls teaching our prevention education workshops to teens in D.C. and Maryland schools. Within three years of launching the school program, we've educated over 2,000 kids.

Alyssa was only fourteen when her traffickers began selling her on websites like Craigslist and Backpage. She was from Boston but had been trafficked across the country. When her trafficker and other women tried to kill her, she nearly died. Instead, she ended up in the hospital where a Boston detective who was leading the city's efforts to stop sex traffickers found her. Alyssa testified against her traffickers, who ended up incarcerated. Alyssa went into hiding with the help of the FBI but struggled with being isolated in a small town hours from Boston.

Alyssa is forceful in her determination to help stop sex trafficking by educating kids on what it is because she had no idea when she was fourteen. She wants to take down the websites that allowed her abuse too. Soon, Alyssa is going with me inside schools around Washington, D.C., and living with a friend of mine while looking for an apartment. Her intense stare and knowledge on sex trafficking online make her a perfect advocate. We make plans to take on Backpage together, alongside Asia and other advocates.

A member of our growing coalition of groups fighting to shut down the adult section of Backpage has a media connection to Nicholas Kristof, a journalist who's been writing about sex trafficking globally for years. He agrees to meet Alyssa and me at his office in the *New York Times* building, a huge, intimidating place.

Alyssa brings all of her court case files in a heavy binder to prove to Mr. Kristof, whom we soon call Nick, that what we say is true. Alyssa points to the scar on her face and tells Nick she received it when her trafficker used a potato peeler to slice her skin. Nick recoils with horror.

That night, we walk around Time Square and Alyssa shows Nick the hotels where she'd been raped. On April 5, 2012, the *New York Times* published his article, titled "Where Pimps Peddle Their Goods," and the next morning Nick calls me early. The Backpage CEOs are trying to discredit our story by saying Alyssa is lying. His response is to call out their investors, including Goldman Sachs, who soon pull their investments. It feels like the beginning of the end for Backpage.

In early summer, a thirteen-year-old girl named Bethany who was trafficked on Backpage and is now four months pregnant wants to share her story to prove what's going on. FAIR Girls doesn't allow children to speak to the media, though. They're too young to understand the lifelong impact of sharing their story. So instead, a supporter helps us hire a twelve-year-old actress, Victoria, to speak Bethany's words in an advertisement that would air on MSNBC, CNN, and the *O'Reilly Show*.

Bethany sits in my office with me and the preteen actress, writing her words and eating pizza. The girls are soon friends, and I hear Victoria say to Bethany, "Girl, we're going to nail those CEOs to the wall!"

I know the CEOs of Backpage will accuse us of lying, but not only is every word true, but Bethany's story also mirrors that of so many survivors who are sold online and came to FAIR Girls.

"Well, bring it," says Victoria when I caution her about the potential backlash.

So, we do. Our ad reads:

> *I thought he was my boyfriend. I thought he loved me for real. But he made me work every day. He threatened me; he made me take drugs. He raped me a bunch of times. And then, he sold me to four, sometimes five, men a day for $100 an hour. One time, there was ten men in one day. I thought they would kill me. I thought I'd never get away. My pimp advertised me online at Backpage.com. That's how these guys would buy me . . .*

The video closes with a close-up of Victoria's face, shadowed by her braids. The faded gray room looks like a hotel room and, as Victoria speaks, she becomes more and more clear while the background fades completely to gray. As she stares into the screen, her eyes glisten and she plays with her plastic bracelets. The video ends with, "I'm thirteen."

MSNBC is the first media outlet to pick it up. My friend Krystal Ball has just launched a new show, *The Cycle*, and she invites me and Victoria to talk about the ad. Sitting on the set with twelve-year-old Victoria, I whisper, "We're about to make some pretty powerful boys mad."

She smiles. "Bring it," she says again.

"Why did you create this advertisement? How does it relate to your work?" asks Krystal as the set lights almost blind me.

"Almost every single sex trafficked girl we have assisted in the U.S. this year was sold by her pimp using the adult section of Backpage.com. In the past year, the number of girls we have assisted has more than doubled. For us, this is not just a campaign. This is about protecting real girls from being victimized," I reply.

By now, we have allies all across the country. Backpage is owned by Village Voice Media, and our "ask" is for the twenty-six major advertisers in Village Voice Media's thirteen local publications to immediately discontinue advertising. If the CEOs of Backpage are only interested in money, we think, then we'll take it from them. Backpage's online advertisements selling sex earn around $27.4 million.

"Basically, we want to take their toys," Victoria says.

"If they want to do business with pimps, then they shouldn't be doing business with anyone else. This is about human rights. This is about showing that no one deserves to be sold, raped, and left behind like an old bike after it's used," I add.

FAIR Girls is joined by fifty attorneys general in a letter from the National Association of Attorneys General, 700 clergy from Auburn Seminary, four U.S. senators, Change.org, and some of the biggest organizations fighting human trafficking in the country, including Polaris Project (which ran the national human trafficking hotline). AT&T,

Barnes & Noble, Best Buy, and IHOP soon follow Goldman Sachs in pulling out.

"Power of the people," declares Victoria as we take a photo outside the NBC building with peace signs. But we both know this fight is far from over. That afternoon, media outlets all over the country want to talk. A reporter named Geraldine Sealey reaches out from *Marie Claire*, a magazine I've been reading since high school. A few weeks later, Geraldine comes to D.C. to shadow Alyssa and me during our outreach on the streets. To preserve the privacy of the teenage girls who visit our drop-in, we wait until they leave to begin the interview.

We plan to walk her through how we searched for victims in online advertisements in our office, and then head out to the K Street track where girls are often sold. While Alyssa shares her story and we search for possible victims on Backpage, a photographer not-so-quietly photographs us. I worry that all this media attention might lead to someone recognizing us. Alyssa's pimps have been in jail for years, but she once told me that they know people who could get to her.

We're scrolling down the ads when I see a girl who doesn't look older than twelve or thirteen. She's lying on a bed in lime-colored babydoll lingerie and furry slippers. She's small with no curves at all. She's staring, with an empty expression, into the camera as she lays on the bed with her legs spread. The bedspread and carpet make me think she's in a cheap hotel on the outskirts of D.C. that I know well from our outreach.

"I have to report this," I say to Alyssa and the reporter. Officer Wilkes answers my call. "Oh crap, she does look young," she agrees as she looks at the ad on her screen. Sometimes I need to convince law enforcement that someone might be a victim, but not this time. Officer Wilkes says they'll go out to see if they can find her. I know that means she and her partner, Officer Melvin, will likely respond to the advertisement, pretending to be a sex buyer.

After I get off the phone with Officer Wilkes, I explain to Geraldine why it's risky to report a possible victim. A lot of the time, police who find girls like this will arrest them, either because they don't know they're victims or because they want to use them to get to the pimp. More and more, Officers Wilkes and Melvin are bringing the girls they find to FAIR Girls. But sometimes they arrest them first to make sure they show up to grand jury and testify against their trafficker.

"Why would you arrest them? That's like arresting a victim of rape," I once argued with Detective Schwalm.

"No, it's different. We need to get to the pimp, and they might run away before we can," he replied.

"It's like serial rape for profit. You're arresting the wrong person."

We still don't see eye to eye on this, but we do find a lot of girls who need help.

There are tattoos on this girl in the ad that look like branding too. Dollar signs, cherries, pimp names, words like "Daddy." Alyssa and I point this out to Geraldine, and she writes it down in her notepad.

"In a city with up to 1,000 ads a night on Backpage alone, it's almost impossible to find all the victims," I tell Geraldine as we head out, walking toward K Street. We'd likely find more possible victims online, but the track was still out there too. We decide to stop at a bar where I know pimps hang out. "This is old school outreach," I say as we settle in amid the glittery lights, liquor, pulsing music, and dancers.

"So, when you send these detectives the ads, they might arrest girls like the one we saw?" Geraldine quizzes me.

"They might. But if a girl like her needs help, I'm not going to just walk away. I don't want her to be arrested either—that's where stories like yours can help. We can stop the arrests and still stop the traffickers. Plus, we show how trafficking really happens."

"So, places like Backpage basically are like an open source to find victims?"

"Yes, but you can't start a fire and then claim to help put it out. Backpage CEOs say they help law enforcement. But I report ads like the one we saw today to them and they do nothing. The same ads show up over and over again after we report them."

I get a text later that morning from Officer Wilkes: "She's eighteen. Said she didn't want help." I wish they would have let me talk to her before just walking away. I text Geraldine the update, saying, "I could have shown her that there were people who could help her."

The pressure of it all is starting to take a toll on me. I feel guilty if I'm out with friends and not answering every call from every girl who reaches out. I feel guilty if I don't open our drop-in on weekends. I bend the rules of our lease at the drop-in, where we're not allowed to have girls stay overnight. We meet the girls at the police station, hotels, or hospitals and wait until 12:30 a.m., when it's technically morning, to let them rest at the office. Our landlord doesn't appreciate my literal interpretation of "overnight," and we're constantly at risk of being evicted. The idea for a safe home has been circling in my head, but I'm not sure how to go about making it a reality.

A few weeks later, we're working with another nineteen-year-old survivor whose violent trafficker is well known for kidnapping girls from other traffickers. He's also known for hurting girls with what's called a "pimp circle."

"Basically," Alyssa explains to me, "this is what happens if a victim does something to break a rule, like trying to keep some of the money they make or walk on the sidewalk and not the streets. A group of pimps makes a circle around you, and they threaten and assault you until you look one of them in the eyes. Then, he owns you."

Alyssa knows what it means to break the rules. That's how she got a scar on her stomach. Her trafficker sent other women to kick her until she lost her baby when she was four months pregnant. Our new nineteen-year-old client had survived a pimp circle, and she quickly bonds with Alyssa.

One afternoon, Alyssa is out buying clothes for our new client when a trafficker walks up to them in the mall. He recognizes both of them. Pimps often work together, and this one knows Alyssa's pimp. Alyssa runs, but our client stays behind. She never comes back to our office. The next day, the trafficker forces her to deliver threats to Alyssa and me by handing messages to a twelve-year-old girl walking into our office.

We shut the whole office down, and my husband meets me so we can walk home together. I beg Alyssa not to leave her apartment. That night, she continues to send me screenshots of text threats from the trafficker, who'd been given her number by our client. He says if we call the police, he will kill our client or us.

My husband knows law enforcement in the area because of his work and insists we call the police even though I desperately don't want to do anything to make Alyssa more at risk. "Andrea, you have to think of yourself and us too. Come on," he pleads. He calls them even though I say no.

The trafficker is never found, and neither is our client. I hide at home for days, sick with worry for her, Alyssa, and myself. The experience scares me so much that I don't want to do any more media. I don't want to do anything to put us out there where traffickers can see us. I'm sick of Backpage and the constant pressure of more and more girls coming to us. I want to go back to having Saturdays free for planting flowers and making dinner.

Will is quiet as we eat Thai carryout a week later. He's like that when he's worried. My phone rings next to my plate. It's Detective Schwalm. "It's probably a new girl he found," I say. I forget to be scared for a moment and get up to go into the other room to talk to him.

"How far are you going to take this, Andrea?" Will asks as I walk away.

The honest answer is, I don't know.

* * *

"How do you know the difference between a victim of sex trafficking and a sex worker?" I ask.

Alyssa and I are standing in front of the green chalkboard, looking at about thirty D.C. high school students. Some are giggling; some are ignoring us. A few stare intently. At least three are sleeping. We're doing another prevention education workshop inside a local high school.

"If only I'd known what trafficking looked like, maybe I wouldn't have fallen for their trap," says Alyssa.

"Wait, so you were a hoe?" a boy asks.

Alyssa's face falters for a moment, her arms going defensively across her chest, but then she narrows her eyes and steps toward the desks. "You have a lot to learn today, so I would listen up," she says to him.

The first time I walked into a D.C. public school to talk to kids and teachers about trafficking, I walked out with two teen girls who needed help. The teacher referred to the girls as "little prostitutes" whom I could "talk sense into" if I met them. Five years later, FAIR Girls has educated over 3,000 students in D.C.

Even other advocates who work to support survivors of trafficking said we were wasting our time. They said American kids weren't being trafficked, or, if they were, it was rare. These were the stereotypes we were up against. But here is Alyssa, an American woman trafficked as a teen in Boston, going into D.C. schools with me to help prevent the exploitation and abuse that happened to her. Being in these classrooms is part of our way of shifting compassion toward kids who are called "runaways" or "lost causes."

After Geraldine's *Marie Claire* article comes out, we have press inquiries about Backpage from across the country. The one that stands out is from a reporter named Yamiche Alcindor from *USA Today*, so we invite her to join us and see how we work.

That day, Yamiche spends hours with Alyssa and me, first following us into the school to watch our training. I'm still battling the fallout from the trafficker who threatened Alyssa and me two months earlier. I'm often too nervous to walk home alone, and Will walks from his law firm on K Street to meet me. Detective Schwalm says he heard our client was back with her pimp and likely in Baltimore. That should mean Alyssa and I are safe, but I still need to sit facing the door when I visit cafes. I take note of all the exits in any room I enter. I feel I need to always be on the lookout.

At the school training, we introduce ourselves and explain the definition of human trafficking. We show them a video created by a survivor and nonprofit leader named Rachel Lloyd to help illustrate. As Rachel narrates the story, we see the point of view of a twelve-year-old girl who lives in New York with her mom who's struggling. She's lured by an older man offering to take care of her, but after buying her gifts, he forces her to dance in a club.

As they watch, we go to the chalkboard and Alyssa writes "Prostitute/ Hoe" in big words on the left side, and on the other she writes "Sexually Exploited Child." She draws a line down the middle.

After the video ends, she asks the kids, "When you think of the words 'prostitute' or 'hoe,' what words come to mind?" After some giggles, a few students start to shout out words like, "dirty, stupid, skank, thirsty, money, trash, dog." The list of insults goes on.

"How old do you think a prostitute is?" Alyssa asks. More giggles. They shout out ages anywhere from twenty to eighty.

The words and ages fill up the left half of the chalkboard.

"So, what words come to mind when you think of 'sexually exploited child,' I ask. Immediately, the teens start shouting out, "sad, scared, abused, foster care, rape, homeless, lonely, hungry."

"So how do you know if the girl or boy you see who you think is selling sex for money is a 'hoe' or a 'sexually exploited child?'" I ask. Silence.

"I don't know," says one boy. The giggling has stopped.

"That's the point," says Alyssa. "You don't know, so instead of judging, you can help. Next class, we're going to give you a list of places you can go for help if you or someone you know needs help."

A week earlier, a thirteen-year-old girl had drawn a picture of a girl's face covered in bruises with notes under each bruise: "She didn't make enough money," "She said no," "She tried to leave him that one time." We've been worried about her. This time, she writes a note in purple marker that reads, "She's really sad because no one cares." Alyssa and I see it on her desk before she folds it up and puts it in her bag.

Alyssa and I look at each other. It's become an unspoken language of ours to send a quiet look to say, *I think this kid needs help.* The girl lingers behind as the bell rings and other kids run to their next class.

"Hey, you have a way of seeing how things really are," I say. "Do you like to draw?" I try to sound positive, so she won't feel like I'm trying to "social work" her. A lot of these kids are well aware of being "social worked"—they fear that telling their worst secrets to a social worker might land them in foster care or get them in trouble with an angry parent who'll take it out on them later.

"I guess I just see stuff. A lot of these girls are really already messed up before they even get out there," she replies.

I hand her my card with my number and tell her that we have a fun jewelry-making group at our drop-in, and she can come try it out if she wants to. She shoves my card in her purple satchel and says, "I'll think about it." But she smiles, just a little.

It's usually girls who're reaching out for our help, but boys leave us notes or call the office too. As I look through the comments box, I find a note from the boy who'd been making jokes. "My dad is in the life. My uncle is a pimp too. I don't want to go down that way. What do I do?"

I don't have an answer.

As the next class trickles in for us to teach, Yamiche is writing in her notebook. Alyssa erases everything under the two phrases: "Prostitute/ Hoe" and "Sexually Exploited Child."

"How do you know the difference?" we ask once the new group settles in. They call out the predictable words for each side. Then I ask how they would know the difference if they saw a girl or boy on the street who looked like they were "a hoe" or a "sexually exploited child." One boy answers, "You can't know the difference, I guess. I mean, not for sure."

"Did you know that the average victim of sex trafficking is fourteen when they're first exploited?" I ask.

"That's so sick. Who does that to kids?" a Latina girl in a hoodie asks, lifting her head off the desk and looking at us. I didn't even realize she was listening because she's been staring down the entire time. Sometimes, the kids ask for help with their body language more than with their words.

Alyssa asks, "So, if the average age is fourteen and the average length of time being sold for sex is four years, you're looking at this: some adult sex workers were once child victims of trafficking. What do you think of that?"

"I guess I see these people out there in a new way," says a boy in a football jersey. "So, what do I do if I think someone needs help?"

I feel a lightness in my heart.

"Our goal is to build up sympathy so that the kids we teach know that there's help out there and that they don't have to be ashamed if something is going on," I share with Yamiche as we ride back on the D.C. metro to the office. My bag is full of the kids' drawings, which we lay out on the table when we return. It paints a picture of just how much these kids already know about trafficking, even if they've never really thought of it as a crime or something that could happen to them. Yamiche takes photos.

Alyssa talks about the fact that another woman groomed her for their pimp. The other woman showed Alyssa, who was sixteen at the time, how to set up dates, take photos, and even decide which sex buyers were "safe" or not. "Soon, I didn't have a choice. He took me out of school, dragged me to parties, and beat me if I didn't do what he said. I ended up in the hospital after he had other girls kick me until I had a miscarriage."

That is when Alyssa finally got out. Alyssa helped put her trafficker in jail, and she was still in witness protection when I met her.

Yamiche takes notes as Alyssa talks about how she was then forced to find more victims like herself. "I'd go to schools, malls, group homes, bus stops, and search online—wherever there were vulnerable girls. And I knew where to look because I was one."

We take a break, and I pull Alyssa out to the hallway to talk alone.

"Be careful. What if she takes all you're saying and makes it out like you're the bad guy?"

Alyssa refuses to stop. "If she doesn't report that, girls will just be trafficked more. They need to know that pimps force their girls to do this because they'll trust another girl more than a guy sometimes."

Alyssa is right. We see it all the time, and people don't want to see the cycle of violence, so it continues. Still, I stare at Yamiche nervously while Alyssa and I show her what trafficking signs we look for on Backpage. Will she believe that there are victims among those willingly selling sex? That some are as young as thirteen?

In mid-September, I'm walking to work and every Starbucks has *USA Today* outside for sale. I had no idea our story would be on the front page, above the fold, with Alyssa's face in the photo. The story is excellent and media inquiries skyrocket, but so do the obscene emails. There continues to be a complete lack of response from Backpage. What I think should have been a tsunami of impact feels like a drop in the bucket, and more and more ads are going up every night.

A month later, I'm alone in my office desperately writing donor letters, hoping we'll make it through another few months. The girls are outside on our patio, where the air already has that warm-fireplace aroma that's a sure sign winter is around the corner. Their chatter is about boys, music, and issues in the shelters or at home. They stay late, waiting on a few boxes of donated coats to arrive. They all need coats. They look like a typical group of friends hanging out with pizza and a huge salad that only I will eat. They're typical girls, but they're also the typical kind of girls that become victims of trafficking, suffering years of abuse, stints in detention, and family homelessness. People passing by on their way home from work or headed to a restaurant will only hear the laughter of a group of teen girls hanging out, though. They won't see the pain.

I would be out there with them, but I'm stuck at my desk, running the numbers over and over to figure out how to pay our rent and salaries. At this point, it's been eight years and those stressors never go away. The girls on our patio depend on us for food, clothes, counseling, and support. We get endless mail from people asking for help. Yesterday, the FBI brought yet another girl to our door who's fifteen and pregnant. My case manager drove her to a local youth shelter, where she'll stay until she finds a long-term foster placement.

Will texts to ask me when I'm coming home. "I don't know but maybe around 6:30," I text back. We both know that won't happen. On my way out the door at 9 p.m., I grab a letter I've been curious about all day. It has a jail inmate stamp.

After dinner, I curl back up on the sofa and tear the letter open. I read the words that opened this book, the first words I received from

Tiffany Simpson. *I am 18 and when I was 17, I was arrested for sex trafficking and I'm doing 20 of 30 years in prison down here in Georgia.* I already knew that she didn't belong in Pulaski State Prison, but I want to know more about her.

I search her name online: "Tiffany Simpson + Georgia + sex trafficking." I find an article about her arrest on a local Georgia TV station website. *My pimp said I was not making enough and he used my phone to convince this other girl to come with us.* All the article says is that she was arrested along with her boyfriend for sex trafficking another teen girl. There's a mugshot too. Her freckled, seventeen-year-old face looks terrified and exhausted in her arrest photo—a picture that shouldn't have been shown online in the first place given she's a minor when she's arrested. The article refers to her as a woman.

So, she's a child who trafficked another child with her boyfriend? Something doesn't add up. My mind is already full of questions.

The article says her boyfriend is thirty-four, twice her age. He looks angry in his arrest photo; his expression hostile and his eyes full of the dull emptiness that those hardened by not caring about life tend to have. I click back to the search results and scroll for more, swapping out my search terms when nothing relevant pops up. But that's the only article about her case I can find. She's been in jail for almost a year.

He said he was going to burn down my grandmother's house and stab our baby out of me if I didn't do it. Well, there it is, I think. A seventeen-year-old girl was trafficked and forced to contact another girl. Sex traffickers often coerce their victims to commit crimes like robbery or recruiting another victim. It's a way of further ensnaring them. They use violence, threats, and promises to ensure that their victims do what they say.

According to the Trafficking Victim's Protection Act and Georgia state law, you don't have to prove coercion when you're talking about a child victim of sex trafficking because a child can't consent to a commercial sex act. Still, even if Tiffany had been eighteen, there's coercion with the threats to burn down her grandmother's home. In the eyes of the law, it's not about whether he would have followed through on his threats, it's about whether Tiffany believed he would. Tiffany doesn't know this. Even most of the police officers we train don't know that fact.

Now, I can't see my son and my pimp's mom is trying to get custody of him from my mom. I'm worried I'll lose him forever. So many sex trafficking victims do lose their children. Her fear is real, and now her trafficker's mother could get her son, whose name is Ayden.

I saw that girl Alyssa's story in that USA Today *story you were in.* My heart flutters—I had felt so discouraged after that article barely ruffled any feathers, but Alyssa's bravery led Tiffany to question her sentence and the narrative the system had pushed on her.

So, I wanted to know. Am I a victim of sex trafficking or a prostitute?

Chapter 5

WHERE SHE BELONGS

Dear Tiffany,
We got your letter yesterday. I read it right away! Thank you for
trusting us with your story. I don't know all the ways we can help
you, but I am going to talk to our team so we can come up with
some ideas.

I dive straight in. First, I tell Tiffany that based on what she wrote, I fully
believe that she was a victim of sex trafficking. I tell her what that actually
means, writing out the Trafficking Victim Protection Act's legal definition
in the way we share it with the kids in our classrooms.

Any child who is involved in a commercial sex act—like prostitu-
tion or pornography—is considered a victim of human traffick-
ing. So, even if you did it not for money but, say, for love, a place
to stay, clothes, or even drugs—it does not matter. And, even if
you thought your trafficker was your boyfriend, it also does not
matter. You were a victim of human trafficking. If you are over
eighteen, you have to prove that your trafficker forced, frauded
(like tricking you), or coerced you (like saying they would burn
your grandmother's house down).

I pause to look up the Georgia law on arresting children for prostitution and trafficking. Your rights are dependent on where you live, not what happened to you. At this time, some states will not arrest children for prostitution, and some even allow for other crimes to be excluded, like running away, if it is related to the child's trafficking.

When I first read the federal Trafficking Victims Protection Act of 2000, it was clear to me that it meant any child involved in commercial sex was a victim of sex trafficking. I didn't understand why individual state laws were needed to enforce this. But in 2009, New York passed the first safe harbor law to codify this effort. Georgia still didn't have any provisions, though.

"Andrea, you have to eat." Will had been to get us pizza before our favorite Italian restaurant closed. I put my pen down and got up to pour two glasses of wine. I try to stay present as Will talks about his latest case and a new jazz show we should go to at the Kennedy Center. Will is the smartest person I've ever met, and he's amazing at his job. Back in graduate school, he would skip classes and still do better than me on exams. But right now, I can't stop thinking about Tiffany's question. *Am I a victim of sex trafficking or a prostitute?* So, after we finish dinner and do the dishes, I slide over next to him on the futon.

"Hey, so just hypothetically, if there was a girl who—"

Will laughs. "Andrea, please, what's her name?"

I smile. He knows me too well. "Okay, so I got this letter from an eighteen-year-old in jail in Georgia. She was arrested for sex trafficking when she was seventeen, and she was sentenced to thirty years in jail. I don't think she should be there. How do we help her get out?"

"Let me see the letter," Will says. I already have it in my hand. He reads it a few times, slowly. He looks up at me. "That's really sad. I feel bad for her. You need to find out more, Andrea. If her story is true, her attorney could try to strike a deal with the prosecutor on a habeas hearing, but we don't really know any facts at all."

He's right and I know it. I'm feeling out of my depth; I don't know what a habeas hearing is. "I know, I guess I'm already a little invested.

I feel bad for her in there alone, and she looks so young in those arrest photos with her ponytail and freckles."

Will kisses me on the cheek and then gets up, heading for bed. "Don't stay up too late writing to the new girl."

I nod. How can a child be arrested for trafficking another child if they were being threatened? It doesn't make sense. I curl up on the futon and keep writing.

There are more donor letters to write and texts from our crisis line to respond to, but it's Tiffany's letter that I can't let go of. I've never written to anyone in jail before and don't know what the requirements are that would allow her to receive mail. So, I decide to use the same kind of lined paper and black ink that she did.

I want Tiffany to know the word "survivor," so I copy passages from other survivors' stories and how they overcame their past.

> *Tiffany, you aren't a prostitute, and you aren't just a victim. You are a survivor and there are others—many others—like you. Just the fact that you wrote to me so bravely and shared some of your hardest truths shows me that some part of you believes in yourself too.*

I don't want Tiffany to sit in that jail feeling like no one cares and sinking into a state of depression because she feels like she's just a victim. Labels can hurt and words matter. I've never liked the term "victim" because it takes away your agency.

The next pages I write are more personal. She told me how she ended up in jail, so I decide to tell her how I started down this path with survivors like her.

Writing about Aischa takes pages. Then, I write about my friend who was bullied in school. I even tell her I've been through some bad things in high school and know what it's like to have someone you love betray your trust, leaving you too ashamed to tell anyone or ask for help. I end the letter by asking Tiffany to write back and tell us more about her life before she met her boyfriend. *What is your most pressing need that we can help with right now?*

I feel myself fading to sleep with the lights on. It's 2 a.m.

The next thing I'm aware of is the sound of the city bus stopping near our door with its distinctive hiss. The robins are singing outside in our holly tree. I open my eyes, the tassels of a plum-colored blanket tickling my cheek, and realize the pen is still clenched in my fist. I see pages of my letter to Tiffany all over the floor. I must have passed out in the living room while I was writing. Will must have turned the light off and put my favorite blanket over me before he headed out to the gym.

My almost-dead phone says it's just after 7 a.m. My head thuds sluggishly, trying to fire up after yet another night of minimal sleep. I call this an "activist hangover," and lately I've been looking "hungover" a lot. Being your own boss means it's up to you say, "Time to clock out," which in my case rarely happens. But I can't go back to sleep. The girls will soon be hanging around the drop-in entrance door waiting for me to let them in by 8 a.m.

Now that I'm awake, I'm wondering if I shared so many things with Tiffany for her sake or for my own. I pull out an envelope and fold the ten double-sided pages of my letter inside. I throw on my black wool coat and knit pink hat and lock the door.

D.C. was never a place I wanted to live, but Will's first job after law school drew us here. It took me two years to feel like this could be home. Now I know all the cafe owners around our Dupont Circle apartment and where to score free day-old food for the girls.

By the time I'm at the office with two bags of bagels, the girls are standing around the drop-in door, waiting with their hands shoved in their pockets as the cold air creates clouds from their exhalations that are making them laugh. Asia grabs one of the bagel bags and mumbles, "You could always ask me to come help you, you know."

"I know," I say as I turn the key. A few minutes later, our first case manager arrives and calls some of the girls to start filling out their rapid housing applications.

"'Rapid' housing. I don't think they get what that word means," says Asia, referring to the people who process and approve the applications. It took three years before Asia got her own place through this process. For some girls, it takes nine months to get a housing voucher, and even then it might be so far away that getting to and from school or work would cost $12 a day on the train. That's too expensive for someone who might be in school and working part-time at a minimum wage job. When donors ask me what survivors need after trafficking, I sometimes reply, "Everything," because it's true.

Some of the girls fall asleep on our donated sofas, which used to be white but now look like an abstract expressionist painting done in Starbucks latte spills. We let the girls sleep if they want to because living in the shelters means always staying a little awake to make sure no one steals your stuff, picks a fight with you, or bullies you, though so much worse can happen.

My program director, Teresa, comes into the office. Teresa had been a *Washington Post* reporter working on a story about Asia and her arrest. When we needed a new director of programs, she applied, and I hired her on the spot. She tells me we might have two more girls from the FBI coming that night. The FBI always gets involved if a child victim of sex trafficking is identified—it's a federal crime. We like this because this means the trafficker may get more years in jail and we'll have more resources for housing and care for our young client.

I know that the D.C. police are doing a sting operation in what is called a "residential brothel," which is basically a run-down apartment where sex trafficking is taking place. They pop up with several women and girls and then disappear when the traffickers move on, making them more difficult for police to find. These brothels are often run by gangs who are also selling drugs or weapons. Most of the victims are from Latin America, especially Mexico and El Salvador. If the girls and traffickers are from El Salvador, as they are in this case, then the sex buyers need to also be from El Salvador. This makes it easier for the traffickers to hide from the police or rival gangs. The women and girls are often forced to have sex twenty to forty times a night, and the men who buy them pay them in tokens worth as little as $15 a sex action. Then, the women give the tokens to the trafficker controlling the brothel so that the trafficker knows how much each woman made for them.

This means the FBI or D.C. police have to find an El Salvadoran undercover detective who can get in the door to figure out if there's trafficking. It's a long shot to say the least. Many women and girls are never found after they disappear into such a brothel, and more and more D.C. brothels are popping up due to the ease of finding buyers on Backpage and other sex sites.

Teresa and I both know this means we'll need to find hotel rooms, food, and pro bono attorneys if the FBI is successful and brings us the girls or women. We can't use shelters because the traffickers likely know where those are. I'm calculating the costs in my head and thinking of our bank account, which contains barely enough for rent.

"We really need our own safe house, like yesterday," says Teresa as she sinks into her chair. "Too bad our grant application to the office of Victims of Crime Assistance was denied because D.C. government thinks that human trafficking isn't enough of a 'gender-based problem' and $60,000 is too much money for us to handle."

I sigh. Everything is piling up. "Teresa, look at this letter we got from a girl in jail in Georgia," I say, pulling Tiffany's letter out of my bag. She reads it while I google the phone number of the sheriff in the county where she was arrested. "Maybe he'll remember Tiffany's case," I say, writing down the number.

Teresa hands the letter back. "That's really screwed up. Are you going to write her back?" I show her my thick envelope and she smiles. "I'll write to her too." I know she will.

"I'm going to call that sheriff and see what he knows."

"He's not going to talk to you, Andrea."

Maybe not, but I'm about to pull out some of my Southern charm.

Teresa is tough—she has strong Italian roots, mixed with growing up in the wild west of Prince George's County, Maryland, and combined with years doing street outreach and working with survivors in the Bronx. She's always the one to go with me at 3 a.m. to police stations, McDonald's, or wherever we find our clients. Her brown hair, darker skin, and big brown eyes make her my physical opposite. As we pulled into the police stations around town to negotiate for the release of our clients after their arrests, we'd joke, "You be a crazy advocate and I'll be a sweet advocate." Like Asia, most of our "older" clients, and even some of the girls who were under eighteen, were arrested on prostitution charges. The youngest girl arrested was thirteen.

Teresa leaves our office to meet with her clients while I call the sheriff's office. My internet search shows that the population of Cairo, Georgia, where Tiffany is from, is only about 9,000, so I feel like he'll remember. I call Grady County first because that's where she and the other victim, Kassie, were first trafficked. Tiffany had faced charges and was sentenced in both Grady and Baker County, though. I dial and it just rings and rings. I hang up and try again ten minutes later. Finally, the secretary answers and transfers me to his line.

When the Sheriff answers, he says, "What can I do for you?"

My heart is racing a little. *Why am I so nervous*, I think to myself.

"Thank you for the time. I'm Andrea Powell and I'm the director of a nonprofit called FAIR Girls. We serve young women and girls who are survivors of sex trafficking."

"We received a letter from a teenage girl named Tiffany Simpson who was arrested in Baker and Grady County on, well, several charges, but also sex trafficking. I think she's a victim though."

I know I'm overstepping. Detective Schwalm often says overstepping is a form of exercise for me because I constantly ask for things he can't do. My favorite overstep is trying to get my client's phones back before he's done processing them for evidence. Sometimes I win though, so I keep on overstepping.

He's silent for a moment, but I can hear fingers on a keyboard. "I don't recall her case. Are you sure she was arrested in Grady?" he asks.

I have the arrest charges in front of me from their criminal database. *He doesn't recall a seventeen-year-old girl arrested for sex trafficking? It was even in the news. How many police officers do they even have there?* My mind is running in circles.

"I'm sure, sir."

"Do you have her arrest information?"

"I do. Her case number is 2257768. Tiffany wrote to me that she was trafficked by her then thirty-four-year-old pimp, Yarnell Donald. He would have been arrested along with four other men who paid to rape her and another teenage girl."

He sucks in his breath. "I see. So how do you know this Tiffany Simpson? I mean, how did she find you?"

"She said she was reading a *USA Today* article that featured me, my organization, and a survivor colleague of mine. She wondered if we could help her."

"I see, but I don't see how I can help you."

"I'm concerned Tiffany was a victim of child sex trafficking. She was arrested and sent to jail for twenty years but should have gotten help like the other girl." My heartbeat continues to pound.

"Sounds like she's right where she belongs. She's a child molester. She helped her Black boyfriend rape a girl and they got caught."

Now I'm the one sucking in my breath. Teresa was right, he's not going to help us. I'm not sure what I really want from him anyway. He can't un-arrest Tiffany. He can't give her a year of her life back. But he also can't make her disappear—we see she's there.

"Sir, maybe it's better I learn more about her case from someone else."

"Good luck," is all he says before the phone clicks and I'm left in silence.

What does Yarnell being Black have to do with Tiffany's being arrested for sex trafficking? I wonder. No cop in D.C. would have said that to me. Unlike the sheriff I just spoke to, D.C. police know they'll get in trouble at even the hint of racism. But even though in D.C. they have whole units like LGBTQ, Sexual Assault, Youth, and Human Trafficking, police still arrest victims. Now, I'm faced with a small, Deep South town in Georgia and all the racial and gender-based baggage that comes with that.

I wonder what Tiffany is doing right now. I wonder if she thinks I'll ever write her back. I take my letter out of my bag again, pull out the last page, and write one more line.

Tiffany, we will do everything we can to help you get out of there. I promise. Then, I seal the envelope and walk to the mailbox.

I'd no idea how long it would take to make that promise come true, or how hard it would be to keep, but at that moment, I felt my life intertwining with Tiffany's. I wasn't going to let her fade away.

Chapter 6

HOW TO BE A MOM

Over a month later, I haven't heard anything back from Tiffany. Her original letter is still stuffed in my journal, and I see it every day.

Maybe she changed her mind and doesn't want help, I muse. *Or maybe I scared her off with my massively long letter.* Not to mention Teresa wrote to her too, along with our case manager, Priya, who has an infectious laugh and joyful energy that all our clients love. Priya is an Indian American who grew up in Georgia, so she understands well the prejudices that women deal with in the Peach State.

Asia says I should write to Tiffany again. I'm thinking about it but don't want to come across as pushy. *What if she didn't get our letters, though?* It's the day before I'm leaving for Thanksgiving weekend with Will and his parents, and as I'm collecting my things from our office, I decide to write another letter to her on the flight.

D.C. is already a ghost town. Many people flee the city to see family and friends on weekends and especially on holidays. Most of my clients are stuck here though, many without family. We've just finished our Thanksgiving lunch for the girls and are quickly cleaning up the mess of secretly vegan yam pie crumbs. I learned years ago that calling any food "vegan," even if it's just an apple, would result in the girls refusing to eat it. They don't ask if my yam pies are vegan though, and I don't tell.

"Girls, we have to go," I say to the last few. "It's getting dark." They groan as they grab their bags of leftover food and new knit mittens a sweet grandmother has made them. Most are heading to youth shelters or to their foster group homes. Their stuff is often stolen by other girls in the group homes, so they carry their bags full of clothes and makeup and anything else they value everywhere they go. Some are laughing as they head out, plugging in their headphones.

Two girls remain after the others leave. Sisters Lisa and Anita are giggling and whispering, "He's a cuuuutie."

I walk in just as they snap a selfie, presumably to send to the latest guy they found online. "Girls, no location services are on your phones, right?" I'm still hypervigilant as neither Lisa's nor Anita's traffickers have been arrested.

"I know," they mumble in unison. They haven't been out of their trafficking situations even a year.

"Mom, it's fine," says Anita. She's been calling me "mom" for months. Sometimes people stare when we're out in public. A girl with blonde hair and a backpack isn't who they expect when they turn to see who Lisa is talking to. In the months I've known Lisa, I've never met her real mom, even though she lives only a few miles from our office. Lisa never mentions her. So, if calling me "mom" helps her heal, I'm okay with that. Everyone needs a mom. Plus, I care about these girls so much.

No, it's actually not fine, I think as they turn back to their phones. Pimps use social media to find girls, and they know how to pick out the ones who will fall for their scams.

Lisa is nineteen now, but emotionally she's about eight or nine years old. This is what trauma does to the brain of a child, what's also known as "arrested development." Emotions and reasoning abilities don't mature beyond the age that the child was at the time of their trauma. These children have heightened stress responses and find it difficult to control their emotions. Anita is the same. I'm in awe of Lisa and Anita's ability to thrive despite their traumas.

Lisa and Anita were also both born with fetal alcohol syndrome, and their mother continued to drink throughout their childhood. When Lisa was four and Anita was five, their father would have sex with one while the other helped hold her down. He said he was training them for what it was like to "be with a man." When Lisa was fourteen, a teacher finally figured out something was wrong and convinced Lisa to report her father to the police. Lisa testified against her father, and he was convicted and sentenced to forty-five years in jail.

Despite this victory over their first abuser, the girls were basically easy targets on the streets and online because making money through sex became normal to them. One Saturday while taking Lisa to get a cupcake for her birthday, we stopped in a clothing store. As we walked around, I noticed a younger man following us up and down the three-story building, watching Lisa.

"Lisa, do you know that guy?" I whispered.

"Yes, Mom. He's a pimp. He knows who I am."

"Why do you think he's following us? Is he going to tell your pimp where we are?"

"No, he just wants to get me working for him."

I knew it was crazy to do, but I asked Lisa to wait for me. I walked up to him slowly, not wanting others to notice.

"I know what you are. You think you can just walk up here and pull your game on us? You need to stop following us. Also, you're like a vampire. You don't belong outside during the daylight."

He smiled and stared at me without saying anything. Then, he left, and I returned to Lisa.

"Mom, you're crazy."

"What's he going to do, Lisa? People are everywhere."

We finished shopping and went to the cupcake cafe, enjoying her birthday. As I walked Lisa to the metro, I said, "You deserve cupcakes on all your birthdays." She just smiled and hugged me before running down the metro escalator. I still think about her pimp, luring other girls and hurting them like he hurt her. Lisa deserves so much more than cupcakes.

I met Lisa on a Tuesday morning like any other, when Priya and I raced in from the metro and grabbed chairs at the Department of Justice building where we held our monthly D.C. Human Trafficking Task Force meeting. This group brings together law enforcement, the FBI, nonprofits like FAIR Girls, and advocates to find and help victims. For the previous six years, I'd been co-chair of the training committee for the Task Force, and each month we talked about trainings, cases, outreach events, and what's going on in D.C. to fight trafficking. Now there are Task Forces like this all over the country, though ours was one of the first.

Like always, I checked in at the lobby, went to the fifth floor, showed my ID and went through a security check, then waited for a guard to let us go down to the third floor. Before I could sit down, Ari Redbord, a prosecutor and the chair of the Task Force, ran over to me and said, "I have something going on in my office, and I need your help." I knew this was about a case before he even said it.

We walked back to his office and there was Lisa, curled up asleep on his black leather sofa with what looked like his suit jacket over her. He leaned over to her and said, "The woman I told you could help you is here." She sat up slowly, not looking at me. She had on a tiny, worn, black sweater, and I could see bruises on her arms through it. As I introduced myself, I heard her stomach growling.

"Are you hungry?"

She nodded. "I would like a banana."

I don't like bananas, but I knew who would have one. I went back to the Task Force meeting and asked Priya for her banana. She always has one in her bag with other snacks.

"Hey, I need that banana I know you have in your bag," I whispered.

"What? Why?" she whispered back.

"I'll tell you later. We have a new case."

Priya got up and followed me out while whispering, "And the case involves you needing my banana?"

"Yes, it does."

Priya and I walked back to Ari's office together. Lisa took the banana and my strawberry breakfast bar. While she ate, we went out into the hall with Ari.

"How did this girl end up in your office?" I asked while giving him my *you have some serious explaining to do* look.

"Yeah, I know this looks weird. She was a victim in a case I had a few years ago against her father, who was molesting her and her sister, Anita. She must have had my work cell phone memorized." Ari told us that Lisa had managed to escape her trafficker after he left her alone on the highway to make money. When she called, Ari and his boss went to get her. That was five hours ago.

"You know, I have a cell phone, so you could have called me when you found her," I gently scolded. He ignored my jibe, but the fear and concern in his eyes were real.

"You really care for her, don't you?"

"I do. Her life has been so unfair."

Looking at Lisa through the door, I could see the softness of her features, small, wide-set eyes, and thin upper lip—signs of fetal alcohol syndrome. Lisa didn't feel safe going back home to her grandmother's house because her trafficker knew how to find her there. She needed food, clothes, and pretty much everything. I traded her Ari's jacket for my coat, and we went to get a taxi so she could come to the drop-in to shower and rest. Ari called Detective Schwalm to begin the process of finding the trafficker. In the taxi, Lisa slept on my shoulder, her tiny body still shaking.

After her shower and more food, Lisa and I sat on the sofa, where she told me a little bit about how she met Superior, the man who trafficked her from D.C. to Virginia. Lisa was living with her maternal grandmother and had graduated high school but couldn't find a job. While she was at the supermarket one day, a guy came up to her and told her she was pretty. When he offered to take her to lunch, she agreed.

As soon as she was in his car, he told her she now worked for him. Lisa didn't fight because she was scared. That night, he posted her on

Backpage and took her to a motel. Man after man came to have sex with her. Five months later, Superior finally left the motel for a while and she ran. He texted her that she better make him money or she would be punished when she got back.

Lisa was eighteen when we found her, so by D.C. law she had to prove that someone forced, frauded, or coerced her into commercial sex to be considered a victim of sex trafficking. There are not always physical signs of abuse, but the bruises on Lisa's arms were pretty strong indicators of force. For now though, we needed a place to keep her safe.

Not only did the trafficker know where to find her at her grandmother's, but Lisa's grandmother would also take her monthly $750 social security checks. Her mom, who drank heavily, wouldn't allow Lisa to live with her either. We found a bed at the local youth shelter, though I worried she'd be found and trafficked again.

Lisa struggled with speaking due to her fetal alcohol syndrome and I had to listen closely to understand her soft voice. She also forgot things easily and had trouble with eye contact.

After hearing her story, I said, "You rescued yourself, Lisa. I admire your courage."

She smiled for the first time. "I didn't think I would get away from him. He made me change my name to Paris," she said. He'd been trying to erase her identity and condition her to think he owned her, but it didn't work.

Over the next two days, I made sure someone from FAIR Girls would drop off and pick up Lisa from the shelter. I always had a banana and bagel ready when she walked into the office.

Will got up at six, and by the time I was up and on my way to get Lisa, he'd already left the apartment. When I got home, he was out with friends, and by the time he got home, I was asleep. I was starting to wonder if we were living in different worlds.

As Will began to play more and more jazz shows on the weekends, I found myself alone in our apartment searching for possible victims. Will and I had been together over a decade, but more and more I felt like I lived with a roommate instead of a husband. Every time I wanted to tell

Will my worries about how we were growing apart, I was too scared. I was exhausted from the girls needing me and FAIR Girls always being on the edge of not making it through another month. Talking about my fears for our marriage felt like too much, and Will didn't seem unhappy, though I never asked him directly.

Detective Schwalm established a plan to lure Lisa's trafficker to D.C. to meet her at a McDonald's near our drop-in center. It's a place where traffickers find victims like Lisa who will go there to get cheap food. Schwalm had Lisa text the trafficker that she wanted to come back. The detective assured Lisa that he'd be nearby, and he was determined to arrest Superior.

I felt uneasy. I secretly texted her, "You don't have to do this, Lisa," so Schwalm wouldn't know I was making sure she truly wanted to do this. Lisa was easily talked into anything. That was a part of her condition with fetal alcohol syndrome. I'd only known her for a day, but I could tell she would do anything she was asked to do, and that made me fear for her safety. Superior was violent and had beat Lisa regularly if she didn't make enough money.

"You're so white that you're like a glow stick in the night, Schwalm. Think the pimp might notice you in that McDonald's?" I whispered as Schwalm got out of the van.

"You're one to talk, Rescue Barbie," he quipped back.

Lisa stood right outside the McDonald's, texting the messages that Schwalm dictated to her, and finally, her pimp agreed to meet her. The operation was in motion. I hid in the backseat of the police van, Schwalm lingered nearby, and Lisa walked inside the restaurant to wait. Maybe he got spooked or maybe he didn't really care if Lisa was gone, but after two hours of a no-show, we took Lisa back to the shelter.

But Schwalm still wanted to catch Superior.

The next day, he and Ari showed Lisa a series of photos of men who could be her pimp. Lisa didn't know his real name, but if she could positively identify the man she knew as Superior in the photos, Schwalm would have the probable cause to pick him up. Schwalm was positive one of the photos in the array was Superior, but Lisa said he wasn't there. Schwalm asked several times, and Lisa continued to say she didn't recognize any of the men. Schwalm was furious and confident that she was lying. I was equally confident that Lisa was afraid she would have to testify against her pimp like she had to with her father. Though he'd been put away, her life hadn't gotten any better because of it. I assured Lisa she did a good job, and we went back to the drop-in where she fell asleep on the sofa.

When my childhood best friend, Kristie, and I were in junior high, we would spend lots of time analyzing the words and actions of the boys in our class, trying to figure out if they liked us. We wished that if a guy had a crush on us, he would have a blue dot on his forehead that only we could see. Now, I wish that blue dot could apply to pimps. It would make photo arrays like the one Lisa was confronted with so easy. Lisa wanted love and romance just like most people, which, unfairly, only added to her vulnerability. Pimps can see that weakness on their faces immediately, no blue dot required.

A few days later, Lisa came to me and said, "I think my sister, Anita, is out there like I was. I haven't heard from her." We sat together, scrolling through my usual sources for finding sex trafficking victims: Backpage.

"Stop, that's her!" Lisa's eyes welled up with tears as we came across an ad based in Virginia with her sister's image.

"I'm sorry, Lisa. I know you wanted to find her, but this must hurt a lot."

She nodded and put her arms around me. Like pretty much every other survivor whose ads I'd seen, Anita's ad read, "I'm new to town, looking to have fun. Roses for your time." And then, "no cops, no black men." Like Lisa, she looked young, and it was plain she had a cognitive disability.

"Do you think Anita wants our help?" I asked. If Anita was in love with her pimp, she might refuse help. Lisa thought Anita thought her pimp was her boyfriend and would defend him. As a consequence, in Virginia, where I didn't have a Detective Schwalm, it was very likely

Anita would be arrested for prostitution. She could go to court and end up in jail, I warned Lisa.

"I don't care if she wants your help, she's getting it," Lisa said.

I called Detective Schwalm, who agreed to call a detective in Virginia. They made arrangements for an undercover detective from Virginia to answer the Backpage advertisement where Anita was posted. But when they arrived, they didn't help Anita like we'd hoped. Instead, they arrested her for prostitution. She was booked and taken to the station in Alexandria, Virginia.

"What? How did this happen?" I asked Schwalm in the morning. "We called them to help Anita get away from her pimp, not arrest her!"

"Well, that's how they do it in Virginia."

"Did she say she wanted to help?"

"It doesn't matter. She's a nineteen-year-old prostitute according to them."

I appreciated Detective Schwalm more and more. I didn't ask him directly, but I just knew he would not have arrested her. Now, she was facing real jail time.

After being released from central booking, Anita was free to go until her court date. We arranged a taxi to bring her to FAIR Girls. Reunited in our office, Lisa and Anita cried together, this time from joy.

"How could they arrest a girl who clearly can't even understand her legal rights?" I asked Anita's pro bono attorney, Stacie. I'd immediately seen that Anita, like Lisa, had the widely spaced eyes and slow slur of speech that indicated fetal alcohol syndrome. The cops didn't even ask Anita if she was a victim of sex trafficking, and even though Detective Schwalm had spoken to them, they didn't believe she was one either.

Just as we had with Asia, FAIR Girls wrote letters and spoke in court, hoping the prosecutor would realize she wasn't capable of accepting a plea deal because of her disability. The court didn't agree, and though she didn't end up in jail, Anita was required to pay a fine and do community service. The prostitution charge would also stick on her record. Anita cried throughout the entire court hearing. So did Lisa.

"We'll fight to get this off your record, Anita," I said as we took the metro back to the office with Stacie.

Two traffickers walked free, and two girls were in shelters. *How is this fair?* I wrote in my journal that night.

Since then, Lisa and Anita had come to the drop-in office almost every day we were open. Both girls have their high school diplomas, and though they got part-time jobs, they were never able to keep them. Most jobs available to them were at fast food restaurants where they would have to work quickly, deal with angry customers, and use a cash register. They were often confused, would forget to charge customers, or would not understand orders. The managers didn't want to spare any time or patience, so they got fired.

Last month, Anita found out she has HIV, and she struggles to remember to take her medication and Lisa struggles to remind her. When I told Ari, he almost cried. It felt like a slow death sentence.

I once asked Lisa if she ever thought about her father.

"Yes, and I'd like to see him," she said.

That surprised me after all he'd done to her and Anita.

"What would you like to say to him if you saw him?"

Lisa looked me straight in the eyes this time. "I'd like to tell him that when Anita dies, I will know he's actually the person who killed my sister and my best friend."

* * *

Back in the office, as the minutes tick down on my Thanksgiving holiday flight and I'm packing up to leave, I take a moment to watch them together. I feel wistful and anxious—I'm happy they've made it this far in life and are together now, but it makes me sad to know they'll always live with the impact of their mother's drinking and their father's horrible sexual abuse.

"Come on, girls, I'm literally turning off the lights and you'll be in the dark." That makes them laugh harder. Lisa has panic attacks when I go on trips. We talk for hours each time before I leave so I can assure her I'm coming back. She says she knows, but still there are tears.

I promise Lisa I'll text her every day to check in. It's better to check in once a day than to have a crisis on my hands when I get back a week later because I was out of touch. Somehow, when I go on trips, there always seems to be crisis with the girls who I'm personally supporting. I used to think it was because I'd not done enough to help them feel bonded to our other staff who'd be available while I was gone. But by now, I know it's deeper than that. My leaving brings up the feelings of abandonment that they've all experienced at one point or another. I know it isn't healthy to promise Lisa I'd check in every day, as she needs to learn to spend time on her own and be more independent, but I don't want her to lose the progress she's been making.

As she's getting her coat on, Lisa hands me a folded letter with hearts and swirls designing the outside. She tells me not to open it until I'm on the plane. I thank her and hand them both little goodie bags with food and some new knit gloves.

"Aw, thanks, Mom!" says Lisa, and the sisters hurry out the door.

Then, as I reach for the light switch, I see the mail on Teresa's desk. The loopy handwriting is somehow already so instantly recognizable to me. I fist pump as I see the faded "Pulaski State Prison" stamp on the back. *It's Tiffany!*

"Yes! There she is!" I shout, though no one is around to see me smiling at this tiny envelope. I grab the letter off Teresa's desk and put it in my bag, storing it safely next to Lisa's, before dashing off to meet Will for dinner.

While waiting for Will to show up at the restaurant—for once, I'm not the one who's late—I pull out Lisa's letter, running my fingers over the little illustrations she's drawn. I can't wait until the flight.

> *Dear Mom, I will miss you a lot. You came into my life when I didn't have anybody. You get me food, you talk to me, and you make me feel loved. I sometimes wonder what my life would have been like if God had let you be my real mom. I hope you*

have a nice trip and I'll be here when you come home. I love
you, Mom! Love, Lisa

My tears well up as I look at the little flowers she's drawn around the entire letter. The letter is sweet, but the heaviness of her question to God pulls my heart down. Why did fate give Lisa an alcoholic mother and abusive, rapist father? What happened to her mom that this came to be?

Will shows up, a big smile on his face because we're having a rare sit-down meal with just each other. But it's hard for me to focus. People talk about survivor's guilt, and I feel something similar to that. Sitting there, at a candlelit table in a Turkish cafe with a person who truly loves me, I keep thinking of the girls. Lisa and Anita are in a shelter instead of at home with loving parents. Tiffany is in jail. Will Tiffany get Thanksgiving food? Will her mother visit her?

The next morning at the airport, I pull out Tiffany's letter.

Dear Andrea,
I received your letter and I was so happy that you wrote me back.
I haven't gotten a real letter like that in a long time. Now I have
three! Tell Teresa and Priya that I'll write them back later too.

Tiffany's father is in jail, so maybe he can't write to her too often, but where is Tiffany's mom? Friends? Do people get to visit her? There are always so many questions, but no way to ask Tiffany as I think of them.

My dad sometimes writes to me, but I haven't heard from him
since he sent that article. My mom's kind of back at drinking
and stuff so who knows what is going on with her. Actually,
that is kind of the problem in a way. My mom had custody of
my son and now he's with Yarnell's mom. My mom always puts
the bottle first.
I don't really have a way to stop this because I don't really
have any rights here in jail. I lost custody when I went to jail.

I need help to protect my son. I don't want him being raised by Yarnell's mom. She won't even let me see him.

I'm already wondering if we can find an attorney for Tiffany. This can't be right. I email Priya while we sit at the gate. Maybe she knows an attorney in Atlanta who would work pro bono for Tiffany. How can Tiffany lose her rights to Ayden? Being in jail doesn't mean she doesn't love her son.

I don't know anything about the law in this situation, so I look it up. In Georgia, if a mother is convicted of a violent crime, she loses her child. We'll have to start with getting Yarnell's mother to let Tiffany and Ayden see each other. How did Yarnell become the kind of man who rapes, sells, stabs, and beats teenage girls? What scares his mother about having Tiffany in her own baby's life? Just like last time, Tiffany's letter leaves me with more questions than answers.

In my response, I ask her what Yarnell had thought when he found out she was pregnant with their son last year. She writes back two weeks later.

He was angry. He didn't want a baby. I did and anyway, I didn't want to kill a baby.

So many of the teenage girls who come to FAIR Girls have children.

Yarnell kept me working, though. He just shoved more drugs down my mouth to keep me from trying to run. I finally tried it when I was about eight months pregnant.

Didn't even one person see a pregnant teenage girl who was on the streets as maybe someone who needed help? What about the men who bought her? Didn't they feel bad for her and her unborn child?

I was worried that if I kept having sex that I'd hurt my baby. Yarnell didn't care and kept taking me to trailers full of men to have sex.

Despite all the pain, suffering, and trauma that she's been through, I'm starting to see a light, hopeful, joyous side to Tiffany too.

> *I think my baby boy is the one who taught me what love really means. Do you have any kids?*

I think of Lisa's letter, of the way she calls me "mom." I think of the other girls, their smiles and laughter, their tears and worries.

Will and I have been talking about having a baby, which is something I've always dreamed of. He doesn't think we can afford it, and he also thinks I'm too wrapped up in helping survivors to really focus on being a mom. Sometimes I think he's right. It's hard to hear my own voice when he's arguing so loudly against it. And I don't want to be raising a child if he would be resentful of how I continue to focus on FAIR Girls. We've promised to talk more about it on this Thanksgiving trip.

No, Tiffany, I think. *I don't have any kids. I just feel like I do every time I open the FAIR Girls drop-in center.*

Chapter 7

DAMAGED GOODS

*A*lyssa and I are on a train heading to New York to meet Nick Kristof of the *New York Times* again.

While on the way, Ari calls me. He has a twenty-year-old woman who's been violently raped and left to die in an area of D.C. known for sex trafficking.

"Her name is Phoebe. The sex offense detective wanted me to call you, but she's not a victim. I told him this isn't your case, but he still wants to talk to you."

"What makes you say she's not a victim of sex trafficking?" I ask as I rush to find a quiet place to talk. Alyssa follows me and listens in, despite me asking her to watch our things.

"She's a victim of sexual assault, not sex trafficking. She was a victim of trafficking in a prior case, that's why the detective called you. This is just a sex offense case. I need you on trafficking cases."

"We'll see. Priya will go meet her tomorrow morning at the hospital."

"We aren't going to step back because it might *just* be a sexual assault," I say to Alyssa after hanging up.

Alyssa and I agree that this doesn't add up. I've never heard of this detective from sex offense before, but he got my number from Detective Schwalm, who wouldn't have referred this to us if he didn't think it was trafficking. When Detective Alex McBean calls a few minutes later, I can tell from the way he speaks that he really cares about Phoebe's safety.

"The detective said that Phoebe was found by a guard in a hospital parking lot after she ran to him. Her clothes were torn, and she was screaming for help at about 2 a.m.," I whisper to Alyssa while people walk past us in Penn Station. I always worry that hearing this kind of thing will bring Alyssa's memories of her own assault back.

"Not only that, but the hospital is also near a known area for sex trafficking that leads from Maryland to D.C.," replies Alyssa. She's right. We often do street outreach there.

Phoebe is in our office a few days later. She sits quietly, tears running down her face most of the first few days. Finally, she starts to speak to me, but she still refuses the bagels and fruit I offer. When she speaks, she looks down at her hands, which she folds over and over until I pass her a stress ball to squeeze and pick at instead.

"I have nightmares about him even when I'm wide awake. I feel it. I smell him as if he's still behind me," she says, before telling me about the night that almost ended her life.

Her rapist had picked her up at a gas station where she was waiting for men to stop. "I was going in and out of the gas station getting hot coffee to stay awake because I had to make $500 and only had $200 so far." Pimps force their victims to meet quotas, or they risk being beaten or even worse. "When he pulled up in the van, I was just thinking I needed the money. I didn't really even look at him too close, not that it would have mattered."

She got in and thought that he would want to take her somewhere behind the storage units where a lot of men go. As he started to drive, Phoebe suggested they go behind a hotel, but he kept driving. The farther he drove, the more nervous she got. Why was he driving so far away? She felt a chill down her spine and asked to get out. He pulled a knife and grabbed her phone. She looked into the back of the van and saw torn black sheets and black trash bags crumpled next to them. She knew she was in danger.

"When he pulled over, he waved the knife at me and told me not to scream." After he raped her, he beat her so badly that she thought she would die. She could barely see as her face swelled.

"I saw a *Law & Order SVU* where the dead prostitute had the DNA of her killer under her nails. So I fought as hard as I could and I scratched him." Phoebe speaks rapidly as if she needs to tell me everything. She's shaking so hard that I think she's about to have a panic attack.

"You don't have to talk, Phoebe. Let's just take it day by day. We have time, okay?"

She keeps picking at the yellow stress ball, but then stops talking and lays back down. When she falls asleep, I get up to talk to Priya about finding Phoebe a place to truly sleep for the night. We arrange with the housing manager at the youth shelter for Phoebe to have a bed there. She leaves the office that day but never shows up at the youth shelter. We call her over and over, but she doesn't answer. We fear she's been found by her pimp, or worse, the man who almost killed her. We try to keep it quiet but Lisa, Anita, and the other girls ask where she is. They can sense when another survivor is in danger because they've been through it too.

A week later, Phoebe returns to the office, and I feel the pain in my chest unclench a little. She starts coming in more and more to the drop-in to shower, eat, and sleep. She doesn't talk to the other girls and refuses to talk to our therapist. When she's not with us, she sleeps in the parks in downtown D.C. One morning, after a scary night in the cold when a pimp harassed her, Phoebe finally says, "You're right. This life is going to kill me out there. I'll go to the shelter." We set it up and arrange for Phoebe to also speak with the detective on her case, who's been calling us daily. He has news: they caught Phoebe's rapist.

We get Detective McBean on the phone, and he tells us about even more women Phoebe's rapist has assaulted. He wants Phoebe to help him with the case to prosecute this man. "This is a serial rapist targeting women and girls who he thinks no one will care about if they disappear."

"So, I guess he thought I was some trash he could throw away when he was done," Phoebe says.

I guess he did. We see stories all the time of girls going missing and never being found. What's often not talked about is that there are girls like Phoebe who no one even reports missing. The rapist's calculations were evil but not incorrect. He just met the wrong victim when he chose Phoebe. She fought back.

"We're not trying to tell you what to do, Phoebe. We'll help you no matter what," I tell her.

Phoebe decides to help after learning there were at least three other young women who were victims of the same man. FAIR Girls joins as her advocate alongside the prosecutor, detective, and a court-appointed victim advocate.

This wasn't the first time that Phoebe had to report a sexual assault or testify in court.

Phoebe was seventeen the first time she was trafficked from her home state of Oregon. Her trafficker had forced her to stand in downtown Seattle and she was picked up by police and charged with prostitution. Those charges still stand. She was eventually found by the FBI in a raid in Texas after her trafficker forced her and other victims to work in a bar where an undercover FBI agent figured out she was a victim of sex trafficking. After testifying against her traffickers and helping put them in prison, Phoebe went to Maryland where she tried to get help for her trauma and rebuild her life. Only, she was struggling to survive and soon met a man through a friend who she thought wanted to date her. He didn't. When she shared her past with him, he began to sell her on the streets of D.C. with the threat of beatings if she didn't make money each night.

Phoebe thought that when she was raped in D.C. the police wouldn't believe her because she'd been arrested for prostitution when she was seventeen. There was no "record" they could pull up saying she was a victim of trafficking or that she had put her traffickers away with her testimony. She thought they would think she was stupid for being back on the streets again. A few weeks after she came to us, an FBI agent from El Paso called about her because he wanted to ensure she could keep testifying against other traffickers in her case in Texas.

"I didn't think anyone would care about one more raped prostitute because, when I was arrested, the cop said prostitutes can't be raped. This is like a recurring nightmare. It's like men just see me as their personal stomping ground," Phoebe says, speaking to the FBI agent on the phone.

Finally, one fall morning in October of 2013, a few years after Phoebe had escaped trafficking in Texas, it's time for the trial of her rapist in D.C. As we walk from her secure hotel where the prosecutor has placed her during the trial, Phoebe feels sick. Her stomach is a mess, and she goes straight to the bathroom at the courthouse. Even now, years later, when I think of the man who sexually assaulted me when I was fourteen, I feel sick to my own stomach. I push that memory back into the dark hole where I keep it and smile at Phoebe as she comes back from the bathroom.

"You okay now?"

Her nod is unconvincing.

The courtroom aisles are almost empty except for the jury, attorneys, Phoebe, Priya, and me. I'm staring at her alleged rapist as Phoebe walks up to the witness stand and sits down. The prosecutor looks back at me. She prepared Phoebe well, but this is the hardest moment. Phoebe looks calm at first, even as she sits only ten feet away from the man who almost murdered her a year and a half earlier, only a mile from the U.S. Capitol.

"He pulled up in a van with tinted windows and motioned me to walk over," says Phoebe on the stand. "I walked over and asked him what he wanted to do. I didn't like his van." Trust me, there are countless things a man might want to do to a girl he's buying off the street. "A quickie is what he wanted. That means fifteen minutes or less," says Phoebe flatly as she fidgets with her sweater and stares blankly past the prosecutor and into the mainly empty courtroom. She's still maintaining a stoic calm.

"I got in the car and told him to pull into the Howard Johnson Hotel parking lot because they don't care what happens there. But he said he had a regular spot just around the corner."

Phoebe recounts how she asked if she could have the $120 he owed her up front. He gave it to her and kept driving. She always did it that way because it was her pimp's rule. She already had $180 in her small, black, patent leather clutch from the last guy who had bought her for a "full job" an hour earlier.

Phoebe says she asked him to stop. She asked him to pull over. He said no and kept driving without looking at her. She was getting nervous, but there was nothing she could do. He pulled up behind the parking lot of a medical center. She told him she didn't want to do it anymore and tried to give the money back. Phoebe had a feeling he was what girls like her call a "bad date," which means a girl gets beaten, brutally raped, or robbed. He pulled out a knife and put it to her throat. He told her if she screamed or fought that he would kill her. He told her to crawl into the back seat of the van, and that's when she noticed the black sheets covering the seats. She knew he was going to do something truly terrible.

At this point in her testimony, Phoebe's voice starts to falter. Her eyes water and she looks down.

"Can you describe the knife to me?" asks the prosecutor. Phoebe's hands fly up and cover her face. I can feel my own tears start to slide down my cheeks.

Her rapist just sits there, cool and distant in his gray-striped suit next to his closely shaved attorney.

"The knife was a thin silver blade with a black handle. He held it to my throat as I climbed over and he crawled on top of me," Phoebe stutters in a whisper.

Phoebe's instincts were right. He did do something terrible. He raped Phoebe without a condom, beat her severely, took her money, and threw her on the ground outside the van. There was no one around to hear her scream. She thought she was going to die.

He thought no one would notice if Phoebe disappeared, and if she survived, no one would believe her. He was wrong. The judge reads each count one by one. The jury convicts Phoebe's rapist to decades in jail. He will never get out.

In her victim impact statement, Phoebe said:

In my life you're one thing I fear, and before you die, this you must hear.

    I can't talk to nobody, I feel like they don't understand.
    You see me smile but only if you knew, the things I hold on to.
    And just can't seem to let it go.
    I know I must forgive and I said that I do, but you just don't understand all the pain you put me through.
    I used to replay the thought of that knife to my neck over and over again, at this moment I think about it every now and then.

We go across the street with Detective McBean to celebrate the outcome of the sentencing. *For once, there was just a little bit of justice*, I write that night in my journal. Of course, Phoebe's pimp is still walking free as if he had nothing to do with what happened to her, and her arrest record lingers like a black eye over her life.

* * *

When the White House's Office on Women and Girls, and Valerie Jarrett, Senior Advisor to President Obama, reach out and ask me to come to the Eisenhower Executive Office Building to show them how Backpage helps pimps sell their victims, I feel like it's a breakthrough. Our national media campaign is working!

My friend and colleague, Bradley Myles—CEO of Polaris Project, which runs the national human trafficking hotline—joins us. We have to screenshot ads to show Valerie because the site is deemed inappropriate for the White House's server. Ad after ad, we show her all the words and signs that Asia had explained to me five years earlier.

"Amid those women selling sex on their own are children being trafficked for sex. But there are hundreds of ads just in D.C. every night and only one detective who looks for victims. These websites are making millions off these ads and don't care if it's a child victim or a willing adult." Bradley and I leave the meeting hoping Valerie will relay everything to President Obama.

Three months later, followed by a not-super-discreet security detail, Valerie joins me and the FAIR Girls team at our drop-in center to meet the women and girls in our program. We order the obligatory pizza and salad while the girls work on their jewelry projects, a favorite art therapy outlet and small source of income for them.

Phoebe cries through her entire conversation with Valerie. "I can't believe someone that important would even listen to me," she says the next day.

"No, Phoebe, she came to learn from you. You were the important person in that conversation. You are the expert on this, not her." Phoebe's story that day made a significant impact.

"I'm proud of that, but it's hard to feel when I can't even afford rent," Phoebe replies.

In a White House statement on human trafficking after her visit, Valerie writes:

> *Everyone should be equipped to address and respond to traffick-ing. So, we educated and provided tools to federal, state, and local officials to help them identify human trafficking and be more attuned to the needs of survivors. As a result of this train-ing, we will be better equipped to detect and stop trafficking as well as to ensure that survivors are never treated as criminals.*

Still, survivors like Phoebe are being treated like criminals, not just by law enforcement but by employers, educational institutions, and even hous-ing programs. Phoebe struggles to find work, then loses her scholarship to college because of the arrest on her record. We need an attorney to clear her record, which I initially think will be an easy process, like writing a little memo.

"Dear Judge, you accidentally convicted a victim of trafficking for prostitution. Do you mind clearing her record?"

As it turns out, they usually do mind. When the judge finally agrees to vacate Phoebe's prostitution charge from when she was seventeen, she's required to do community service. She chooses to write an op ed for the the *Guardian* to educate others about human trafficking. It's our way of using her community service for good, but still, the message from the legal system is clear: Phoebe is being treated like she committed a crime. Her article, written under an alias, is published in October 2015, two and a half years after we'd first met.

> *Even after leaving my traffickers, I felt like I had no options to rebuild a normal life: my arrest made it difficult to find work, and I didn't feel like I could go home even when I finally had one to return to. I ended up back in the life of sex work, in part because, after years of being abused and only experiencing that life, I felt like that's all I knew how to do or to be.*

Dealing with the court system and arguing that our clients' trafficking was a crime against them, not one done by them, is now a standard part of what we do.

* * *

Tiffany and I are always writing. We're growing close through our letters, and my heart sings every time I see the familiar Pulaski Prison stamp on an envelope. I share with her the stories of the girls we're trying to help, my worries about the nonprofit, and my personal struggles. We have a deep connection that lights me up, and learning about her story keeps me curious and open, always thinking about how being a survivor was not as black and white as the movies or media want to portray it. Tiffany starts to share more and more about how she met Yarnell.

> *I first met him because a friend of mine who was older intro-duced me to him. I felt like I had nowhere else to go and no one I could trust to help me. She said he was cool.*

He played the Romeo card. I can relate. Love is the most addictive of all drugs. A child like Tiffany can't be expected to know how to get help, even if there was any in the small southern Georgia town where she was being sold in broad daylight.

> *I was so hooked on the idea he could love me even though I felt like, who could love a girl like me who had nothing. It felt so good to hear it. I didn't feel like I had anywhere I could turn, so I was living with him soon. By that time, I was not in school so no one really noticed me with him. He really made me feel like I was special.*

Traffickers are experts in making their victims feel no one else understands them. They say no one else will accept them or love them.

> *That sweet stuff didn't last too long, though. It was like my heart was where he deposited all his sweet talk and took out all his anger and abuse.*

In another letter, Tiffany writes how she once tried to call her grandmother to come get her, but by the time she got there, Yarnell was home.

> *He was holding me by my hair. I told my grandmother I was fine and she left.*
>
> *Yarnell said if I ever tried that again, he would burn my grandmother's house down by pouring gasoline around it and setting a cigarette on fire. I heard once from a former girlfriend of his that he actually burned some girl's house down and she was killed. So, I believed him.*

A few weeks later, Yarnell was high, and she finally tried to run out of the house while they were at a party. Yarnell caught her and dragged her across the dirt road. He pushed her into the car and stabbed her in the leg with a knife.

At first he would not take me to the hospital. But there was so
much blood that he finally did. He was next to me the whole
time. When the nurses asked me if I needed help, I said I was
fine. I was so ashamed of myself for having sex for money. Yarnell
said if I told anyone, I'd be arrested for being a prostitute.

As I read her words, I mentally add nurses to the list of people who
need to be trained on recognizing victims of sex trafficking. It seems so
obvious to me. A teenage girl with a stab wound who's pregnant and beat
up? A man twice her age looming over her?

"Come on, that's insane," I fuss as I read her letters in the office.

I wish I'd risked it all and tried to get help. Maybe I'd not be
in jail. Maybe Kassie would be okay.

Being on the streets led Tiffany straight to Yarnell, but shame played
a big role in keeping her there.

I was so ashamed of what I was doing. I didn't want anyone tell-
ing my grandmother I was with guys. Or that I was doing drugs.

Reading those words is one of the first times I think about how damaging the shame of being trafficked is to survivors' ability to get help.
Shame led to Tiffany putting up with a lot more abuse.

Even my attorney called me "damaged goods" when I was in
court.

So, that was her defense? Why was that allowed? I feel the tears of
frustration welling up in my eyes again.

Who are all these cops, lawyers, and judges who think it's okay to
lock up a girl like Tiffany? They seem like the damaged ones to me. But
I was determined to change their mindsets. I have a plan to expand our

trainings to law enforcement, and with Detective Schwalm's help, we start lining them up.

"The United States passed the Trafficking Victims Protection Act in 2000. That was thirteen years ago. Now, here we are still arresting child victims for prostitution," I explain in a training for thirty-five D.C. police officers and detectives. Detective Schwalm gives his law enforcement side of the story and explains how to investigate and understand the signs of trafficking. I explain what it's like working with advocates and teach the way trafficking really happens.

Not understanding why they should stop arresting these women is always a sticking point.

"Arresting them is better than having them out on the streets where they will just run back to their pimp," says one police officer at a training. A lot of people think this way.

"It's like if you were to go to a couple's house on a domestic disturbance, and instead of arresting the man who's beating his wife, you arrest her because, if you don't, you think she'll just go back to him, so jail will be safer for her," I reply. It's victim blaming in the highest form.

There has to be a better way, a third option beyond leaving them on the streets or locking them up. This is a pervasive issue, and one that Tiffany writes to me about too.

> *The police knew who I was and that I was fourteen or fifteen years old. They'd just call me a prostitute. Then, send me back to my grandmother's house. One cop actually would have sex with me in exchange for not arresting me, and then send me to my grandmother's. Soon, I'd get in a fight with my grandmother, and I'd run away again with the next guy who showed me some attention.*

In a way, this proved that cop's point. Dropping a kid back home or in some foster group home after they were raped and exploited didn't help them stay safe or escape exploitation. In addition, most of our young clients were actually being arrested on other charges, like truancy or running away. So, on the surface, it looked like child victims of sex trafficking were not being arrested because of their trafficking. But our clients' lives painted a different picture. Their trafficking was a pathway to a life inside the juvenile justice system.

Though it's a start, going to the court meetings and training law enforcement is not enough. We have to reach probation officers, social workers, and foster group homes. We have to dig deeper if we're going to stop the arrests that often lead to years of abuse and exploitation because no one believes they're survivors, not criminals.

Part Two

CEMENT BOXES

Chapter 8

A SAFE PLACE TO LIVE

The entire office is covered in ads printed out from Backpage, random bags of old clothes, drawings by kids in our trafficking prevention school classes, and toys for our therapy dog, Jewel, a Cavalier King Charles Spaniel and Boston Terrier mix. We're preparing an art installation to show the community what sex trafficking really looks like from the eyes of survivors. It's October 11, 2013, and we time our artist installation to happen on the International Day of the Girl, designated by the United Nations. This same month, the D.C. City Council sign a proclamation to name October 11th the D.C. Day of the Girl to demonstrate their support of girls' empowerment.

One month earlier, we'd begun plotting how we could convince the D.C. City Council to finally pass the Sex Trafficking of Minors Prevention Act to stop the arrest of children for prostitution and solicitation. This proclamation was part of the plan. Council members listened and a few op eds came out, but it felt like the bill was dying in the judiciary committee as they debated what level of crime it really was and if it would cost money to implement. We needed to show them what was really happening to girls—and women—all over D.C. That's how Night of the Girl came to life. Our second aim with this event is to raise money to start a safe home, a place that can house girls in need.

We have four media outlets coming to cover the event. "This event is either going to be amazing or a total fail," I say to Teresa, Priya, and Alyssa as we stuff more printed ads into our bags. We've been printing out these ads for days and marking out faces, phone numbers, and any other identifying information to protect the women and girls in the Backpage advertisements.

"Safe harbor laws don't go far enough. I wish we could stop the arrest of everyone for prostitution because most adults were trafficked already as kids," says Alyssa.

She's right. "We have to start somewhere. Other states are passing laws like this, so we just push that D.C. is behind the curve," I reply. We tried in 2010 to include safe harbor provisions into D.C.'s Prohibition Against Human Trafficking Amendment Act of 2010, but the council shot it down with the usual flawed logic that if we "let them go," they will just "run back to their pimps or get in more trouble." We chose to pass the law without that provision so we would have at least something to hold traffickers accountable. The law also required training for D.C. law enforcement, and it criminalized all forms of human trafficking. It was a bittersweet win as I kept going in and out of D.C. court with my minor clients who were arrested on charges of prostitution or truancy. Locking them into detention didn't help. It usually just taught them no one believed them, and they would run away as soon as they could, becoming harder to find and help. More and more, I used Backpage to look for them since that's where their traffickers sold them.

We need people in charge to see that it's about more than just not arresting children for prostitution. We need every single one of the 3,000-plus D.C. police officers to be trained on how to spot human trafficking. Maybe that will help adult survivors too.

We load up a car with the ads to take to the seedy hotel where we're mounting the art installation. We know exploitation occurs here most every night because it's a place where Lisa, Asia, Anita, and so many other survivors were kept while the men who bought them came to rape them.

When we get there, the hotel manager looks at us suspiciously as we drag in six large suitcases.

"We might have a few friends drop by," I say as we walk past the manager's desk, hiding Jewel in Teresa's jacket.

We tape the ads and slips of paper with quotes of survivors to every part of the walls and even the ceiling. We want visitors to the room to feel trapped and overwhelmed. We use red lipstick to write on the mirror, *What have you done to contribute to human trafficking?* and leave pads of sticky notes for visitors to write their answers on and add to the walls.

I didn't ask her if she needed help.

I laughed when I saw a male prostitute on the street.

I watched porn and didn't even think about if the girl was there willingly.

The next room simulates a bedroom in the safe home we hope to build if we can raise support for it. Showing how the home could look to young survivors might help people see how they can help survivors too. There are new blankets, plants, donated clothing, and pretty photos. There's also a wall where people can sign up to help us advocate for the safe harbor bill or donate funds and supplies to support our home.

We counted over 200 "friends" who dropped by that night, including members of the D.C. City Council. We finally shut down at midnight. I leave a thank you note with the hotel manager that includes a big tip. As I wait on our taxi to go home, I see a young woman in flip flops and pink glitter halter top stumbling on the sidewalk nearby. A car pulls up and, before she gets in, she looks back as if someone is watching her.

It takes months, and things continue to move slowly, but those D.C. Council members begin drafting a D.C. bill on stopping the arrest of child victims of sex trafficking. Then, a donor gives us thousands of dollars in support, and we're on our way to opening our safe home, which will open its doors in summer of 2014—less than a year away.

* * *

The media stories help, but what really persuades lawmakers and the public is when a survivor speaks out about what they experience when they are arrested.

Ashley Lowe is a young woman who embodies what a little love and hope can do for a survivor. I met Ashley in 2013, and she's an example of some common themes among the exploited. Ashley had been in and out of juvenile detention since she was thirteen years old. Her trafficker lured her with the idea that he could be a father to her after her own dad died. She had a sixth-grade education, nowhere to live, and no better offers. Alyssa and Teresa met her in the D.C. juvenile detention facility and she started coming to our drop-in. What I instantly saw in Ashley was a hope for a better life for herself and, later, for her young daughter. I wanted that better life for her too.

Now, two years later, Ashley has been asking how she can help and volunteers to tell her story on camera.

"I have to warn you, Ashley curses like it's an art form," I text to the reporter prior to their visit. The reporter replies that it's fine.

The back room of the news studio is painted hot pink and filled with shaggy yellow and purple pillows. Ashley sinks into the sofa after they put the mics on her. The reporter sits across from her as Ashley fidgets with her long red hair. Even though I've asked the reporters to block out her face, Ashley is still on edge.

"Do I look at you or the camera? This is my first interview. I'm all nervous," she says. I smile at her as the reporter answers her questions, and she takes a deep breath before beginning. "After my dad died, it was just me and my mom and older sister. There was a lot of pain and anger. My mom ended up doing drugs and I told the school. They didn't do anything."

Ashley had previously told us that she left home after child services came and didn't believe her about the abuse from her mother. She ran away from home to escape it all.

"An older girl came up to me and said she could help me out because she knew what it was like to be alone on the streets. I was scared of how

I'd survive so I went home with her. She said her father was nice and a foster parent." He was a registered foster parent named Shelby Lewis.

"So you were recruited by another girl?" the reporter asks.

"I guess. I never thought of it like that. I liked her," Ashley replies after looking down at her hands for a moment.

"I'm sorry. I didn't mean to sound like I thought any of this was your fault," says the reporter.

I appreciate his thoughtfulness. Reliving their stories can be really difficult for the girls, and self-blame and the shame of being trafficked leaves so many of them trapped in a loop of pain and anger.

Just a couple of days later, Shelby forced the other girl to show Ashley how to walk the track and post herself online.

"She was so sophisticated and, like, she just knew what she was doing. I didn't want to be back on the street, so I was going to do it. I didn't think I could say no anyway. He had guns and said we had to make $500 a day or else."

The $500 is a common quota. The "or else" meant starvation, beatings, or threats of being arrested.

After she was with Lewis for a few weeks, a police sting operation downtown found Ashley walking the streets at 3 a.m. with the other girl, who was only seventeen and had been Shelby's victim for two years. I knew that downtown area well. It's part of the K Street track where pimps sit in the park and their victims walk around, waiting on men to buy them.

"I was scared when the police caught me on the streets. They kept pressing me on my age, but I was told to say I was eighteen. Then, the cop lady said they were just going to send me to central booking with the other adults. So I had to say my real age. I was thirteen."

They arrested Ashley anyway, I tell the reporter. "They charged her with prostitution because by law in D.C., it's still a criminal offense even though federal law defines any child involved in commercial sex as a victim, even if they want to be there. Even if there's no physical force, fraud, or coercion. That's why we have to pass this bill to stop these arrests."

"The cops interviewed me for hours," Ashley shares. "I was cold and hungry and scared. I just finally broke down and told them what they wanted to know. They never asked me if I was tired or hungry. They just wanted to get information out of me like I was some kind of vending machine."

Ashley felt loyalty to the other girl and didn't want her to go to jail. She was also scared because she'd been threatened that talking meant Lewis would beat them both. But a thirteen-year-old girl can only hold out for so long when she's tired and hungry. The cops knew that. They only wanted her for intelligence on Lewis.

"When I got to juvenile jail, I was ashamed. I felt so embarrassed. Here all these other girls are there for, like, little stuff like truancy. I was in there for prostitution. I felt dirty. That's embarrassing."

When Ashley went to court, they sent her to a registered foster parent because they determined she couldn't be safe at home. Soon, she ran again. Her probation officer found her and sent her to Utah to another locked residential program. She bounced from locked facility to locked facility until she was eighteen. We met shortly before she was to be homeless with a sixth-grade education.

"It's not like we just want to stop the arrests from happening. We want services for girls like Ashley before they end up in and out of jail because they were trafficked," I say.

Ashley adds, "I wasn't offered counseling or anyone to talk to about what I'd been through. I was just being locked up so I wouldn't run. It's like I was a stray dog to them. I was so angry. I lashed out at everyone. I missed my dad."

"Anything else that you want to add?" asks the reporter.

"I'm wondering how the nation's capital and the center of our justice system can still be arresting thirteen-year-olds for sex trafficking," I say. "It's not even in compliance with the federal Trafficking Victims Protection Act. That's why we want to pass a law to prevent the arrest of children like Ashley for prostitution and solicitation."

The reporter thanks us and leaves soon after. I worry that Ashley will not like it when the story comes out. Ashley is only twenty years old, and who knows what her life might be like five years from now. What if she doesn't want a boyfriend or a boss to know about her past? We talked about all this beforehand, but she insisted she wanted to help.

"Even if this law doesn't help me, I want to give back what I never got when I was a kid," she says as we decompress in the office. Out in the main room of the drop-in, our Thanksgiving dinner party is going on. Jewel is running around begging for food, the sofas are full of laughing girls, and volunteers are serving plates of food. Ashley gets up to make a giant, well-deserved plate for herself. Like always, she packs a box of extra food to take to her grandmother.

The next night, I'm eager to leave for overnight duty at our safe house, Vida Home, named after the first girl who inspired the JewelGirls program in Belgrade. It's been open less than two years, and already over thirty survivors have stayed there. The night before Thanksgiving, all six beds are full. We don't have the funding for overnight staff, so the day staff takes turns staying, including me.

The walk from the metro station takes me by the U.S. Capitol and Senate buildings, nestled in a stately glow. From there, I turn the corner to walk into a neighborhood where the houses slowly turn into apartment blocks and convenience stores. Our safe home is in the basement of a tiny, vintage row house. It takes some work to open the door because the metal gate often sticks.

Our safe home was inspired by a girl named Justina who came to us two years earlier from Michigan. She was seventeen, almost eighteen, when we met. That age where child shelters won't take them, and adult shelters are often very unsafe.

Justina and I stayed in hotels for four nights until a bed at a shelter became available. We sang to Taylor Swift and Billie Holiday. We got our nails done. We went to my husband's jazz show and drank Shirley Temples. She tried her hand at drumming after the show, which made us all laugh. She reminded me of my little cousins. "Little Miss Sparkle Eyes" was what the Vietnamese lady at the bagel shop across the street called her when we'd go in for breakfast. Every morning, Justina asked me where she was going to stay that night and my accountant badgered me about how many nights we were paying for the hotel room.

A month after moving into the shelter where she shared a room with three other young women, Justina was still doing well. Alyssa and I had connected her to a restaurant owner who was familiar with us, and he hired her without question. She enrolled in a GED program. She came to every support group and was the life of our jewelry-making program. I started to relax a little on the evening texts I sent her to make sure she got home okay after work.

Then, she met a young man in the shelter who gained her trust. She confided in him and visited his family. But then he tried to sell her to some friends for weed money. Justina fought back, and he forced her to eat a used condom as punishment.

The next day, everyone in the shelter had heard the story. The shelter manager soon threatened to throw Justina out for fighting the other girls who taunted her for being a "dirty prostitute." Justina had to wait in line to do bag checks to get out of the shelter, but now she was avoiding coming and going with the residents, making her late for work. If she lost her job, the shelter wouldn't allow her to stay.

She stopped showing up for work and stopped coming to the drop-in. The adult shelter threw her out. We were out of options. She was homeless and unresponsive to my calls. We'd lost Justina. My heart hurt so much, and I still don't know what happened to her.

We had to do more. A survivor of trafficking like Justina deserves more love, more safety, more care.

"We have to do it. We have to open a shelter," I said to Teresa, who smiled as Priya came in from the office. She nodded. It was on. FAIR Girls was going to open the first shelter specifically for young women survivors of human trafficking and sexual exploitation. We were determined not to lose another young woman like Justina because we didn't have a safe home for them.

Two months later, we applied for a grant from the Office of Victims of Crime in D.C. for the second time. This time they gave us a $62,000 grant to open a safe home for young women aged eighteen to twenty-six. That amount would only cover rent and part of the time for one case manager to support our clients as they navigated court, welfare, jobs, and finding therapy. But it was somewhere to start. Then, we had to find a place.

"Who will live in this apartment?" was the worst question on the rental applications we filled out.

"Six to eight teenage girls, one puppy, and some overnight guests," we wrote on the form. We weren't having much luck finding a place, even without mentioning the whole "pimps might come to the house" problem.

The first studio apartment Teresa found let us stay for a month, and then we finally found a small, one-bedroom apartment in a part of D.C. where it was somewhat safe to walk at night—unless you were a girl, in a gang, or walking alone. We were well aware of the shootings in the area, but it was the only place we could afford to put our safe house and the neighbors seemed like nice older people who wouldn't mind if we were there.

My life had changed a lot in those six months leading to the opening of our safe home. I went from being married to separated. More and more, Will had been angry at me for being out late or traveling for work, which was fair, but there was always something that needed my attention. I felt on edge at home because Will didn't want me to talk about work. He wasn't wrong—it was true that we both needed a break from the terrible stories—but I felt alone all the time without him to confide in. By the time we realized we'd drifted apart, we were living in two separate worlds.

I moved out of our home of eight years to stay with a friend before finding a tiny efficiency apartment a mile from the FAIR Girls drop-in center. Our separation was a deeply painful decision that left me in a state of depression. There were days I couldn't stop crying and texted Teresa that it was best I stayed home.

Shortly afterward, at an art festival in Colorado, I fell for a man who was an artist and filmmaker whose passions to bring joy to survivors of trafficking matched mine. He listened, he showered me with affection, and I felt truly understood and seen. I was shocked by the idea that I could meet someone and be happy again.

About twenty weeks later, I learned I was pregnant with a little girl. I found out the same night we discovered we had gotten the grant to open the safe house. I knew my baby immediately. I'd always wanted a little girl named Veronika, which means a "true life."

I had my daughter prematurely on Christmas Day, the same month we opened the safe home. "Now, I have an actual baby *and* a safe home baby to take care of," I said to Teresa on the phone while Veronika and I lay in the hospital. Veronika stayed in the hospital for five weeks until she weighed five pounds.

I was back at work right after New Year's to help with the safe home. I wrote to Tiffany to tell her about Veronika, and I wondered if it brought her memories of holding her own baby boy, before she lived with Yarnell's mother, who refused Tiffany any contact with the child. It hurt and amazed me that anyone could deny a mother and child the opportunity to have a relationship. Now as a new mom, I felt it on an animal level. I could never imagine not holding Veronika's tiny body as I fell asleep with her in my arms in our rocking chair.

I like arriving at the safe home an hour or so before the young women arrive. That way, I can clean and organize activities and movie night. That night after the Thanksgiving dinner at the drop-in, they all show up right at 6 p.m., just after sunset. The first step is always checking their bags for weapons. It's my least favorite part of the night, but we have to be safe. After being trafficked and abused, many survivors don't think of safety the same way other people do. Plus, the bonds with their traffickers, many of whom used a blend of false promises of love and abuse, are strong. Many survivors of sex trafficking think they were in a loving relationship with their trafficker.

The concept of the "trauma bond" emerged in 1997 when the term was coined by Dr. Patrick Carnes. He defined it as a "dysfunctional attachment that occurs in the presence of danger, shame, or exploitation." The brain tries to make sense of the trauma, and the bond is based on how someone responds to the severity and length of the trauma.

Everyone has a need for human attachment. Almost all survivors of sex trafficking who come to FAIR Girls have broken bonds with their parents though, and they have already endured cycles of abuse, neglect, and trauma. They are perfect victims for traffickers, whose abuse creates a trauma bond rooted in a cycle of abuse, apologies, and promises of love. Even if they get away, they sometimes go back, hoping it will be better, or not feeling that they have any better options. Once the girls make their way to us, it can take months or years to find relief from the desperate feeling of wanting to recreate the cycle of the trauma bond. This is compounded with low esteem, self-destructive coping like addictions, depression, and feelings of suicide.

The nights I stay at the safe home, I stay awake, listening to the struggles of these young women trying to understand how someone who promised them love would also abuse them. Our goal is that the support and care we provide will prevent them from returning to their trafficker or another abusive situation that might wound them so badly that they can't get help even if they want to.

Each night as we cook, I talk to the girls about how to create a home together that we can be proud of and enjoy. Many have been homeless or sleeping in hotels and don't have experience taking care of living spaces. We experience some issues with rats in the drop-in center, so cleanliness is always top of my mind. But though I'd thought keeping the drop-in center clean was hard, a single bathroom apartment with six young women is a hundred times harder. "If we don't clean this shower, the fur babies you left will start a bathroom residents union," I say about the hair accumulating in the drain. The girls roll their eyes at me. The sink is always full of dirty dishes and cleaning schedules are largely ignored.

Still, I'm proud of what we're creating. Most of what we use to decorate the apartment is donated by Teresa's friends and family. The metal bunk beds, two old fabric sofas, lava lamps, and artwork give the place a freshman dorm room vibe. It's home, and it makes me proud to see the girls really living.

We have strict rules for keeping the safe house location confidential, so if a survivor violates that, we have to ask her to leave. I always feel guilty, but we only have one shot to make this safe house truly the refuge we want it to be. One pimp showing up could ruin that and put us all at risk.

Traffickers also condition their victims not to trust other women. They get their victims to recruit other girls either by threatening them or convincing them that they're getting help through offers to join the "family." It's an intoxicating blend involving a sense of family and romantic love that preys on the very human desire to feel safe and loved. Each young woman thinks she's the special one, the one he loves, so they rat out the other girls to stay in the trafficker's good graces.

It's the same basic psychological trap that's used in prison camps. In reality, the trafficker never chooses one of his victims to be at the top of the hierarchy. He makes them all think that spot is theirs, and they'll do anything to keep it. This strategy means the victims monitor and control each other and themselves. Even if two victims bond as friends, the threat of betrayal is always there. On top of that, he keeps his hands clean by having his victims control the money, take the photos, and recruit other girls. Even if they are all arrested, he can walk away free or with lesser charges.

Coming out of that kind of dynamic of abuse and manipulation means that going into a home full of other young women feels like a threat to safety. The arguments over lost toothbrushes and borrowed clothes are always brewing. Still, I love spending nights at the safe home. Before we watch movies or stay up too late talking, we make dinner from donated food and our limited budget.

I show them the way my East Texas grandmother made cornbread, with a little splash of orange juice and a hint of nutmeg to bring out the flavor of the cornmeal. A girl named Tannie protests, "That's so weird, Miss Andrea." Then she eats three squares. Everyone shares stories of their first time eating cornbread. Most of the cornbread they've eaten has come from a box, and everyone agrees that this version is so much better. We'd started to keep a little recipe collection, including pancakes, jambalaya, tacos, and pasta, and the cornbread recipe is added.

Every night, the lights go out at 11 p.m. Whoever is on "overnight" shift is to remain awake in case there's a crisis. Tonight, I play "Who snores the loudest?" to stay awake. After a few hours, I can tell "Three Slices Tannie" will win.

I have to stay up anyway, as Ashley and I are due to give testimony to the D.C. City Council for our version of the safe harbor bill in a few days. I'm behind, as usual. I need to write my testimony and an op ed for the *Washington Post*. I also want to write to Tiffany. I'll have no problem staying busy until 7 a.m., when the girls wake up.

I pull out Tiffany's latest letter. It's been two years since we started writing. The pro bono attorney we found for her isn't optimistic that she could ever be granted a release or even a retrial, especially as the same judge and prosecutor are still working in that district. "They think they locked up a child predator," he said.

The four men who raped Tiffany and Kassie at the construction site Yarnell took them to went to jail. But there were so many other buyers of sex trafficking victims who did not. I'd written to Tiffany that we were trying to pass a bill that would stop the arrest of children for prostitution. I'm continually trying to show Tiffany the injustice done to her.

> *I had to have sex with so many men. I was so ashamed. One of them was even a cop. Why am I here in this box and they are not? I was a child. The police would pick me up and drive me back to my grandmother's house. They never asked me if I was okay or if I needed help.*
>
> *I was so angry at my mom and dad. I knew I'd never be that kind of kid who gets to have a mom and a dad and a puppy and stuff. The only people who paid attention to me were the guys having sex with me or the cops who drove me home. No one cared about me, so I didn't care about myself.*

Tiffany is angry, and she should be. I can't help but wonder: if safe harbor laws had existed in Georgia when Tiffany was being picked up by the cops, would they have helped her? At least she would have had a better shot. The laws are only as good as the people who implement them correctly.

We need more than laws; we need a total revolution of compassion, I write to her.

There are so many moving pieces, and it feels daunting as we try to align them in our favor. For example, I think the Department of Child and Family Services for D.C. will be supportive of the safe harbor law, but they aren't. They don't want to have child trafficking classified as a form of child abuse, as that would require them to investigate cases like Ashley's or Tiffany's in which the trafficking was not directly done by a guardian. Currently, they can decline our calls when a child is a victim of trafficking simply if their trafficker is not their guardian.

Council members' support is also critical. But they wonder whether the police will be able get these children away from traffickers if they can't arrest them for prostitution and hold them. They also don't want to approve a budget for services for child victims of trafficking, which would include all children involved in commercial sex, because they think it's too expensive. They want the cost of serving a child victim of trafficking to be covered by organizations like FAIR Girls, as if we aren't stretched thin enough already.

We also want every single D.C. police officer trained in how to identify and assist a victim of trafficking instead of arresting them. They would be required to refer victims to child welfare services, who would then work with us. We don't want child victims arrested. We also don't want them left in their trauma and continuing to be trafficked, like Tiffany, who only got away from Yarnell when she was arrested—not much of a victory when you consider it ruined her chance at a normal life with her son.

I spread out my papers and computer on the desk, the safe house quiet around me as these thoughts churn through my mind. It's going to be a long night.

Chapter 9

BILLS, BILLS, BILLS

The D.C. City Council judicial hearing finally arrives. We've been advocating for the passing of the D.C. Sex Trafficking Prevention Act for fifteen months. Teresa and I watch the live feed while she wraps presents for a Christmas party and I write 850 personalized donor emails. We're on edge.

"Arresting me didn't make me trust the police or feel worthy of support. It pushed me into the margins of society where I lived in shame for five years as a minor being put in one group home after another. I didn't know I was a victim for years, even though I helped lock up a child sex trafficker for decades. Where is justice in that?" asks Ashley in her testimony.

After hours of the hearing, the D.C. City Council moves to pass the bill. It happens so fast that I'm confused.

"Wait, did they just pass the bill?" I holler to Teresa across the office. She smiles. We did it! Youth in D.C. can no longer be arrested on charges of prostitution, and the Child and Family Services Agency and Department of Youth Rehabilitation Services has to screen youth who come into their agencies for trafficking. This is key because so many kids are being arrested on charges that aren't prostitution but are still a result of their trafficking, such as running away.

The victory is hard-won, but that doesn't mean we're finished. Building off the success of the safe harbor bill, we join a coalition of advocates from across the U.S. to pass a national piece of legislation that would do some of the same things—and even help us deal with Backpage once and for all.

Veronika is starting to crawl, and the late nights are becoming harder and harder for me to manage. Raising a daughter on a nonprofit salary is almost impossible when I need childcare during the day and occasionally at night. My mom comes in February 2015 to help me through it, but money is a constant issue. On top of that, my daughter's father and I begin a custody battle that terrifies me. My best friend, Alia, loans me $5,000 to find an attorney who can help. There are days I'm so overwhelmed that I feel the only safe space is working with survivors, who, despite the fact I don't share details of my personal story, understand me. I keep everything bottled up. I don't want the staff or board to see I'm sinking in stress because they count on me to guide the ship.

I'm invited to testify before the Senate Judiciary Committee for the Justice for Victims of Trafficking Act of 2015 (JVTA). I ask Ashley if she wants to join me for this bigger, national version of safe harbor. I walk her through the elements of the bill: mandatory law enforcement trainings, funding for direct care and counseling, efforts to hold everyone who buys a child for sex accountable, and requiring police to screen and connect potential child victims to child welfare, who would then be required to investigate.

"That is a lot of stuff, Miss Andrea. I'm down, though!" Ashley exclaims.

Ashley is too shy to testify when she finds out "actual senators are literally going to be there" on Capitol Hill, so Senator Kirsten Gillibrand, a Democrat from New York, agrees to read Ashley's story in front of the Senate Judiciary Committee.

We take a taxi from the drop-in center to the Russell Senate Office Building across town. No matter how many times I go there, I always get lost amid those marble staircases and entrances that all look the same.

"I'm kind of scared I'm going to fall and bust my tail on this floor," Ashley says as we navigate the slippery expanse of marble flooring. I don't confess that I know someone that'd happened to, and that someone was me.

"Well, we need to run if we want to get a seat."

Ashley and I run down the hall and into the elevator. After going to three wrong floors of a building that had only five, we find the right hallway for us to continue our run. We make it just as the door is closing and grab some seats.

"Yo, Miss Andrea, everyone is in dresses and suits. I feel kind of stupid in my jeans," Ashley whispers.

Well, now *I* feel stupid. I should have told Ashley what to wear. I just didn't want to stress her. "Ashley, you're good. It's Senator Gillibrand who has to bring it today. You did your part. You shared your story. Be proud." She smiles. I add a note to my ongoing mental list: *we need a partnership with the nonprofit Dress for Success immediately.*

"I'm nervous, Miss Andrea," Ashley whispers to me. "Senators Murkowski, Klobuchar, and Gillibrand are powerhouse women senators."

"We got this, Ashley," I reply, even though I'm nervous too.

"When Ashley was thirteen," Senator Gillibrand begins, "she ran away from home and lived on the streets. She went into a foster home, but a trafficker found her and started selling her. Ashley went out every night and risked a beating if she didn't take home at least five hundred dollars. When the police finally found her, she was arrested on charges of prostitution and solicitation. For the next five years, Ashley bounced between sexual predators, who continued to traffic her. She ended up in New York City with a violent pimp." She got most of the facts right except that Ashley was lured into a foster home by another young victim.

Senator Klobuchar comments that no girl would ever willingly post herself on Backpage. "That senator got that one wrong because I had to a few times, though," Ashley whispers, this time not so quietly.

That really hits me in my chest. Three words. "I. Had. To." She had to because she needed food and a place to stay, and she didn't have anyone to rely on. In ten years of building FAIR Girls, I learned that in the advocacy world around sex trafficking, there are often two camps. First, there are those who believe that anyone who's in prostitution is simply a victim of trafficking and there's no such thing as someone willingly engaging in prostitution. On the other side, there are those who believe that prostitution is a choice and should be valid work where it's legal.

Where does that leave Ashley? Since we met, Ashley has tried living with the grandmother of a friend. She has sometimes stayed with her mom, but her mom's housing voucher does not allow Ashley to live there. She struggles to get a job and keep it. Her sixth-grade education doesn't give her many options. Ashley knows what it's like to be hungry, and she doesn't want to go back to the streets.

Economic coercion is real in the lives of many survivors and women who are not legally victims of trafficking. Where else are they to turn when men will pay them for sex but working at a fast-food restaurant won't even pay for their rent? Still, sitting next to Ashley, I know today is not the day for this level of nuance. Our goal is to pass a bill that will protect child victims.

"Ashley, these senators sometimes get a little passionate and don't always understand the real ways trafficking happens. But I know you've always done what you had to in order to survive."

After the hearing ends, Senator Gillibrand walks out and Ashley and I push through the crowd to catch up with her. After thanking Ashley for allowing her to read her story, Senator Gillibrand asks what she could do to help survivors of sex trafficking.

"Survivors need more than just not being arrested like we're trying to do with this bill," Ashley says. "We need deep support like counseling and job training and a chance to just be kids. And survivors need their records cleared. That's how you stop child survivors from becoming victims as adults."

Senator Gillibrand's chief legal counsel promises that they'll follow up. In the taxi back to the office, Ashley is on fire. "Miss Andrea, I never thought anyone would care about my story and now literally all those senators did. I want to keep doing this with you. I love it!"

Even though this fight is tiring me out, her passion is infectious. I feel an uprising of hope.

The Justice for Victims of Trafficking Act is passed a month later, clarifying that any child involved in commercial sex is legally a victim of sex trafficking, making them eligible for services and protection. This also means that law enforcement has to be trained and are required to screen children they pick up for possible trafficking rather than arresting them for charges like truancy or running away and labeling them as juvenile delinquents who are then placed in detention centers.

Everything in that bill could have made the difference between Ashley spending five years in and out of detention and locked residential treatment programs and having the support she needed to heal, finish school, and even go to college.

"God has led me to this place, though. I'm going to help other kids not go through all this pain like I did," Ashley says when I tell her the bill passed.

Teresa and I now have a new agenda. Most of our clients were arrested before they were identified as victims of trafficking, and some—like Phoebe, who was seventeen when she was arrested—were still children. They now have trouble finding jobs, lose housing opportunities, and are treated like criminals when they apply to college. It's a legal black eye. For Tiffany, her arrest, and the fact that the entire court system didn't treat her as a victim, has led to losing custody of her child and facing a minimum of twenty years in prison.

After the JVTA is passed, Teresa and I meet with Senator Gillibrand's staff again, and I'm thinking of Tiffany the whole taxi ride over. Three years have passed since we first began to write letters. Her pro bono attorney rarely talks to us anymore. Tiffany is focused on her GED and trying to have a relationship with Ayden.

For our clients who were arrested for prostitution at age eighteen, like Asia, the consequences are dire. Even though Asia spent only a single night in jail, she cannot follow her professional dreams of being a cosmetologist or apply for certain housing programs.

"I'm forever just a little less free because of these charges always hanging over my head," she told me once.

I share Tiffany's story with Senator Gillibrand's staff, even though it happened in Georgia. "Tiffany was charged with a twenty-count indictment that included most of the crimes Yarnell committed against her. We need federal legislation for adults that will be a model for addressing not just prostitution charges but any charge at all that's a result of a trafficking victim's own exploitation." Most cases I knew of were state cases, but a federal bill could help ensure that survivors like Tiffany were included.

Tiffany's sentencing document shows how a lack of trauma-informed and trained judges and court systems can lead to trafficking victims being charged instead of protected. We won't be able to train every single court in the country to avoid this injustice, even if we try. This is why a vacatur—a legal annulment—is essential to clear survivors' records so that they can lead full lives after they are released.

In my letter next to Tiffany, I write about this, knowing the issue is deeper than what even a law could mitigate.

> *Tiffany, I feel sometimes like these laws are just like us trying to build a safe house with leaves and sticks. We need to dig into the foundation of our society to reach people who think even for a second that it's okay to arrest someone who is already suffering so much at the hands of a trafficker, from men who pay to own their bodies, and from living in a world of abuse, neglect, and poverty.*

In my personal life, money continues to be a constant struggle. Just a few months ago, I had to ask my landlord if I could be late with the rent payment. I stand in Trader Joe's and quietly calculate how I can get enough food for Veronika on $25 a week. FAIR Girls' financial struggles have resulted in having a small staff and regularly not paying myself so that I can pay others or keep the lights on. I go to events and receptions at night with Veronika so that we can get food, and we go to the farmers' market for free samples on the weekends. I even take extra rolls of toilet paper from cafes. I'm too ashamed to tell anyone, even my new boyfriend. I listen to Ashley and other young women in our office and quietly relate to their fears of not making rent or having food for their kids. I understand how turning to a life that's familiar, even if it's not something they really want to do, would seem logical in the face of having no other options.

"Maybe, by the time Tiffany is free, Georgia will have followed suit and passed their own vacatur legislation to clear survivors' records," I conclude to Senator Gillibrand's team in our third meeting together in less than two weeks.

A legal staff member says they will work on this with us, and ideas for a federal law to allow victims of human trafficking to expunge or vacate their records begins to coalesce. The biggest challenge is that some legislators feel it should only apply to the charge of prostitution or not allow for vacating "violent crimes." This still wouldn't help Tiffany and so many others like her. Survivors like Tiffany don't have a shot in a legal system that doesn't understand what trafficking truly is or how victims can be forced to be offenders.

Tiffany's sentencing document started with four counts of rape, one for each of the men who raped Kassie. Those charges were considered violent because Kassie was a child and it was a sex crime. This was despite the fact that the men also raped Tiffany, who was a child herself at the time. Why didn't the laws that protected Kassie protect Tiffany from being sentenced in 2012? No one was ever sentenced for the rape and trafficking of Tiffany.

Tiffany was then charged with child molestation and cruelty to children for the abuse that Kassie endured at the hands of the same four men and Yarnell. She was also charged with "trafficking in persons for sexual servitude in one count" and "kidnapping in one count." All these charges were read out at her sentencing and, when asked, Tiffany said she understood them, but I've long felt she didn't understand at all.

When asked by the judge, Judge Cato, if she was under the care of a therapist, Tiffany replied, "No, sir."

She was seventeen years old and had years of sexual abuse, neglect, and child abuse inflicted on her. Her mother lost custody of her due to her own trauma and drug use. Tiffany never got to see her father. Her ability to process her own abuse, let alone express it to others, seemed buried under all this unresolved trauma. Sitting there with a group of men in suits referring to her as a "prostitute" wasn't the place where she would suddenly be able to speak up and advocate for herself. A counselor would have helped Tiffany advocate for herself and find a therapist.

Why did no one come to Tiffany's defense while she signed thirty years to life away? There was no advocacy organization or victim advocate by her side. All she had was a court-appointed attorney. Could a seventeen-year-old really process the concept of life in prison?

Tiffany waived her right to a jury trial. At the start of the sentencing, Judge Cato asked Tiffany, "Do you understand that you could be imprisoned for as much as life or twenty-five to fifty years and given a fine not to exceed $100,000? A total of possible life plus thirty years?"

All Tiffany said was, "Yes, sir."

The state prosecutor began his case for sentencing with, "She scoped this child out."

Tiffany had tried to stop Yarnell, but he dragged her by her hair and took her phone from her. If anyone was scoping, it sounded like Yarnell was scoping which of Tiffany's friends was the best possible victim.

Tiffany's attorney asked Judge Cato if he could illuminate some factors that "led my client to commit these crimes." The court allowed him to proceed.

"From the same age, from almost the same age, as this young victim in this case, Tiffany was also pimped out by this Yarnell Donald."

Judge Cato didn't take this information as evidence of Tiffany's own abuse and exploitation. Instead, he turned her own trauma against her. "So then she would have understood the trauma involved in such?"

Her attorney continued, "Indeed, your honor, I think a sense of arrested development of moral—a moral compass, for that matter—this young girl trusted her, was a runaway looking for alternatives, and they offered her for sex to these Mexican gentlemen who, for whatever reason, paid the money and had sex with her."

So, calling his client devoid of a moral compass was his idea of saying what? That Tiffany didn't know right from wrong? I've been watching Tiffany stay free from trouble and get her GED. She writes most often about missing her son and worrying what's happening to him. She has a relationship with her father and has forgiven him. I completely disagree that she has no moral compass.

"Just like that," replied Judge Cato.

Tiffany's attorney replied, "It's not that simple, and I would not want to diminish that act at all. As far as her role, she understands the consequences of her actions, but not perhaps fully as far as understanding just how wrong it is. But this is going to have an effect on her life."

"On the victim's life?" asked Judge Cato.

"On the victim's life. It's going to impact her for the rest of her life," Tiffany's attorney replied.

"Sure, it's a life sentence. She has got a life sentence." Judge Cato understood that Kassie would endure a lifetime of trauma from being trafficked and raped by Yarnell. He understood she was a child. His understanding stopped there.

Tiffany's attorney replied, "And, if the state is interested, Yarnell did this to her at the age as well. And—I'm . . . she is damaged goods but fully understands now what she is facing."

That was the strongest effort her attorney made for her at sentencing. The goal was not to keep Tiffany out of jail, but to keep her from a life sentence. His recommendation was to go with the state's own recommendation to the maximum standard of twenty years with fifteen to serve.

"I'm done," said Judge Cato. "All right. I'm not going to follow the recommendation. I'm going to give you thirty years, twenty to serve, the balance to be served on probation."

Judge Cato went ten years over the recommendations of the state, and Tiffany was charged with thirty years in prison. This was after he'd asked her where she prostituted at age fifteen. Yarnell got forty years. In the end, everyone got a life sentence, but only Kassie was treated like a victim. Tiffany's life sentence assured that she was silenced as a victim and deemed a criminal not worthy of being in society.

She was now three years into her twenty years in prison. She would be thirty-eight when she could be released.

Senator Gillibrand's office worked with Teresa and me alongside other advocacy groups to craft the Trafficking Survivors Relief Act. It took over a year to draft and find Republican co-sponsors. Along the way, we were pushing the D.C. City Council for similar legislation.

On September 26, 2016, Senator Gillibrand's office released a statement on the Justice for Victims of Trafficking Act. "Senators Gillibrand, Portman, And Blumenthal And U.S. Representatives Wagner, Gabbard, And Jolly Announce Bipartisan Legislation To Clear Criminal Records Of Human Trafficking Victims."

I think of Asia, Phoebe, and more than half the survivors I served who were arrested for charges like prostitution. This bill, and state legislation like it, will help them. But, as I'd feared, it won't help Tiffany or survivors like her who had been forced to commit "violent criminal offenses."

Once again, the law is focusing on the crime and not the whole person who was convicted. This logic is not so different from Judge Cato only seeing the crime Tiffany was forced to commit and not Tiffany's life story of suffering and exploitation and how that had affected her decision.

"In many cases, when trafficked people—including children—are forced into slavery, they are tagged with criminal charges that stay with them for the rest of their lives, even though they have absolutely no freedom to say no to their captors, who force them to commit crimes," Senator Gillibrand wrote in the statement on the potential legislation. "I urge all of my colleagues to support this legislation to clear nonviolent criminal convictions of trafficking victims who were forced to break the law while in captivity. We all have a responsibility to take care of the most vulnerable Americans."

I know that getting legislation passed is always a game of compromises and that this Act is a huge step forward, but it's been four years since Tiffany first wrote me. They still don't believe she's a victim. I can't let go of the thought that Tiffany will be placed on the sex offender registry upon her release. She won't be able to live in a household with any children under the age of eighteen. She must submit to regular drug testing. She may not work or volunteer in any place where there are children. She cannot leave the state of Georgia without her probation officer's consent. She must "submit to a search of your person, property, residence, and vehicle at any time of the day or night with or without consent or a search warrant whenever requested to do so by a probation officer."

Tiffany was one of those "most vulnerable Americans" before she was trafficked. When she's released, she will be even more vulnerable because of laws that refuse to see her as a victim.

I have to keep fighting. *If we can't free Tiffany now, I want legislation that will help her in the future to be free of the bars that her sentence carries,* I think.

Thanks to Mr. Kristof at the *New York Times*, I get the chance to write an op ed in his weekly column. This is especially meaningful because Senator Gillibrand is from New York.

> *Jail or juvenile detention is no place for a victim of sex trafficking. Instead, survivors need services, housing, and real job and educational opportunities. Senator Gillibrand's legislation is critical to restoring the lives of survivors who are caught in the broad net cast to catch sex traffickers. Survivors should be treated with dignity while we continue to hold the real criminals, the traffickers, accountable.*

Meanwhile, the Trafficking Survivors Relief Act is caught in a heated debate, with Republican senators opposing it due to an inability to arrive at a conclusion about what a violent crime is.

"What do they mean that they can't figure out what a violent crime is?" I ask Phoebe, who's living in our safe home after having to leave her father's house again. We keep our foot on the pedal though, leveraging our connections to get an op ed on the subject published in the *Guardian*.

"The same Republicans who are saying Backpage CEOs should go to jail for facilitating trafficking are opposing a bill that would give survivors their lives back after trafficking. I don't understand how they can play both sides. Do they support survivors or not?" Phoebe asks as I work with her to write the article.

She has a hard time sleeping at night with the nightmares of her trafficking and rape from five years earlier still fresh in her mind. She stays up all night and sleeps during the day.

Believing in survivors and getting their lives back on track is one side of the coin. But the other side is at-risk kids who haven't been put in the system yet. After years of advocating for teenage victims of sex trafficking who were sent to detention for charges that were because of their trafficking and abuse, we want to work on stopping the cycle. Emboldened by the passages of the D.C. Safe Harbor Act and the Justice for Victims of Trafficking Act, FAIR Girls joins a D.C. Superior Court program to divert kids to services and support rather than just charging them until they end up in serious trouble, like Tiffany.

The Safe Harbor Act means law enforcement officers are required to refer all youth who are screened as high risk of trafficking to child welfare. In turn, they are referred to groups like FAIR Girls. In two years, the number of teenage girls referred to us from child welfare agencies doubles. Some are trafficked by family, some by pimps posing as boyfriends, and others are trying to survive on their own. Now, they are all considered victims of trafficking, not "child prostitutes." That does not mean they don't need care or that the trauma is gone. One barrier done, many more to go.

Chapter 10

GIRLS AREN'T FOR SALE,
BUT THEY ARE ON BACKPAGE

Ashley is dragging her little girl's stroller up the four flights of broken wooden stairs into the drop-in. This is a perilous journey I know well from dragging Veronika's stroller around too.

"Strollers are heavy! How do you get them up here with a baby in your arms?" Ashley is breathing heavily as she walks through the drop-in doors.

Ashley moved into our safe home in July 2016 after being trafficked by a man she thought loved her. She managed to escape him in downtown L.A., jumping out of his car with her baby. A friend of mine helped her get an airline ticket home to D.C. Now, she's living with her friend's grandmother, but the train ride is a full hour, with plenty of perilous stairs in the metro stations. She settles into the sofa with her baby, taking the water I hand her.

"I gotta run, Ashley. We have that Backpage hearing."

She smiles. "Those guys should be packing up because you'll nail them, Miss Andrea."

"Oh, no, I'm not testifying. Even better though: parents of survivors are going to!"

"That's what's up!" Ashley is jazzed. "I look at my little girl, and I never want her to go through what I was going through. I feel it."

My own little girl is almost four years old. We still live in a tiny one-bedroom a few blocks from the drop-in center. We'd moved to another drop-in six months after Veronika was born, and she thinks Mommy "plays with lots of friends" in a big place that is painted "rainbow." It's true. We did paint the new drop-in every possible color we could find. Now it's 2017 and the rainbow walls are covered in stickers, affirmations, and lots of scratches from Jewel. *We will not be getting our deposit back*, I sometimes think to myself when looking around at the disarray.

It's the morning of the Senate Judiciary Committee's hearing on Backpage, and one of the same Senate co-sponsors of our Justice for Victims of Trafficking Act, Rob Portman, a Republican from Ohio, is presiding. The parents of a young woman who was sold on Backpage at age fifteen are also here to testify. The Senate subcommittee has been investigating Backpage for twenty-one months. All the media, the advocacy meetings with Congressional representatives, and survivor's suing Backpage are coming together. A new documentary, *I Am Jane Doe*, has lit a fire under Arizona's Republican senator, John McCain, and this investigation is the accumulation of over ten years of advocacy. The goal is to prove that the owners of Backpage knowingly facilitate online sex trafficking on the "adult" section of its website.

Almost every survivor I know has been sold by their trafficker online. "Our goal is justice for survivors, and to put other online publishers on notice that instead of thwarting the efforts to find victims of trafficking, they should help," I say to a reporter who's outside the hearing proceedings.

Sex workers' rights groups are largely standing by Backpage, as they see the website as their best place to advertise themselves for sex. I don't want to harm them or judge their choices, but Backpage's business practices are designed to profit off victims of trafficking and sex workers alike. It's not a safe haven. They work with traffickers and men who pay to rape victims, and do nothing to protect possible victims other than a little disclaimer that they don't tolerate sex trafficking. Yeah, right: they not only tolerate it but actively profit from it. Now, we need to prove that the people behind the business know they're profiting off the rape of victims of sex trafficking.

"I was raped by a man who found me on Backpage.com. It's not safer for me than the streets. It's just that it was easier to find me online. They could buy me while sitting in a board meeting rather than prowling the streets at night. So, it's safer for them and my pimp," says Ashley in a CNN article I write about the legislation.

The Senate report finds that Backpage knowingly facilitated sex trafficking by filtering the text of advertisements to remove words like "Lolita" or "school girl"—words that clearly signaled underage girls—before posting them for their advertisers. They also hire screeners in the Philippines who scrub ads along with keeping their money offshore in the Netherlands. "They were effectively helping pimps avoid law enforcement raids instead of referring the suspect ads to law enforcement for help," I write.

Did they screen words from Alyssa's ads? Or Asia's? Or Ashley's when she was thirteen years old?

The day before the Senate hearing, Backpage closes their adult section and, in its place, posts a screen saying "CENSORED" in large, all-red capital letters. Beneath that, it reads: "The government has unconstitutionally censored this content." This is almost exactly what Craigslist had done in 2010, over seven years prior. The government didn't close the section; Craigslist did it as a publicity stunt. Besides, it didn't change anything. Immediately, the sex ads began to migrate to other sections of the website. Closing Backpage's adult section will not stop traffickers from using the site or elsewhere on the internet to advertise victims. Just like when Craigslist closed their adult section, we'll just see another website take over.

The solution is to make it clear that those who knowingly profit from trafficking ads will be held legally accountable. If trafficking victims like Asia, Tiffany, and Ashley are arrested for prostitution, why would those who knowingly and willingly profit from the same crime not be held accountable? Unlike trafficking victims, no one is using force, fraud, or coercion to make the CEOs of Backpage facilitate trafficking.

Mike Lacey, Jim Larkin, and Carl Ferrer, the owners of Backpage, sit before the Senate Judiciary Committee and refuse to speak. Their faces look as stiff as their suits while Senator Portman questions them about Backpage's business practices. They refuse to testify.

Their silence cannot drown out the voices of the survivors or their families who are here speaking out. Nacole and Tom, the parents of Natalie, a young survivor who's suing Backpage, speak about the damage and destruction to their family after their daughter was trafficked by her pimp on their website. I've become close to Nacole in the three years since we met. More than once, Nacole sat with me and cried, showing me the binders she put together about her daughter's case.

"Suing Backpage isn't about money," Nacole told me. "It's about holding them accountable. Natalie helped put her trafficker in jail, and these men need to pay too. Natalie needs to heal, and she can't until they pay for what they've done."

Seeing her shake in fear as she reads her testimony puts a weight in my chest. As a mother of a little girl myself, I feel the pain of this mom in a new, deeper way. A way I know Ashley understands too.

"All it will take is a few small words to make the Communications Decency Act of 1996 in alignment with the realities that traffickers sell girls like my daughter on websites like Backpage.com," testifies Nacole. As always, survivors' voices—and now their parents'—are the ones that had the greatest impact. The Communications Decency Act of 1996 was passed to protect internet users. In particular, Section 230 focuses on protecting internet service providers by providing immunity for what others publish on their platforms. It's easy to think that it's about freedom of speech; however, it gives these internet service providers a way to do nothing when traffickers are creating ads and selling sex trafficking victims. It's at the core of how the Backpage owners have avoided liability for the many trafficking victims, like Nacole's daughter, being advertised on their website. As long as they can claim they don't control the content published on their website, they could walk away free.

In 2014, I thought we had a smoking gun against Backpage's claim that they didn't control content. Backpage's defense was built around the claim that they were merely a publishing platform that didn't monitor or censor the free speech of anyone who wanted to advertise there. But we could prove that Backpage did control the content that was posted.

Three years earlier, Teresa, Ashley, and I wrote an outreach poem to place in the adult section of Backpage. The goal was to do virtual outreach. We reasoned that if traffickers were going to use Backpage to sell their victims, we would use it to find them. The ad read:

A GIRL JUST LIKE YOU

SHE WAS CAUGHT IN SEX TRAFFICKING, THE SECOND BIGGEST CRIME IN AMERICA

ONLY 19

HELD BY INVISIBLE CHAINS, PRETENDING TO BE LOVE

SHE WAS TRAPPED IN A CRIME

THAT HUNTED HER.

SHE WAS SOLD ON THE STREETS BUT MAINLY ONLINE.

SHE WAS SOLD OFTEN.

SHE GOT NOTHING.

EXCEPT ABUSE. BAD DATES. NOTHING.

DOES THIS SOUND LIKE YOU OR SOMEONE YOU KNOW?

If so, here is where YOU can get help. No Judgement. Totally Confidential. We are here 24/7. We are NOT law enforcement.

WE BELIEVE YOU.

Backpage refused to let us post the ad, responding that it didn't comply with their standards of use. They even returned our $10 we paid in posting the ad. At first, I was angry. "They don't want us to help find victims," I told Detective Schwalm. He gave me the email address of Backpage's CFO, Tony Ortega, who wrote, "Your ad is in the wrong section. It belongs in the community section."

For the Senate hearing, we'd prepared an amicus brief, a legal document that provides pertinent information about a case from someone who isn't directly involved in the case. We shared how Backpage refused to post our outreach poem, which offered clear evidence that they know what's being published on their website.

Senator Portman ends the hearing after Nacole and Tom testify. The Backpage owners and management get up and walk out of the hearing and back to their lives. They had claimed the Fifth Amendment and refused to testify the entire time. Nacole and Tom leave to return to caring for their trafficked daughter. I go back to my office to help survivors who cannot find jobs or housing as a result of their arrests. That night, I count over 300 sex ads on Backpage. How many are trafficking victims is impossible to know, but the survivors I've met who were advertised by their traffickers were often sold on Backpage multiple times a night.

Backpage senior staff write a letter saying that "human trafficking" is "abhorrent." They claim to have spent "thousands of hours and millions of dollars" to bring traffickers to justice. That could be true, and yet they still also help traffickers by scrubbing ads of words they know might tip off law enforcement.

For the past seven years, advocates like me have been asking Backpage to institute clear age and identity verification, proactively remove and report flagged sex ads to law enforcement, and adopt a consistent, nationwide child sex trafficking victim identification and reporting mechanism. These steps could prevent sex trafficking without interfering with consensual sex workers' safety or harming internet freedom. They continue to refuse. That shows me they don't care about the free speech of the sex workers either. They only care about profit.

It won't be until 2018, one year later, that the CEOs of Backpage are arrested for money laundering and facilitating prostitution. Hundreds of survivors and advocates are prepared to testify in their Arizona trial. The FBI asks me to meet with them several times, and I'm subpoenaed to testify alongside survivors and others who can show that Backpage's CEOs knew that they published illegal content. They're not on trial for knowingly facilitating sex trafficking, even though many of the witnesses were themselves survivors of sex trafficking and sold on their website.

One week into the Backpage trial in September 2021, the judge calls a mistrial because a young survivor refers to herself as being a victim of sex trafficking. The judge says that it's not what the defendants are charged with in this case. They are charged with facilitating prostitution and laundering money.

It's like these guys are Teflon because justice seems to just bounce right off them and they get to walk, I write to Tiffany at the time of the mistrial. Meanwhile, she's still glued to a prison she never should have walked into.

A new trial is set for 2022. I hope Tiffany is free by the time they're locked up where they belong.

Chapter 11

NEW HOPE, OLD PAINS

At the beginning of 2017, the D.C. Superior Court launches the pilot of HOPE Court.

HOPE stands for "Here Opportunities Prepare you for Excellence," but as one client said upon her graduation, it should stand for "Hang On, Pain Ends." Through a multidisciplinary approach, its goal is recognizing and treating child victims of sex trafficking rather than prosecuting them for underlying offenses. It's everything FAIR Girls has been working toward.

Potential clients for the court are nominated by their attorneys, and then they team up with a case manager who works with the juvenile court and law enforcement to connect the youth to mentoring, crisis counseling, health services, or anything else they need. The key part of HOPE Court is that it's youth-led, meaning the clients are guided to engage with their case instead of passively letting their attorneys make all the decisions. The goal is that successful completion of HOPE Court will not only end participants' involvement in the juvenile system but will also start them on a successful path to adulthood.

As it's based on preventing future crime and abuse instead of punishing the child, HOPE Court provides those teens, almost all of them girls, a chance to potentially have their charges dropped and build a community of advocates and support around them. We attend court every week to talk about how each kid is doing and what else we need to do to help them.

The biggest challenge is working with the court-appointed attorneys. They're the ones who have to present the idea of their client joining HOPE Court rather than staying in the juvenile court system. This means teaching them to recognize the signs that a child is at risk for or is already experiencing trafficking. Like Ashley, many kids don't want to admit it. Many of the public defenders don't have training in what human trafficking is or how to represent a young client who's a victim.

"Why doesn't every juvenile court act like HOPE Court?" I mumble to an advocate in a HOPE Court meeting. Then, we'd really have a better chance of preventing trafficking, even one child at a time, rather than just cycling kids over and over again through courts that see the behavior, not the child. But this is progress, and there will soon be more programs like HOPE Court all over the country.

Two months after the launch of HOPE Court in January, the head of the D.C. Metropolitan Police Department's Youth Division, Chanel Dickerson, creates a website for D.C. Missing Persons to list every missing child in the district. There are dozens of Black and Brown missing girls. More than 2,000 kids are reported missing every year, and most are young girls of color. The press picks up the story, and soon the missing girls' faces are all over the TV across the country. Some people say in online comments to social media posts that it "makes sense" that most of the missing kids are girls of color because D.C. has large populations of people of color. But actually, about 50 percent of D.C.'s population is Black or Brown. The Metropolitan Police responds to the stories by stating that the majority of the Black and Brown girls left home voluntarily, so they aren't considered critically missing.

"Critically missing" is a technical term that the police use to determine who's a priority, such as an active child abduction. This nuance doesn't play out well with the public, and soon people are asking why all children aren't considered "critically missing." Tweets of the faces of missing girls and stories make it all the way to the *New York Times*.

Days later, D.C.'s mayor, an attorney and woman of color named Muriel Bowser, says in a press release that she wants to break the cycle of young people who go missing in the nation's capital. She forms a Task Force, and I'm invited to join as FAIR Girls' representative and an expert on the intersection of missing kids and child sex trafficking. The idea of whether someone is critically missing or not is a wall I've run up against many times before. Many of D.C.'s sex trafficked youth have criminal charges, making them juvenile delinquents. So, when they run away or are otherwise missing, they're not listed as critically missing but rather as fugitives. This means no missing person poster and no active search, even if they're known to have been sex trafficked. This doesn't make sense to me because many, if not most, of FAIR Girls' minor clients have also been in the courts for anything from running away to sex trafficking. They're not counted in those 2,000 missing kids in D.C.

A lot of times, it's me and my team who are advocating for missing person's reports and deeming our clients critically missing. "If I know this girl, don't you think that means that it's because she's been exploited already? Doesn't that make her at risk of that being the case right now?" That was the kind of argument I'd have to make if I couldn't get a missing person's report. The Sex Trafficking of Children Prevention Amendment Act of 2014 that Ashley and I worked on was changing that, and so was the Justice for Victims of Trafficking Act. Finally, law enforcement has to report all missing children to the National Center for Missing and Exploited Children. But now the problem is that, first, they have to actually believe the children are missing, not voluntarily leaving home.

I wasn't running toward all those guys; I was running from my own pain. I was running after love that was always just out of reach for me, writes Tiffany when I tell her about the missing girls scandal in D.C.

When Tiffany left home, she was at risk. She was on the streets with a violent trafficker. When Ashley left home, she ended up with a trafficker. Even if a kid leaves "voluntarily," they're still critically missing.

"I knew that if I reported myself to the police, they would lock me up or send me to foster care," says one of our new HOPE Court kids while we wait for her hearing to start. It's a common fear. I've lost a lot of clients that way over the years. They stay on the run, falling further into trafficking, and I don't hear from them again because they know I'm mandated by law to report them to the authorities if I see them. Once again, doing nothing isn't the answer, and arrests aren't either.

The confusion, fear, and anger that so many girls of color are missing in D.C. has created a wave of action in the public, and the D.C. government begins holding town halls in schools, community centers, and group homes. I bring Alona and Tutu, both survivors of sex trafficking who currently live at Vida Home, with me to a local town hall in a part of D.C. where many of the missing girls of color are often trafficked. I've been attending these to gather information for the mayor's Task Force.

The audience is packed with angry parents and youth. My favorite youth services detective is quietly hiding in the back of the auditorium, near the vending machines.

"Guess you don't want to join the chief on stage," I comment after going over to say hi. He nods. Likely he's scouting out some potential cases, so I leave him alone and go back to where Alona and Tutu are standing as the room fills up to standing room only with families, children, teachers, and advocates. Looking around, I see almost only Black and Brown faces.

Washington, D.C. is divided into wards and the town hall is hosted in a local Ward 8 high school, where the council member is a newly elected young Black leader, Trayon White. On the stage alongside Mayor Bowser is Commander Chanel Dickerson and the newly elected chief of police, Peter Newsham. Their stiff faces and uniforms don't help make the night feel more community-minded. Instead, it feels like they're trying to calm everyone down while anger vibrates throughout the room. I stay close to Tutu and Alona as we make our way to the front. I want to record the meeting to show the other girls at FAIR Girls later.

Just as Mayor Bowser begins to speak, my phone buzzes. It's an FBI agent I know only as "Agent Lopez," who's been helping us with the case of a seventeen-year-old girl. Originally from El Salvador, she ran from her foster home after she'd been sexually assaulted by the son of the family. She's now one of the missing girls featured in the D.C. Missing Girls media stories, but I didn't want anyone knowing FAIR Girls was involved because it could compromise her safety if she came back to us. I slip to the side and answer the call. Agent Lopez says he thinks she's in Maryland and asks me if I know anyone she might know there. I don't. I can barely hear him as members of the audience are shouting questions at the mayor. I finish the call and go to sit next to Alona and Tutu, who are taking notes.

A mom jumps up on one of the orange folding chairs and asks the new chief of police why there are no Amber Alerts for her missing daughter.

"Where are her Amber Alerts?" she screams. Other moms are joining in. The mom becomes even more angry when Chief Newsham says the lack of response is likely because her daughter hasn't been abducted. She wasn't considered critically missing—that phrase again—and Amber Alerts are reserved for missing children where there's a real reason to believe they've been abducted and are in life-threatening danger. The mom shouts back, still standing on the chair as two other women hold her arms to keep her from falling. She screams that they don't care because her child is Black.

"He doesn't really understand what she's asking," whispers Alona. She's a twenty-three-year-old Black and Cuban survivor who's hands-down one of the smartest young people I've ever met.

Tutu nods vehemently. She's a young Black transgender survivor and one of our first residents at Vida Home. Tutu knows firsthand what it feels like to be forced to leave home and have no one looking for you because, when she ran away from her father's house after he didn't accept her as a girl, he didn't report her missing. She met her trafficker on the streets while she was trying to make enough money to get a place to live and finish school. She's in nursing school now, but the trauma of her experiences on the streets often leads her to emotional breakdowns that make it hard to go to class. Her sickle cell anemia also means frequent hospital stays, and I've been with her in the E.R. Tutu was seventeen when she escaped her trafficker of two years. A nurse who was caring for her knew about our safe home and connected us. That was three years ago, and now Tutu holds workshops and advocates for other survivors when she's not in school.

There are more tears and shouting, the crowd riled up and the police offering no real answers. A few times, I worry there will be actual fist fights. Alona and Tutu are highly upset that it doesn't seem like there's a solution being offered by the chief of police or mayor.

"We're making progress. Tonight is just one night. We're building HOPE Court for a reason," I say as we drive back to Vida Home. I'm angry and tired too. But I'm also hopeful because, finally, we're talking as a community about what's going on with missing Black and Brown girls in D.C. But for Tutu and Alona, both of whom have been Black and Brown girls who went missing multiple times, this is personal.

"So, if we really want to help solve this problem and bring down the numbers, we have to break the cycle of young people, especially young girls, who repeatedly run away from home," says a spokesperson for the mayor in a *Washington Post* article that's published after one of the town halls. I feel a little hope that some officials are finally starting to hear what we've been saying.

In the next Task Force meeting, I say, "If a minor is a part of the juvenile system and there's a warrant out for them because they ran away or have skipped school, there's no missing person's report. They're not counted in the thousands of missing kids reported in D.C. They're fugitives. If they're found by the police or turned in by social workers or others, they'll be sent to detention. Many of my clients have stayed on the run because of this."

Most of the teens who are missing are either already involved in the child welfare system or the juvenile justice system, which means they have already experienced courts, group homes, and probation officers. It also means something traumatic has happened in their lives. These kids are not at home for a reason after all, whether it be negligent parents or something else. Instead of arresting kids who leave home because of abuse or neglect, we need to provide safe drop-in centers, counseling, and safe housing. It's a point I bring up again and again at the Task Force meetings.

"Every teen who leaves home or is missing should be treated as critically missing. White girls are noticed when they go missing more, but me and most of my friends just disappeared. I had nowhere to go if my parents didn't want me at home. The police didn't find me. I found myself by escaping my trafficker," says Tutu later that week when we're talking in the FAIR Girls drop-in center. She and Alona are still upset from the town hall, and I want to make sure they feel we're hearing them.

Later that month, Tutu and Alona go with me to a meeting with teens who are or have recently been homeless or otherwise not able to live at home. The D.C. director of the Child and Family Services Agency we invited to attend is there. We hope these teens' stories will help demonstrate the need for reforms and increased services.

One teen girl talks about how she went to a social worker to ask for help in finding a safe place to live until she graduated high school and nothing had been done. Another young man talks about living in motels and on the streets rather than in a homeless shelter where he'd already almost been raped at age fourteen. The obligatory pizza and drinks and the comfy chairs are meant to help ease the tension, but their stories are rough to hear. Alona starts to cry and shake.

"No one is listening to teens in crisis because they just think they're out there because they want to be," she says through her tears. Alona had been trafficked for four years before she found an FBI agent who believed her. "It's like we're just being thrown away by society," she screams. Tutu takes her outside to calm her down.

"All those teenage girls who 'just leave home' and are 'out there because they left voluntarily' do need help," I say as we close the meeting. That same night, we admit another teenage girl into Vida Home. She's already been arrested for prostitution by the police before they call us.

Later that month, I learn that D.C. missing youth who are considered fugitives because of their status as juvenile offenders will now be searched for by the police just like any other child. The district is going to open a drop-in center to be managed by the Department of Youth Rehabilitation Services, and nonprofits like FAIR Girls could offer services there. Soon, FAIR Girls starts receiving many, many more referrals for trafficked girls who have been screened by the police and probation officers who are implementing these new laws. It's progress, even though one of the major reasons that girls are going missing is still prevalent. Sex trafficking isn't going to stop, but at least some girls going through it will now have a better chance at getting the help they need.

I cannot stop thinking about the word "runaway," which is used with abandon while talking about these missing kids. But that makes it seem like they had a choice. What will it take to get people to see that "thrown away" is a more accurate term for what's happening to these young people? We need to reach into our roots as a society to change how we see these young girls and boys who are being thrown away.

Tiffany said the same thing about her situation. *I feel like no one wanted to see what was really going on with me. So, they just threw me in jail.*

Does anyone see that society threw her away a long time before she was ever arrested? It's been five years now and society is still looking at Tiffany like she's a runaway who turned into a sex trafficker.

* * *

April 6, 2018. That date sits in my mind like a dark divide that separates my life with FAIR Girls and without FAIR Girls. A month earlier, the FAIR Girls board of directors called me to a meeting in the board chair's office. I didn't realize the entire board would be there, but as soon as I see them, I know they're about to push me out of the organization I've given more than a decade of my life to serving. I try not to cry.

For the past six months, I've been dealing with mounting verbal attacks by another employee who'd been hired to be our director of policy. She was a personal friend of the board chair and came highly recommended.

At first, she's incredible in helping us advance FAIR Girls' policy agendas around vacating federal records for human trafficking survivors. Soon, though, she's critical of everything I do, and I can feel the whispers and notice the closed-door meetings when her phone rings.

In December 2017, the board chair announces this woman will become our executive director and I'll be the president, focusing my time on fundraising and media. They also recommend part of my salary be commission, based on how much money I raise. I point out that this is in direct violation of the IRS and they drop it. Besides being illegal, I can't afford that kind of instability as a single mom. Veronika is a toddler, and childcare is almost as much as my rent. I'm terrified.

Soon, there are accusations that I don't know how to manage our finances, and I'm in and out of meetings about new policies our board wants to create. It's exhausting on top of trying to manage our case managers, help clients, write media articles, advocate and testify in courts, and fundraise, all for an organization that more and more feels like it's not mine.

That day in March, sitting with the board of directors, I've never felt more betrayed or hurt. One of the board members, a personal friend, implies in a question that my ex-husband, who'd been a board member during our marriage, hadn't done his job right. That's the only time I cry in the meeting, defending him and saying he was the most honest board member we'd ever had and that attacking him while he's not present is unfair. They give me a month to write up reports and teach the new executive director the ropes, and then almost immediately erase me from the website. By April 6, I'm out—and it's like I never existed.

Things go from worse to even worse. A few weeks later, my boyfriend of three years, whom I'd planned to move in with in South Carolina, breaks up with me. It's been a year of him repeatedly cheating on me, increasingly picking fights, and breaking up with me only to come back and win me over days or weeks later. This time it's over for good, and while I know the relationship wasn't ideal and he wasn't ever going to fully commit to me, I'm still utterly heartbroken. In our years together, he'd become a father figure to Veronika, and I'd deeply loved him. I cut off all contact with him and FAIR Girls. The future that I saw for myself vanishes.

I immediately get to work finding consulting work training law enforcement on human trafficking across the country, writing short stories to educate teens on human trafficking, and creating trainings for youth and parents to learn about human trafficking, the latter done in tandem with my best friend and then director of a San Francisco nonprofit, Freedom Forward. Our "I Am Jasmine Strong" campaign to support youth in the Bay Area launches in late 2018 and ends up on billboards across San Francisco.

I am making it, I think to myself at night. Only, I can't stop a sinking feeling in my heart as if I am carrying a weight inside me that makes each heartbeat feel like a drum beating in my ears, a clock loudly ticking down the seconds to something—I don't know what, but it isn't good.

In August 2018, I have what I now know is a cardiomyopathy, something that's often called "broken heart syndrome" and results in the heart not being able to pump blood effectively. It can lead to heart failure. This felt like my chest was outside my body when I laid in the hospital bed trying to figure out if I'd be okay. That week, I reach out to a dear friend, Sebastian Lindstrom, who's also the film producer who would later help us produce Tiffany's film, *Lack of Love.* With his help, I find a life coach named Lisa, who says it's time to decide if I want to truly be my fullest self. That day, I stop all contact with my ex-boyfriend and delete every FAIR Girls board member's phone number from my phone. Lisa tells me I deserve the same love and protection as the girls I help, and that I'm worthy of it from myself. I take it in, but I know it'll be a long time before I can truly live my life with that knowledge. I download the healing podcasts Lisa sends me and begin the journey of truly healing. With the occasional chest pains, I know that the boundaries I'm placing will protect me.

That fall, I join survivors I've known for years to create a new nonprofit, Karana Rising. The word "Karana" is the name of a young girl who's the fictional heroine in my favorite childhood book, *Island of the Blue Dolphins.* Like so many survivors, she survived impossible solitude and challenges to stay alive and actually be happy. Our goal is to help survivors like Tiffany who have been wrongfully arrested, and to work with young survivors who are a part of the Department of Youth Rehabilitation Services service center program. We file paperwork to become a nonprofit and, almost a year later in September 2019, we have our IRS status. We organize jewelry-making workshops, invite former FAIR Girls clients to join us, and meet many new young survivors.

One woman who co-founds Karana Rising with me is a Kenyan woman named Fecha Talaso. Fecha came to FAIR Girls in 2012 after a terrible experience led her to seek our help. After Fecha had transitioned from a FAIR Girls client to FAIR Girls staff, she went on to work as an overnight staff at our safe home and later taught prevention education, like Alyssa and I did, in D.C. schools and detention centers. She, like me, left FAIR Girls in spring 2018. Our friendship began to grow deeper and, by the time Karana Rising is being created, I consider Fecha one of my closest friends. Her ability to see life and people as good despite the pain she's experienced is awe-inspiring to me. She's very artistic; I love the way she can look at just an ordinary street and see a chance to take a photo and turn it into art. Fecha also patiently teaches other girls how to make jewelry—she's the best jewelry designer I've ever met. When around the same time we're creating Karana Rising a former FAIR Girls client is shot and murdered, our bond grows deeper. We both believed in this young woman who was so traumatized she didn't remember her real age or where she was truly from when she came to us. Fecha and I grieve her.

Just days after Karana Rising is officially off the ground, I meet a man who lives near me and has a little girl a few years older than Veronika. His wife lost a brave four-year battle to cancer a few years earlier, and I could sense that his little girl was often sad. I love making her laugh and, even though I could never replace her mom, it feels nice to give her some mommy-love. Soon, we start dating and, by December, we're spending holidays together. On New Year's Eve, he looks me in the eyes and whispers, "I love you." I feel like I'm getting my life back together with him and Karana Rising.

Early in 2020, I fall while ice skating and break my right arm. The girls stand over me, fear in their eyes as I lay there, utterly unable to move from the pain. When my boyfriend takes me to emergency care the next day, I've already passed out in his arms twice. With my dominant hand and arm soon in an extensive cast, I can no longer write, or even sit up without assistance. Yet again, I can't take on writing jobs and begin worrying about making ends meet.

As I recover, another illness is coming. When the COVID lockdown takes over D.C. in March, I know, like so many others, that the world is changing forever. Suddenly, there's no school and it's almost impossible to know how to get basics like toilet paper. Both my boyfriend and I are facing at least a year of home-schooling our children. We're not even allowed to go get fresh air on the roof of my building.

When he asks me to move to San Diego, at first I think it's a bit crazy. I've never even been there! But the idea of being near the ocean and starting to build a life with him is beautiful to me. It feels right. In August 2020, in the height of the COVID pandemic, we move across the country to a house where you can hear the ocean at night. We settle in quickly and it feels like home. Likely the neighbors can hear our two little girls hollering in the mornings as they sing songs and run around the house. The first piece of mail we receive is a letter from Tiffany.

A few weeks earlier, on July 29, 2020, I had clicked "publish" on Tiffany's Change.org petition, titled "Free Child Sex Trafficking Survivor Tiffany Simpson." I feel almost exposed. Our years of sharing our stories and fighting together to get her lawyers to advance her case all feel so personal. We've been trying for years to talk her pro bono attorney into a habeas hearing to get her another shot at a trial. We've tried to get her more access to her son. Twice, her attorney has not shown up in court without telling Tiffany he wouldn't come. He simply said he felt we didn't have a shot. Together, Tiffany and I decide it's time to go public. We have to shake people awake who can help free her, and petitions for other survivors like Cyntoia Brown have helped them. It's Tiffany's turn. Now, the world will read Tiffany's story and decide if they want to sign her petition, which we have set to be sent to the Governor of Georgia. Change.org has millions of followers who, in addition to all the people we would try to reach online, could sign. The first person who signs is my mom, followed quickly by my best friend, Alia. We want to get at least 1,000 signatures in the first month to show momentum for when we get a new court hearing.

* * *

In October 2020, Tiffany's emails become fewer and fewer. In the last few months, the petition has gotten to just over 1,500. It's a daily push with social media posts asking for signatures, educating the public, and trying to get Tiffany's case attention. She's been on lockdown because of COVID for months. She's locked in her room almost twenty-four hours a day with no outside air. She begs me to reach her pro bono attorney, but I rarely get him to respond unless I convince him that the media is looking at Tiffany's case.

It's clear that Tiffany needs a new attorney. I write to the ambassador-at-large for the Office to Monitor and Combat Trafficking in Persons, John Richmond. After looking over the petition, Tiffany's arrest files, and all of our work to free Tiffany, he calls and suggests I talk to Susan Coppedge. Susan previously held John's position and was nominated by President Obama, serving from 2015 to 2017. She's now in private practice in Georgia.

This is like trying to call Beyoncé, I write to Tiffany. But to my surprise, Susan responds almost immediately. Within days, I've exchanged several emails with her where I share Tiffany's case, sentencing documents, and more. In our first phone call, Susan agrees to become Tiffany's pro bono attorney for a case that could cost over $100,000 to fight.

Things are finally starting to move. Immediately, Susan calls a retired FBI agent, Barbara Brown, to see what we can learn about the case beyond the court records from 2011. She also calls Tiffany's first attorney, who was her court-appointed attorney. He claims to have lost most of Tiffany's files and provides very little to help us. Shortly after her incarceration, Tiffany wanted to re-call her plea and had written him many times. He never replied. Tiffany's current pro bono attorney is notified in a letter by Tiffany that she no longer wishes for him to be her attorney. I wonder if he's surprised given he's often ignored her emails and my phone calls too. Susan officially takes the case over before Christmas.

We start working through all the potential options for Tiffany's release right away. A pardon by the governor isn't a possibility because the state of Georgia doesn't allow this form of relief. The vacated law at the time didn't allow for someone with a sex offense charge against a child to be eligible. So, Susan thinks her best bet is filing a habeas petition and having a hearing before a judge in the county where Tiffany was sentenced.

A habeas hearing, Susan explains, means we have to get a judge to rule that Tiffany's previous attorney failed to provide effective council. When I look online, I see that less than 3 percent of habeas hearings are granted, with some reports saying less than 1 percent. It isn't very much, but it's still more than the zero chance we have by doing nothing. But it comes with a risk. If the judge grants the habeas petition, it means Tiffany will get a new hearing. Then, there's a chance that they could charge Tiffany with even more years in prison than her original sentencing. We have a long way to go to prepare the paperwork and make sure we know all the facts about her case and what her first attorney did or didn't do.

In January of 2021, we also receive a small grant from a foundation called Dressember to help get justice for Tiffany and other survivors who were wrongfully arrested. Dressember has thousands of donors and advocates who can help us get attention for their cases, which is amazing. With their support, we begin plans to make a short film about Tiffany's story that will help us reach a wider audience. While Susan digs deeper into Tiffany's case, we begin plans to go even more public.

Chapter 12

SURVIVORS ALONE IN THE LONE STAR STATE

I wake up at 5 a.m. It's "Train-A-Cop-Tuesday," so I'm getting ready for the four-hour virtual D.C. police training that Ashley and I lead. While I make breakfast for my second grader and get her ready for virtual schooling courtesy of the COVID pandemic, I also print out my ninety pages of training slides. It's almost Christmas—our first holiday here in San Diego. I'm wondering if there's a giant palm tree somewhere downtown that acts as the holiday tree for the city. I miss the White House holiday events and the ice skating outside on the National Mall. I miss the smell of fireplaces and winter wetness that drifts into the cafes in the mornings in D.C. The ocean—the one that Tiffany so deeply wants to see—soothes me.

Finally, everything is ready. I'm tempted to lie down just for a minute, but I know I'll fall asleep if I do. I feel my phone buzz with a text. "Andrea! I'm so excited. Oh, what's the link? This is going to be so bomb." Ashley, now a lead staff member at Karana Rising, is always excited about law enforcement training. I send her the link to get on to the call. My kitchen is a makeshift studio now with lights, books, and a coffee mug as props to make it look like an office.

In 2014, when Ashley and I helped pass the safe harbor bill in D.C. to protect children from arrest and prosecution for prostitution, we also fought for the requirement that every single one of the 3,000 D.C. police officers would receive training on how to best find and support survivors of human trafficking. The bill only passed once it included a provision that these trainings wouldn't impinge on the police budget. So, the trainings only happen if nonprofits like Karana Rising provide them. This frustrated me. Why would D.C., with one of the highest rates of sex trafficking in the country, not want to financially invest in training the police to effectively find victims of trafficking or arrest traffickers? And why would the D.C. City Council not want to invest in funding services for child victims? Even as the bill passed, I didn't feel that human trafficking was a priority for the city listed by the FBI as a hotbed for sex trafficking.

At the time of the bill passing, FAIR Girls agreed to take on cases that law enforcement flagged and provide the trainings. Our caseload of young survivors doubled within months of the bill passing. That was also back at the beginning of planning for HOPE Court. Now, here we are five years later. Despite being in San Diego, Karana Rising is the go-to trainers for the D.C. police on human trafficking.

"I'm so excited I'm training cops in the same city where I was arrested when I was thirteen. This is like poetic justice, Andrea," Ashley grinned when I asked her to do the trainings with me.

I agree. This feels like a full circle of justice. So, we dial in at 7 a.m. and fifty-two sleepy cadet faces appear. Virtual trainings are not as fun as real-life trainings, and I'm always concerned that the cadets will fall asleep or not pay attention during our four hours together. The first two hours are me explaining what human trafficking is, the laws, and how to engage with courts—all important, though not super exciting stuff. I knew Ashley would wake them up.

"I was so angry at the world when my dad died when I was twelve. I feel like I fell off the porch into adulthood and had to survive all alone while my mom used drugs and drowned in her pain," Ashley says. "No one cared. I just walked out the door."

Ashley has the cadets transfixed as she walks through how she was trafficked. One cadet shares that his little sister was trafficked too. Another shares that she kept snacks and clothes in her car for kids she found who needed help. When Ashley is there, the trainings often evolve into more of a therapy session.

"You want to know how to get a child victim of sex trafficking to talk to you? You have to act like a human. Ask them if they're okay. Or if they're hungry, or what could make them feel more safe. You know, stuff you'd want someone to ask you. I was out there, thirteen years old, on the streets, being threatened with going to jail. So, I was lying and not talking," Ashley explains.

Usually, a few days after the trainings, emails start coming in from cadets finding possible cases. For example, late Friday afternoon, a D.C. police officer from our training that week calls me about a young girl he arrested on theft. I connect him to the prosecutor I work with at HOPE Court to see what we can do for her. Moments like this make the early morning trainings worth it every time.

* * *

That night after the training, I get my book and a glass of white wine and go to lie on our tiny patio under the stars. The beauty of San Diego is slowly healing me. Two months earlier, Veronika and I had moved out of the home my boyfriend and I shared with our little girls. A few months after we'd moved to California, it was clear that my boyfriend wasn't in a good place. Now, Veronika and I have a tiny little apartment a block off the beach, and we walk along the sandy shores most weekends looking for dolphins and whales. Usually, though, we just find seagulls who wonder where we're hiding food. It feels like every time I'm able to take a step forward, I get shoved back a few paces.

At night, I listen to podcasts and read books about relationships. They talk about attachment styles, how childhood trauma impacts adult relationships, how love and abuse can sometimes feel the same when you're trauma-bonded to someone. I knew all this from my work with survivors, but to live it is another experience that brings up shame for moving out, shame for failing, and shame for hurting my little girl by us having to leave.

I considered his little girl my stepdaughter despite us not having married, and she and Veronika had grown close. But I couldn't handle the yelling, the insults, and the increasing outbursts, even if there were nights of love between them. During those first few months together, I lived on eggshells and often took walks alone to just get some peace before returning to a home of chaos and screaming. Yet, we love each other. I still want to be with him. I want to see him happy and healing. I want to help him heal, but even though it hurts, I understand that this is something he has to want for himself. I want to forgive the past and also make a better future. That night, alone on the patio, I wonder if he knows my moving out was about self-love and protection, not about not wanting him.

As I read, I hear the familiar ping from my Facebook messenger. I think it might be one of the survivors reaching out, but it's an old friend named Dave Gratz.

Dave Gratz. I haven't heard from him in about twenty years. How odd. Dave was an assistant debate coach when I was a freshman in high school back in Texas. He helped me win my first debate round against two seniors, and that's when my love of justice and debate began.

"Hey, Andrea, long time. I see what you are doing with Tiffany. Bravo! So, a friend of mine here in Killeen has a case with two teenagers and she thinks they might benefit from your help. Mind if I connect you? Her name is Anna Harris, and she runs a local group here called JUST-US Participatory Defense. Here is a link to the story about the kids."

I write back immediately. "Yes! I would be very happy and interested to speak with Anna."

Then, I click the article link. A fifteen-year-old boy and his eighteen-year-old sister had been arrested six months earlier with a twenty-four-year-old woman in Killeen, Texas. They were charged with murder in relation to a robbery. The victim was a former Army technician, Shareef Raekwon Ali-Barnett. I google the name of the eighteen-year-old girl, Jessica Hampton. Articles come up about the alleged crime and a $500,000 bond on Jessica.

The next morning, my phone rings before I even get Veronika settled into schoolwork. "Hey, so the twenty-four-year-old was pimping them straight out. They've been in jail six months and, trust me, they could face capital murder."

"Uh, who is this?"

"Anna Harris, JUST-US Participatory Defense."

Okay. Maybe I should have known, but usually I start calls with "Hello, my name is . . ." I guess Anna isn't into pleasantries.

"I gather the twenty-four-year-old was pimping the eighteen-year-old girl? Or were they both being pimped by someone else? How did her little brother get into this too?"

"The twenty-four-year-old, named Breez, is the pimp. Jessica and Jordan are siblings, and they are both her victims. She was having a sexual relationship with Jordan. The murder victim was there to have sex with Breez, and I guess Jessica too. But Breez's real plan was to rob him, and it went bad. Also, there's no evidence other than her text messages, which can be easily altered anyway. Jessica had been trafficked out before to Colorado and in L.A. when she was fourteen. There was an FBI raid and she was rescued from Colorado, went to California, and then ran from the group home and landed in the hands of a gang member who was raping her. So, there's some gang involvement here too."

That's a lot of trauma and abuse, I think.

"Did Jessica get help when she got home? Where was she living?"

Anna talks so fast I can barely keep up. "I'm not sure about it all, but her mom tried to get her help. She started working in a thrift store and that's where she met Breez. Jessica had been sober and was on probation and doing pretty good, but then she started hanging out with Breez and Breez already had other girls working for her for money and drugs. I think there might have been another pimp too. Then, Jordan, her fourteen-year-old brother, got involved and Breez convinced him they were in love. So, he started getting into it."

Ugh. Ugh. Ugh. What a mess. What twenty-four-year-old thinks having sex with a fourteen-year-old is okay? *Their mother must have been going crazy with worry*, I think. I would have been.

"So, did Dave tell you what I do?" I ask. "I'm assuming he told you about our work with a survivor named Tiffany Simpson?"

"Yea, that's why I'm calling you. This is crazy. I usually do death row cases. They need better attorneys and to make their bond. Girl, they have $500,000 on Jessica, and it may go up to $1,000,000. What can you do?"

Whoa. This case is pre-plea, which means they haven't been charged yet. We could stop them from being sentenced like Tiffany was almost ten years ago! I know Killeen, though—it's about two and half hours from where I grew up. It's a town near Fort Hood's military base, and people love their military. Not only that, but lately there's been a lot of media about military shootings. The fact that the victim was in the military wasn't going to go over well in this Texas town.

"Do you have any of the arrest reports or interviews? I'd like to learn more about Jessica and Jordan. Also, how are their parents? Are they involved?"

Anna says the kids are half-siblings, and I'm not surprised when she tells me that neither of their fathers is around. That means they both have attachment and abandonment issues. Sometimes, I want to scream. Almost all of our clients don't have a dad in their lives. So, girls like Jessica are easy prey if they're looking for a sense of family. But Breez is a woman. She must have used the "I'll be your best friend" card, sensing that Jessica felt she had no real friends.

"Amy, their mom, is a great advocate, though. She needs a lot of attention, but she could give you documents on Jessica's previous trafficking cases and all her past abuse before that by an uncle who was never charged."

I get Amy's number and send her a message. Within minutes, she calls. She's scared, I can tell.

"They don't treat them right in jail. Their attorneys don't care that they were trafficked. What if my babies spend their lives in jail?"

"Amy, I think the first step is to get them new pro bono attorneys who know how to defend trafficking survivors. Anna thinks the same. I just did this with a client in Georgia named Tiffany Simpson, and her case is finally moving. I mean, it's different because she had already taken a plea. But I think this could help us with the bond and to get them out of jail."

We're on the phone for two hours that night, and it's after 1 a.m. when I finally get to bed.

Amy emails me thirty pages of FBI police reports and documents about Jessica's prior trafficking. What I read in her files is tragic, including letters from the FBI victim advocate assigned to her case. She was fourteen when an older girl convinced her to run away from her home in Killeen and go to Colorado. I already knew from Anna that Jessica had been sexually abused by her uncle before she was in junior high. Her mom was struggling with two other younger siblings, Jessica was lost, and Jordan wanted to protect her. Their story reminds me of Tiffany, Ashley, and so many others.

Jessica was almost set on fire by the trafficker she was sold to in Colorado. She was rescued in a raid and sent to a treatment program, but she ran away. The shelter with the treatment program was later accused of abuse, so I'm not surprised by Jessica's flight. She went to California and was lured by another teen girl who, according to Amy's call last night, offered her friendship to run away once again. Within days, her new friend's pimp tried to sell her. Jessica fled to the streets of L.A.

Soon, another gang trafficker found her and offered her shelter. She was scared of being found by the police and sent to another locked shelter, so she agreed. He almost killed her when she refused to engage in sex for money. Finally, a detective found her. She was so thin she could not stand up on her own. Her trafficker was arrested, and Jessica was sent home to her mom in Killeen.

"I didn't know how to help Jessica," Amy tells me. "I felt so alone and scared. She was depressed, lost, addicted to the drugs they gave her, and wouldn't talk to anyone. She felt like no one understood her and she wouldn't even look me in the eyes. Men were constantly bothering her. She thought people using drugs or running around the streets were the only ones who understood. Our neighbors knew her story, but then they started picking her up and taking her out. I couldn't control her."

Traffickers know how to find victims. They know how to target vulnerabilities and isolate their victims from everyone who loves them. Tiffany often told me about her shame and anger and how she felt like no one but her trafficker understood her.

"Jordan started following Jessica around because he was worried she would disappear again," continues Amy. When Jessica got a job at a thrift store, she became friends with Breez, who was a victim of child trafficking too. This woman had begun to sell other girls. Soon, she had Jessica using drugs again.

"I'd been calling the police about some of Breez's friends coming to our house to try to take Jessica with them and threatening us, but the police didn't ever respond. One night, they were outside our apartment door trying to get to Jessica. I fought back in our front yard, and they beat me so badly in the head that I have skull fractures. Jordan was twelve years old and jumped in to save me and stop them from taking Jessica." After that, she said, Jordan never left Jessica's side. Breez started having sex with Jordan and convinced him he was her only love.

"Jessica needs to talk to someone who can relate to what she's going through in jail," I tell Amy. "So does Jordan. I think Tiffany, along with one of my team members, Ashley, would be open to being survivor mentors to Jessica."

Amy gives me both their addresses, and I write to Jessica to see if she might like to hear from us.

> Dear Jessica,
> My name is Andrea. I know your mom. She told me what happened to you and I'm so sorry. I'd love to be able to support you. I know this amazing young woman named Tiffany who is a survivor like you, and she is really sweet. We are trying to help her get out of prison too. Would you be interested to have letters from her? We really want to support you. Do you like books or writing?

I finish my letter by sharing more with her about myself and our work and how we can help. Then, I write to Jordan.

I know Tiffany is interested in helping survivors, and I feel like she could help Jessica, even if only through letters from prison. Ashley had been writing Tiffany, so maybe Ashley could write Jessica too. This could be the chance for Tiffany to finally mentor other survivors.

I pull out some more paper and write Tiffany a letter. After years of writing and sharing so many details of our lives, we'd started to refer to each other as "Sis."

> *Hey Sis!*
> *So, we have two new survivors who we are helping. I think that you could really help this teen girl named Jessica who has been in jail waiting on trial for about six months. Would you be open to writing to her and just being a bit of a mentor since you know what it's like to deal with lawyers and court and just all these emotions?*

Jessica's letter comes back two weeks later.

> *Hey Miss Andrea,*
> *Thank you for writing to me. I think it's amazing you are an advocate. I agree with what you wrote about how your past should not define you. I believe it's an opportunity to grow and help others. I'm so happy I'm part of Karana Rising. Tell Tiffany I'll write her back. I got her letter too!*

Ashley had also written Jessica. "Do you think we are doing too much, Andrea?" asks Ashley on our team call. I think about the call I got from an investigator who was hired by Jessica's defense attorney. He called Jessica and Jordan "thugs," saying we'd never get them out. He was also drunk. Jessica and Jordan need all the help they can get.

Soon, Tiffany tells me how she's bonding with Jessica through their letters, but she also senses that Jessica is having a rough time in jail.

> *Andrea, I worry Jessica is going to explode in there. It's going to be intense. I wish she could get therapy. She's sad but that is going to turn to anger. I know because it happened to me.*

I worry about Jessica, and Jordan too. They are two more victims being disappeared by the system that was supposed to help them. I feel a lot of urgency to move quickly on their cases.

On January 11, 2021, we launch a Change.org petition for Jessica and Jordan titled "Free Teen Sex Trafficking Victims Jessica and Jordan Hampton." We have 1,000 signatures in a few weeks. Now, we have two public campaigns. The next step is finding them pro bono attorneys, which turns out to be a lot harder than I'd hoped. Finally, Anna and I find an attorney for Jordan named Seth Fuller, who's really involved in supporting juvenile cases. No one seems interested in Jessica's case, even though there are law firms in Killeen and surrounding Texas cities who said they cared about supporting survivors of trafficking. I notice some advocates in Texas aren't responding to my calls for help with Jessica and Jordan.

"Do you think that people just don't believe that Jessica and Jordan are innocent?" asks Ashley.

"I don't think it's that. They want perfect victims, and they don't think Jessica and Jordan are perfect enough. Their cases are messy, and these lawyers don't want to dig into the real facts. But they were children being sold for sex. That's all they should need to know to assert Jessica and Jordan were victims." Just as in Tiffany's case, their trafficking is not being investigated at all.

But I believe Jessica and Jordan, even when they don't believe in themselves.

I didn't feel worthy of anyone being nice to me, Jessica writes me in a letter. *Thank you to you and Tiffany for believing in me and supporting my mom. I feel so guilty because I've caused her so much pain. I hope I can make it up to her someday.*

My heart breaks for this young girl getting beat down by the system that should have helped her. I'm not going to stop fighting.

* * *

In March 2021, I get together with Susan and John, former and current U.S. ambassadors respectively, to create a program for survivors of human trafficking who've been wrongfully arrested, charged, or incarcerated. We've been finding more cases like Tiffany's, and throughout my entire time at FAIR Girls and now Karana Rising, the theme of arresting victims as a way to find them keeps coming up. Law enforcement refers survivors to us only after they arrest them. Sometimes we would get court referrals. Or, like Tiffany, they would find us on their own. I know there's more we can do to get to the roots of these arrests and stop the injustice of a victim being arrested as a result of their own victimization.

"I want to do more than sit here in the river with all these survivors sinking from their injustice," I say on our first call. Ashley is also on the call; I hope that someday she'll be able to lead the program we're building for survivors who've been imprisoned like her.

"We should focus on expanding the burden of proof to the state to prove that someone who committed a crime didn't do so as a result of their own trafficking," Susan replies. "We need to take that burden off the survivors. Basically, we need to expand the concept of affirmative defense."

Affirmative defense is used as a legal argument that if someone commits a crime while being a victim of a crime themselves, they can be found innocent. At least, that was my non-legal way of trying to explain it to Ashley when she quietly texted me during our call. Ashley doesn't like asking questions when Susan is on the phone because she, like me, is in awe of her. Again, it's like being on the phone with the anti-trafficking version of Beyoncé.

A few years ago, I wouldn't have known what Susan was talking about, but learning how to advocate for Tiffany has taught me a lot. I keep notes on every legal concept around Tiffany's case, hoping to someday decode a path toward her release.

Right now, the way affirmative defense works is that survivors like Tiffany or Jessica have to prove that they were trafficked. They have to show that they had no free will and no choice to not commit a crime because they were being trafficked. Affirmative defense is already a law, but if the courts don't recognize human trafficking in a case, they can't use it. Basically, defense attorneys must advocate for affirmative defense for victims, which can be time-consuming and costly, something they're always hoping to avoid.

That means our program also needs to train the defense attorneys who might take these cases. We need to get into wherever these public defenders get their trainings. Susan explains that this would be any training with "continued legal education." I'm not a lawyer, so we need to partner with lawyers. As we are plotting, Ashley texts again.

"Miss Andrea, what if survivors help train those lawyers. I can do what I do for those little police cadets. You know, get them in the real."

How many cases like Tiffany's or Jessica's just fade away? People often say Tiffany was lucky to find me. I think it's the other way around. I'm lucky Tiffany found me because now I know what has to be done.

I text Ashley back, "Yea, I agree. Let's say it out loud now."

Ashley texts, "You do it. I'm nervous."

We need a national movement to ignite defense attorneys to see their clients as victims. I know we can do it.

"It's more than just affirmative defense laws that need to be clarified. We need attorneys who know how and are willing to fight for their clients," I say, jumping back into the conversation.

"We should call this the non-punitive project," John says.

"No!" cry Susan, Ashley, and I in unison.

"John, you're not allowed to name anything. That was horrible," says Susan. We're all laughing.

"It's about survivors and justice," Ashley adds.

That was it. The Survivor Justice Initiative was born. As soon as we're off the call with Susan and John, Ashley and I call Fecha and start to dream up the concept. We'd help survivors like Ashley create case studies and partner with law schools to train law school students. We'd find a way to get to cases by working with courts and public defenders, and we'd be sure that there could be a way to screen clients to see if they were arrested while being trafficked. Then, we could partner with the lawyers to help get their clients freed from charges. It's basically what we're trying to do with Jessica and Jordan's case. It's what we could have done for Tiffany. Fecha immediately starts creating logos and taglines for the Survivor Justice Initiative.

For the rest of the day, I feel in awe that U.S. ambassadors were bantering with Ashley and me. I'm sitting on the sunlit patio of my apartment. The hummingbirds dangle in the air while my new baby bunny, Eponine, dances in circles around me. She's named after the character in Victor Hugo's classic novel, *Les Miserables*, who was forced to steal food and left by her parents on the streets. She died taking a bullet for the man she loved. My Eponine, however, just hops around and eats blueberries and bok choy. She fills my heart with small moments of quiet joy. Taking time to notice nature and find happiness in pockets throughout the day helps me sustain the darkness of our cases. Though I often miss my life in D.C., talking about trafficked children in jail is less stressful when I'm surrounded by the beautiful nature here on the West Coast.

* * *

One night, Amy calls me crying. Jordan has been raped by two female guards and placed in isolation without enough warm blankets. Recently, he'd also been beaten to the ground while naked in the shower. She's especially worried because there's an ice storm hitting central Texas. My own parents are collecting snow to heat up to make water to take baths amid electricity blackouts.

"Jordan is a good kid. He was always laughing and making me and Jessica smile. He loves to please people. Now when I visit, he just stares at his feet, never smiling or looking me in the eyes. I barely get to see him because he's so often in isolation," Amy says.

My stomach clenches. I catch myself holding my breath, which I learned is a sign I'm starting to go into a state of fight-or-flight. I listen quietly to Amy and Eponine, my not-quite therapy bunny, who's looking at me as we speak.

"Are you there, Andrea?"

"Yes, I'm here, Amy. I'm listening."

"I don't know what to do. I don't. No one listens to me here. Jessica is so scared that Breez is going to jump her in there." Jessica was imprisoned in the same facility as her trafficker, which is something that haunted me and Amy. "Why is she still in there with her trafficker? I swear there is a gang in there."

As Amy cries into the phone, I have an idea.

"Amy, what if you wrote to people in your own words? You tell the world what Jessica and Jordan are going through. People will listen to you more than me."

Amy agrees, and for the next week we message back and forth to create a blog post to be shared with the thousands of people who follow Dressember and Karana Rising.

> *There is nothing sadder than seeing your children hurt. When they have a fever or break a bone, you feel helpless watching them suffer. During the last ten months, my two teenage children have been sitting in Texas jails after being sex trafficked. I do not have time to feel hopeless or cry. I have to fight for their lives. That is what a mother does.*

* * *

On April 25, 2021, Bell County holds a hearing for Jordan in which I testify on his behalf. COVID was disastrous in so many ways, but it made going to court weirdly easy. The virtual link leads me straight into the courtroom, where I see Seth Fuller, Jordan's mom, the judge, and the prosecutor. I put my computer on speaker so Fecha and Ashley can listen in to the audio. I want them to learn how to testify in these cases too.

Ashley and I wrote letters in support of Jordan, but I've no idea if Seth will use them. I have written dozens of letters in support of my clients, but never before have I needed to explain to a judge why a sex trafficked teenage boy shouldn't be tried for capital murder as an adult.

Prior to his victimization through sex trafficking, Jordan experienced myriad traumas including witnessing his own mother's assault, having his sister sex trafficked and missing for an extended period of time, and having to effectively become the man of the house when he was twelve years old. Though Jordan can legally be certified as an adult at the age of fifteen, the fact remains he is psychologically a child. While Texas state law can legislate his childhood away and turn him into a legal adult, he is still a child on every level. He makes choices like a child. He processes trauma like a child. Trauma, such as assaults and rape, stunts emotional growth for children. He has not received the healing care he deserves and needs.

Texas is a leading state addressing child sex trafficking. This includes Governor Abbott's Child Sex Trafficking Team (CSTT) created by the 84th Legislature (2015) to ensure and coordinate a holistic response to child sex trafficking in Texas. Their five-star approach includes justice for child victims. However, Jordan was not identified as a child victim despite the fact that according to Texas state law, any child involved in the commercial sex trade is automatically a victim of sex trafficking. One need not prove force, fraud, or coercion, as would be the case for an adult victim.

As an attorney, Seth is dedicated to Jordan, but the prosecutor still sees him and his sister as criminals, killers. She refers to them as "child prostitutes" and "prostitutes" in court. I fear that jail will turn Jordan into the violent offender that they accuse him of being. If Jordan is certified as an adult, the consequences would possibly mean life in jail without parole.

The prosecutor reads out the list of dozens of alleged infractions Jordan has acquired during his months in jail. He's sixteen now. They say he's fighting guards, refusing to do as he's told, and trying to steal food. During the horrific ice storms, he was cited as violating the juvenile detention facility rules for pretending to want to kill himself just so that he could get the much warmer blanket that was given to children demonstrating suicidal thoughts.

I text Amy. "Is Jordan getting counseling now?"

He isn't. For the past year, we've advocated in hearings for Jordan's bond to be reduced so he could be released to a treatment program where he would receive inpatient therapy and secure support. The judge denies it every single time. Jordan has told his mom several times he doesn't want to live if he has to stay in jail too much longer.

"He's losing the light in his eyes," Amy texts back. She's often denied access to Jordan because guards say he's in isolation for acting up. This doesn't make sense because Amy told me he was on the honor roll at school and praised for his good behavior. I feel sure the guards are up to no good.

Seth's arguments are strong. He clearly and succinctly tells the court about Jordan's trafficking, his prior abuse, and the conditions in the jail that were pushing him to do things like beg for blankets and allegedly steal food. He's a child. He was sexually abused. He didn't know what was going on. Fecha, Ashley, and I are hopeful as we listen through our Zoom link. But as soon as Seth makes his closing remarks, the female judge in Bell County certifies Jordan as an adult, paving the way for a now sixteen-year-old boy to spend the rest of his life in jail. All that hope we had is gone. I feel like someone punched me in the gut, and I don't even have a way to ask Jordan how he feels.

Amy calls me immediately and we spend the next two hours strategizing. And crying. We could write the governor, but he can't get involved in a prosecution. We could advocate for more Change.org petitions. We could try to get more media and pressure the judge. Only, we both know there's no going back. Jordan is now considered an adult, and the path toward life in prison is now clear.

"How can this prosecutor fight to put a child in adult court when she knows he's a victim of trafficking?" Amy sobs.

She's right. The prosecutor knows because she referred to Jessica and Jordan as being involved in prostitution. Just like in Georgia, Texas has a law stating that any child who's involved in commercial sex is a victim of trafficking. So, here's yet another prosecutor who's willingly not accepting affirmative defense of a trafficked child.

I'm too tired to go on the date I'd planned that night. After we say good-bye, I remain, emptied out, on my patio amid the flowers, a candle, and the soft sound of ocean waves. I watch my bunny jump joyfully around her toys and feel guilty to be here, feeling the freedom of the soft night air knowing that Jessica and Jordan don't have that luxury. Neither does Tiffany.

I write in my journal that the poor outcome of Jordan's hearing feels like the beginning of the end of our chances to stop Jessica and Jordan from spending their lives in jail. The prosecutor has taken the possibility of the death penalty off the possible sentencing, but I can't help but think that there were other ways to die in there. Tiffany has lasted almost ten years, but would Jessica and Jordan be as lucky?

I don't like giving in to the pain of it all, but I cry until I fall asleep on my patio sofa, waking up at 1 a.m. to crawl into bed.

There is not time for giving up, I tell myself the next day, looking out at another beautiful, sunny California day.

I text Amy. "This is crazy maybe, but I might have a friend who knows an actor named Justin Baldoni who cares about helping men overcome their shame of sexual abuse. We need more public attention on the case. Do you mind if I try to reach him?"

Amy says yes immediately, and soon Justin is on board. We put things in motion to do an Instagram Live with the weight of Justin's followers. I also reach out to Jose Alfaro, a male survivor of sex trafficking from Texas who I know can help us unpack what's going on with Jordan and how a boy can be trafficked. A few days later, Justin, Jose, Amy, and I lead an Instagram Live with over 2,000 people watching. Within hours, more than a 1,000 people sign Jordan's Change.org petition, and Justin offers to stay connected to support Jordan.

It's perhaps a small victory, but every step up this mountain is one worth taking. Every person we reach, every signature, moves the cause forward, however incrementally. But that doesn't necessarily mean much to these kids locked up in prison. I'm frustrated to learn, for example, that none of the letters and books I send have made it to Jordan. He doesn't know that there are thousands of people supporting him and Jessica. I imagine him trapped in there with predators, cold and fading away as he wonders if anyone cares about him.

As soon as Jordan turns seventeen, he'll be moved to the adult prison, which is the situation Jessica is already dealing with. She was a few weeks past her eighteenth birthday when she was arrested alongside Jordan and has been telling us about threats she's been receiving in lockup. Just days after Jordan is certified as an adult, Jessica's first pre-trial hearing is happening. Her attorney, a local court appointed defender, never brings up her trafficking in court no matter how many times I ask him to do it on phone calls and emails. He never even investigates it as a line of affirmative defense. I also have no idea if he received the letter I wrote sharing Jessica's trafficking story or passed it on to the judge.

I wake up at 6 a.m. to prepare to testify for Jessica's hearing in Texas, which is two hours ahead of me in San Diego. After I testify, the district attorney continues to call Jessica a prostitute. She even tries to ask questions about my own sexual history or exploitation, but the judge overrules her. I'm frustrated and feeling especially beat down.

"Amy, I feel like nothing happened at all in court. We have no new court dates. No expert witnesses certified. Nothing."

At this point, Amy and I are speaking as two moms. I worry for her health—she's been fighting nonstop by filing lawsuits and creating petitions about the injustices children like Jordan are facing in the Bell County juvenile facility. She has constant anxiety for both her children, not only for the outcome of their cases but for their immediate safety in lockup. I'm also worried about Amy's safety—people think her children murdered a military man, and I fear potential retaliation.

"Andrea, we have to find Jessica an attorney who cares about her. Her attorney isn't doing anything. She isn't going to make it in there with all these threats of being beat. She's going to just drown."

I agree, but I've already written dozens of attorneys, pleading for them to help Jessica. At this point, I've been on the phone for hours with Amy. My voice is faltering from the dryness in my throat. I have one more idea.

Two years earlier, I'd met a *Washington Post* reporter named Jessica Contrera who was working on a story about a young survivor of child sex trafficking, Chrystul Kizer, who was charged with killing her sex trafficker. Randy Volar was a forty-three-year-old who had previously been charged with the sexual assault of children. He was released by the police the same day he was arrested despite possessing photos of sexual abuse of girls, including then sixteen-year-old Chrystul. As we spoke in a D.C. hotel lobby that had become my de facto office after I left FAIR Girls, I told her about Tiffany's case. Since then, I've kept Contrera updated on Tiffany, but with nothing new happening in Tiffany's case, she was focused on other more current and active cases where there was a fight for their freedom, such as Alexis Martin, a fifteen-year-old who was charged for the fatal shooting of the man who was trafficking her. I felt like she could be the one to report on Jessica and Jordan's case in Texas.

Through calls and texts from December 2020 and through the spring of 2021, I keep Contrera up to date, hoping she might report on Jordan and Jessica and get the public to care for them as she did with Chrystul and Alexis. I share how Jordan has been placed in choke holds over and over, stripped naked while handcuffed, and raped by two female guards in the juvenile facility. I recount how he's often placed in isolation without adequate blankets, once even during an ice storm where much of Texas was without power.

On June 1, 2021, almost a year after Jordan Hampton was arrested, he's featured in Jessica Contreras story, "The State of Ohio vs. A Sex-Trafficked Teenager" as yet another child sex trafficking survivor arrested and charged while being trafficked. The caption under his photo reads, "Jordan Hampton, 15: Charged with murder, being tried as an adult. Facing: Life in prison with the possibility of parole after 40 years. Status: awaiting trial." The article mentions that Jessica Hampton could face the death penalty.

Seeing it laid out there for everyone to read was scary because I feared no one would believe us that Jordan and Jessica were being sex trafficked and didn't have the free will to commit the crime they were accused of. I call Fecha as soon as Jessica sends me the article.

"It's not like we need to say they did or did not shoot Shareef Raekwon Ali-Barnett. We have to convince the jury that they were being trafficked." Fecha does what she does best and immediately creates a social media post to alert our growing petition signers about Jessica and Jordan. We only have 2,000 signatures, but with the *Washington Post* article, we could maybe get more and finally grab the attention of the Bell County prosecutor who I'd already seen in court virtually. She did not seem to view Jessica or Jordan as victims at all.

* * *

When Anna from JUST-US Participatory Defense writes to me about another sex trafficking survivor in jail in Bowie County, Texas, I don't know if we can handle more cases. I'm working basically full-time for free at Karana Rising and trying to stay afloat with consulting gigs. I worry about paying rent and childcare and making sure we keep the lights on—literally. Even just a few cases feels overwhelming.

"I don't want to say yes if I can't do it, Anna." She sends links to articles about a woman named Alana anyway. As I read, I realize it's the same story. No one believes Alana. Just like Tiffany. Just like Jessica and Jordan.

I agree to talk to Alana with Anna on the phone. Just like Tiffany and Jessica, Alana had experienced sexual abuse as a child before she was ever trafficked. She had a baby by her trafficker, just like Tiffany. She was being tried for allegedly killing a man who had beaten and raped her. Also, just like Jessica and Tiffany, Alana had a court-appointed attorney who wanted her to plea to life in prison. Her own trafficking was not investigated at all and there was no mention of affirmative defense.

Through the prison video phone, I see a petite girl with dark blonde hair in an orange jumpsuit. Alana begins to tell me her story. Her trafficker, who was from Mexico, was a friend of her brother. What started as a romantic relationship soon turned dangerous. He wanted money and began to threaten her to sell herself for sex. She feared him and what he would do to her family, who he threatened to kill if she tried to escape.

One day, he drove Alana to a man who had frequently raped her for money. Only this time the man refused to pay. Alana left but her trafficker said to go back or else he would beat her. When she arrived, demanding he pay, he threw her to the ground and began to assault her. Her trafficker, who was waiting in their car outside, heard her screaming and came in. He killed the man and dragged a traumatized Alana to the car. He held a knife to her, forcing her to drive through the night to Mexico.

The next day, she met his family, who were part of a drug cartel. Months passed, and daily he forced her to have sex with men who came into a bar that his family owned. Then he told her that her mother was dead. Alana was also pregnant and, after her son was born, she felt trapped. Police came in and out of the bar and were friendly with her trafficker, so she didn't trust them to help her. She was constantly monitored by her trafficker's father and cousins, who all told her that if she tried to run, they would keep her son.

Over six years later, Alana's trafficker was murdered—she suspected his father did it. Alana wanted to leave but her trafficker's parents took her son. Then, the apartment where she and the trafficker had lived burned to the ground. She was homeless and alone, sleeping on the beach and trying to find her son. Months later, Alana found him after a relative of the trafficker tipped her off. She finally ran to the U.S. consulate for help.

"I knew I would be arrested and put in jail," she tells me. "It was better than being forced to prostitute and be beaten while my son was groomed to become like his dad. I had no idea that the marshals would not believe me after I told them what really happened. Now, I'm facing trial for first degree murder for the man my trafficker killed right in front of me."

The day that Alana arrived in Houston with her son, she was escorted by two U.S. marshals. Her son was sent to live with her mother, who met them at the airport. That was a year ago. She's been sitting in prison and hasn't seen her son since that day.

Bowie County jail isn't safe, either. Days after we talk for the first time, Alana calls me, frantic.

"The man who raped me when I was sixteen found a way to get to me. I thought I was going to a visit with my mom and when I walked into the visitation room, it was my rapist. I felt like my world was crashing. I started screaming for the guards to come let me out and they just laughed while I screamed. Then, they put me in isolation for screaming."

Texas is a big state, but it's a small world and Alana grew up in the same small town where my parents grew up. When I find out Alana likely had met my grandmother at her store there, I just know I have to take her case. Now, we have three cases in Texas.

"Tiffany, there's another woman in a Texas jail who could use your support. Do you want to start writing to her too?"

Tiffany immediately starts to write letters to Alana and so does Ashley. I worry that doing public advocacy for Alana will be hard though. The media around her case is harsh, calling her a murderer. Alana isn't sure if she wants a petition or for us to publicly speak about her case. She worries her son and family will be at risk. My goal is to find her a better attorney who will want to actually help her and not just force her to take a terrible plea deal.

Alana had been trying to find evidence of her own abuse by her trafficker in Mexico for months. She was looking for records of the shelters and consulate where she'd tried to seek protection but had been turned away due to lack of space. She's willing to fight, but looking at Jessica, Jordan, and now Alana, I'm increasingly coming to the realization that a lack of effective legal defense is a black hole that can ruin a survivor's chances of being free

Part Three

AN OCEAN OF LOVE

Chapter 13

LACK OF LOVE

I get my little girl to school and sit back down at my computer to begin reaching out to other advocates. Tiffany depends on us. The film we'd started is now in full production, with Noel and the production company, What Took You So Long, collaborating with our team on every piece. I see Tiffany's story as the catalytic butterfly that could change how survivors are treated by our criminal punishment system. We also have a social media campaign and 5K walk to plan to help raise money for Tiffany, Jessica, and Jordan's cases.

I'm looking for photos of Tiffany for the film. I don't want people to just see Tiffany with her prison uniform on. I want people to see the girl I know. She likes writing, reading, and swimming, and loves her mom and son. She's a regular girl who's caught up in an extraordinary act of injustice by the Georgia legal system. Though most of our relationship has been on paper, we've had the ability to talk through fifteen-minute phone calls for months, and now we can finally have twenty-minute video calls for $3.95 through the jail communications system, JPay. I hate that call-end notice, though: "You have one minute remaining." Tiffany laughs at how mad I get when we hear it. We always stop talking before we get cut off to say, "Love you, Sis." Saying goodbye on our terms is better than being cut off.

After we hang up, the silence always lands on me like stale air. I feel like I'm re-entering a world with color, having come back from a time and place painted gray by the metal chains in Tiffany's world. I try to infuse some color in her world, sometimes taking her "to the beach" by going to the overlook at Beacon's Beach near my home for our pre-scheduled calls.

In a call, I ask Tiffany about photos. She's doubtful but gives me her mom's phone number and her dad's inmate information. When I reach Tiffany's mom, she's sweet, warm, and open to me.

"Do you have any photos of Tiffany?" I ask hopefully.

"I'm so sorry, honey, I don't. I guess they got lost along the way in life."

I send her father a letter. Tiffany's father had been in prison for twenty-one years after being convicted of murder when Tiffany was six. Though they write, they've not seen each other in all that time because the prison system doesn't allow inmates across different prisons to video chat, even if they're related.

The idea he'll have photos seems improbable, but I want to talk to him anyway. After all, he's the one who gave Tiffany the *USA Today* article that brought us together. His reply comes four days later.

> Dear Andrea,
>
> Tiffany has told me all about you. Thank you for all you do for her. I came to jail on May 31, 2000. I've regretted my crime for 21 years. I think about trafficking a lot even if I don't know all the facts. I believe Tiffany has gone through it. No girl deserves this. I regret not being there for her as her dad when she was going through it.
>
> I don't have any photos like you asked but I really thank you from a father's heart. I would love you to send me anything you can about Tiffany. I miss her. Thank you.
>
> In Jesus name,
> I love you both,
> Donald Simpson, Tiffany Simpson's Dad

He clearly loves Tiffany. I can feel it. I think about my own dad. All my memories of us in the woods, on walks, on the boat, cooking at the grill. All precious moments that never happened for Tiffany and her dad.

I'm not going to give up on finding photos. Next, I reach out to Tiffany's Aunt Brenda, whom she hasn't seen since she was much younger. I don't know how much Brenda knows about Tiffany's trafficking or how she feels about Tiffany now, but Tiffany describes her as loving and supportive.

On the phone, Brenda starts to cry. She's seen our Change.org petition.

"If I'd known what was really happening to my baby girl, I'd have fought for her."

Six photos soon come through from Brenda. The first is of Tiffany smiling in her fifth-grade school photo. Her light reddish-brown hair is long with bangs. Another photo is of Tiffany baking a cake with who I think must be Brenda. The most recent photo is of Tiffany after giving birth, lounging in an aboveground backyard swimming pool. It must have been taken after her arrest but before her sentencing. She looks so peaceful floating there in the pool.

"This is going to be like a magic trick, Noel. We have to make Tiffany reappear in the world with only a few photos," I say after sending her what I was able to find.

Noel has a better idea. We decide to create an animated film because we simply don't have enough images of Tiffany, even for our five-minute film. Things are starting to come together now. Each sentence in the script is shaped from something Tiffany has written or said in an email, letter, or phone call with me. We debate using a voiceover actress or perhaps Ashley to speak for Tiffany, but ultimately we decide to try recording her directly.

Tiffany's voice crackles brokenly through the prison phone. Her face blurs slightly on the video calls because I'm holding my phone to the computer screen, hoping to record her secondhand amid screaming inmates, being hung up on, and poor service. We have three minutes to make each recording before the jail system catches what it deems is a three-way call, which isn't allowed. "This call has been terminated due to a system error. Please hang up and try to call again at a later time."

Pouring Tiffany's voice into this film means countless hours of reviewing the script with her on our short calls. I sit in my daughter's closet with stuffed animals around to buffer the sound. I call them my "sound assistants." My favorite is a large pink dog we call Bubblegum. After each session, I crawl out of the closet with my phone and computer and send the recordings to Noel, hoping it'll be good enough for the documentary. I also hope Tiffany and I don't get caught breaking the rules. I don't think we're allowed to video record our chats. I don't think we're allowed to then share our conversations with the public either. We're doing it anyway. How else will the world see?

Finally, we have enough of Tiffany's voice to create the audio of the film. Noel draws a scene to accompany each recording.

A house of fire with seventeen candles.

Bars around an image of her father.

Tiffany, falling, amid a sea of men's feet.

A flowing ocean.

A beautiful rose that suddenly turns into a mouth with teeth, screaming.

As the film fades into an ocean, Tiffany's voice says, "I have heard that when you die, you see the most beautiful thing. I hope to see myself by the ocean with my son. If you believe survivors today, there will be less victims tomorrow."

We title the film *Lack of Love* to describe the total absence of love in Tiffany's life that led to her trafficking. It's Tiffany's personal story, but the truth is that every survivor experiences the same lack of love and belief. On April 2, 2021, we post the film to YouTube after Noel says we're ready. We share it in reels on Instagram, Facebook, Twitter, and in emails and text messages. Dressember does the same. I wish I could show Tiffany but I can't, as YouTube isn't allowed in prison.

A day later, a Texas-based survivor's mom reaches out. A week after that, a survivor in California emails. Then, another girl in Georgia, and it's like the film throws open a floodgate. We're inundated with stories from incarcerated survivors of how they were teens or barely in their twenties when they were first trafficked. Patterns begin to emerge. If defense attorneys are not defending their clients as survivors of trafficking, then the full extent of the trafficking isn't being investigated. These survivors aren't falling through the cracks; they're desperately clinging to the sides of gaping holes in the justice system.

We need more than a film and a social media campaign to make real change. We need more than law enforcement training. Survivors need to not be incarcerated in the first place, and that can only come about through a national movement.

* * *

The air is cool even though it's a late June evening in San Diego. The sun gleams like a slice of mango sliding into the water as the surfers catch the low-tide waves. It's Friday, and I'm waiting on a friend at a restaurant after a long week of advocacy in L.A. When my phone buzzes, it's lost in my black travel bag, and I don't get to it before it stops ringing. *Oh, no.* I think I've missed a call from Tiffany. I move as far away from the other guests as I can, clutching my phone and hoping Tiffany will call back. It lights up in my hand and I answer it immediately.

"Do you accept—"

I press "1" for "yes" before the automated voice can ask the whole question.

Always yes. We dream of the day when no one tells us when we can or can't talk. The familiar moment of silence, crackling from the landline to my iPhone, means she's there.

"Hey, Sis! What's up?"

Tiffany always says she can hear my smile through the phone.

"Andrea, I got this letter in the mail from the court. My habeas hearing is on July 8. Girl, that's like two weeks away."

I freeze on the restaurant patio. We've wanted this for years. Eight years to be exact.

"Do you think Susan knows?" I ask, trying to sound calm.

"I don't know. Can you write her, Sis? I'm excited, and I'm scared too. I don't want this to get messed up."

"I'll text Susan as soon as we're off. I'm excited and scared too! I'll write you as soon as I know more, okay?"

"Okay, love ya, Sis."

"Love ya, Tiff."

I text Susan immediately. It's already 9 p.m. where she is in Atlanta, but she writes back in five minutes. "I think it's her habeas hearing. We should ask the district attorney to have this pushed out because we're not ready, though."

She's right. We haven't found the other teenager, Kassie, and we need to know what she would say if she were to testify. Susan says she'll get back to me.

My heart is racing. If we do have the hearing and we win, could Tiffany be out in a matter of weeks? I start a letter to Tiffany with the information Susan texted to me.

Later that night, I think about Tiffany being free. We'll go to the ocean so she can have that first swim she's dreamed of. I'll be there with floaties and a big smile for her. We'll tour college campuses, and she can find her first job out of prison. I'm even already eyeing cafes around town for her to check out. I want her to have all the experiences that I'm having.

"Tiffany, you have to try avocado toast," I tell her next time we talk. It's a California classic and favorite of mine.

"What's an avocado?"

Oh. Okay. "Hmm, it's like a bag of spinach, a mango, and a banana made a food baby."

Avocado goes on our list of "firsts" that Tiffany wants to try.

We've just passed the ten-year mark of Tiffany's arrest in June 2011. Her thirty charges and arrest photo are still online in the Baker and Grady County court systems.

Soon, I hear from Susan that the habeas hearing will be rescheduled to October. The hearing is out of my hands, but I'm itching to do something more.

For years, I've known actress and advocate Mira Sorvino, and I so admire her work toward justice for herself and so many survivors of the now-convicted media mogul and sexual predator, Harvey Weinstein. Sometimes, I can see the hurt in Mira's eyes when we speak. It's an aura unique to survivors of sexual trauma and often something only other survivors can see or feel when they meet.

"Mira," I text, "would you do an Instagram Live with me to help get more signatures for the Change.org petition and awareness for Tiffany's case?"

Mira writes back immediately that she'll do it and asks for as much information as I can share about Tiffany's case. I trust Mira and send her Tiffany's court documents and the detailed six-page story I'd put together of her life both before and after being trafficked and arrested.

Mira has over 140,000 followers. I'm determined to get us to 10,000 signatures before Tiffany's habeas hearing. I'm not sure exactly how all this will help, but if the district attorney sees all this support for Tiffany pouring in, maybe he'll finally believe there's something true about her story. We set everything up quickly and, along with another survivor advocate from Georgia, Mira and I chat for more than half an hour on Instagram Live about Tiffany's story and the lack of justice in sex trafficking convictions like hers.

I get a text from Mira soon afterward. "Did you see Sharon Stone wants to help Tiffany?" She also lets me know that our petition and the Instagram Live were shared with Marty Kemp, the governor of Georgia's wife.

"Yes! The power of social media," I text Fecha after we post the video. I don't yet know what Marty Kemp could do to help, but having her aware of Tiffany and her case could help lead to other powerful women in Georgia knowing what's going on. Maybe this could get to the district attorney in Tiffany's case somehow.

Susan doesn't want us to get too loud with our national campaign before the habeas hearing, but even she's impressed with the reach of the video. "The district attorney won't care about a liberal celebrity, but he might care if the wife of the governor supports Tiffany."

Of course, social media has a dark side. There were places like Backpage, and we'd been hearing more and more about survivors being lured into video chats or forced to share sexualized photos. Then they were told that if they didn't comply by providing more photos or video, the images they'd already been coerced into sharing would be sent to their family and school. One little girl in such a case was only eight.

But, this time, we're using social media to show people what's going on with Tiffany, Jessica, and Jordan, and it's working in our favor.

* * *

We now have six weeks before Tiffany's habeas hearing on October 27. Fecha and I buy tickets to Georgia. Karana Rising's funding is next to zero and I'm working as a volunteer. I try not to let the stress of paying my own rent break me down. Over the next two weeks though, Tiffany's Change.org petition goes from about 10,000 to 25,000 signatures. For once, something is going right.

"Tiffany, I don't know what we did but I feel it! It's working! We'll get there!"

On October 25, Susan calls. "Andrea, I hope your tickets are refundable."

They aren't. My heart sinks.

"Why?"

"I just learned her former attorney didn't give me all the documents from Tiffany's case. I can't walk into a hearing like that without all the facts. I'm sorry. We have to move this."

"Does Tiffany know?"

"No, not yet. I plan to call her tomorrow."

"When's the hearing going to happen now?"

"I believe December 3."

Just five weeks, roughly. Five more weeks in a ten-year fight. I feel a heavy, deflating feeling in my chest. I try to hide my disappointment, but the tears, the quiet kind, are falling as Susan and I speak.

"Thank you for telling me, Susan. I'm just frustrated. How can this attorney continue to hurt Tiffany? I'm grateful for you. I'm grateful, but I'm angry too. What kind of attorney loses files in an active case where he knows there will eventually be a hearing? What is he hiding?"

Two days later, Tiffany can finally call. She seems in some ways less upset than me, but by now I know Tiffany sometimes shuts down when she's upset.

"I've learned that, to survive, sometimes you have to just find the positive, no matter what. You can't let things bring you down. That is when you get weak, and people in here smell weakness," she says.

The next day, an article I wrote for the *Washington Post*'s online magazine that focuses on issues of gender and identity, *The Lily*, comes out. It's their featured article of the day, with a big image of Tiffany with black bars drawn around her face. It was one of the first photos she had taken with the camera in the prison kiosk.

"She was a victim of child sex trafficking—and sent to prison. Now she has a chance at freedom," reads the headline of the article.

I'd gotten in contact with the editors in late June, when Tiffany first told me about her habeas hearing. They agreed and I had a one-week deadline over the Fourth of July. I spent the nights writing until dawn so it could be published right before Tiffany's court date. That way, there was a chance someone who could make a difference in Tiffany's case would read it. Then, Tiffany's hearing was moved to October. Now it's December. Her freedom is feeling more and more like a moving target, but the article is out, so I want to see what kind of support we can drum up.

I text Mira Sorvino, who's continued to share Tiffany's story online to her thousands of followers. "I want to warm that district attorney's heart. Can you get this to Governor Kemp's wife, Marty? I think she can really help Tiffany."

In addition, Fecha sends the article to the 25,000 Change.org petition signers and posts it all over social media. Support for Tiffany has grown a lot since we launched her petition over a year and a half ago.

A few days later, Susan is back in touch, letting me know that Tiffany's habeas hearing is delayed again—this time until January 4, 2022—because of a conflict with the judge's schedule.

I actually cry thinking about how to tell Tiffany. A month isn't that long, but now it's been over half a year of delays. Plus, the petition for this hearing was first filed in 2013, nine years ago. I wonder how many times it could get pushed back before she stops believing we can get her out of there.

I write Tiffany. "I'm so sorry. I know Susan will do the right thing. I'm going to sign up for us to talk on Thanksgiving."

In her next letter, Tiffany says she understands, but I worry she's losing faith in us and sinking into depression.

The fights are really bad. Inmates are going crazy, and the guards are always screaming about lockdowns. An older woman was raped with some kind of object and now she's gone. I think she's dead. The warden walks around with mace. It's degrading and I miss seeing the sunshine and fresh air. It's so close and now it's just another month but I can't do this much longer.

Having the video chat on Thanksgiving evening is something for all of us—Veronika included—to look forward to. Now eight years old, Veronika calls Tiffany her "aunt." She's been sending Tiffany cards and drawings for years, but this will be the first time they'll get to meet on video.

"I'm going to read her some stories too," Veronika tells me excitedly.

Veronika made Jessica and Jordan cards as well, but she doesn't know that their jails never let them have them. Her third-grade teacher once asked me why she kept talking about wanting a "reduced sentence" when she would get in trouble for talking too much in class. I just smiled and said, "Must be something she heard on TV."

We sit around the Thanksgiving dinner table with friends and family. After, I take my computer upstairs for the call with Tiffany. I let Veronika come in to say hi. She immediately begins singing a song to Tiffany, who smiles and asks for another one when she's done.

After Veronika goes back downstairs to wait for pumpkin pie, our conversation turns back to advocacy. The number of survivors in jail who need support is growing, I tell Tiffany. Through our efforts and those of other advocates and survivors telling their stories, survivors are realizing that they're victims who don't deserve the sentences they're facing or serving.

"This is a movement we're making, Tiffany," I tell her.

"Girl, I'm so into what we're building. I want to be out there helping all the way. They can't keep me in this prison forever."

The video goes dead two minutes before it should, and I sit in my room, staring at the blank screen before closing it down and going back to join my family.

As I walk downstairs, I think to myself, *No, Tiffany, they can't. But they're certainly trying.*

Chapter 14

TIFFANY TAKES THE STAND

*T*he sun streams through the six-seat law library in the Pulaski County Courthouse. It's January 4, the day of Tiffany's habeas hearing—finally. The day before, I fly from San Diego to Atlanta, meeting Fecha at the airport.

"This is quite the road trip," Fecha says. A road trip that's been nine years in the making. Nine years and three months, to be exact, since Tiffany's first letter to me. I have the letter with me in the sleeve of my journal along with letters from Jessica, Alana, and others. Though my focus is on Tiffany, other cases are still ongoing.

"I can't believe we're finally here," I reply as we wait for Susan to pick us up outside airport arrivals. On the plane, I'd had nervous, uncomfortable dreams of not finding Tiffany's court hearing room. I got lost in a courtroom where cats ambushed us, and then loud rock songs started playing over our testimony. I grabbed Tiffany and we ran. I know they're because of my anxiety, so I try to hold on to the thought that these crazy dreams will make Tiffany laugh when I tell her.

From the car, I see the sun setting over the peach and pecan tree groves that line the highway. The golden hour feels idyllic as we speed toward our motel, even in the face of the next day. Susan confides that Tiffany's previous attorney, Mr. Cleveland, said to her he'd never planned to help Tiffany with her habeas hearing despite saying he would. He'd said, "Everyone around here is scared of upsetting Judge Cato."

That seems strange to me. "Isn't he's retired?" I ask.

"Yes, but his influence remains. No one wants to lose his favor."

I think about that for a moment. "I guess all these men have something to lose by admitting Tiffany should be free," I say.

In the morning, we arrive at the courthouse so early that the lights on the second floor aren't even on yet. We've already been up for hours, preparing in our motel. Susan has just dragged up the evidence boxes from the "one person capacity" elevator. It's only 8 a.m., but I keep glancing up, looking for Tiffany, as if the guards might just let her sit around casually in the courthouse. I know better after years of waiting for survivors in courtrooms. This is different, though. This is Tiffany.

"Did you see the confederate statue out the window of the bathroom?" Susan asks as she walks in with the last box.

"Yeah, and did you see the Human Trafficking Hotline poster on the other side?" Fecha replies.

That's right. Pulaski County Courthouse has a symbol of America's slavery on one side and a sign to help survivors of human trafficking to freedom on the other. We all take photos of the ironically inconsistent messaging on view from the second-story women's restroom.

"Her first attorney might not show up today. He has a court conflict," Susan says. He doesn't want to come—I just know it. Last month, he told Barbara Brown, the retired FBI agent donating her time to the case, that he "didn't remember" if Tiffany was a victim of child sex trafficking. Still, he said, he felt like he was a father figure for Tiffany. *Yeah right*, I thought. Tiffany told me she'd only ever met with him once.

At 8:30 a.m., I see an email from Tiffany from the JPay jail message system and pull it up while Susan arranges the evidence boxes and rushes out again. Tiffany must have written it while waiting on the guards to take her to court.

> *Sis, it is 8:20. I'm still in the dorm. We don't have an officer back here and I'm supposed to be at court by now and I'm nervous.*

*I feel like this prison is toying with my freedom. It makes me
mad. I don't know what is going on.*

I reply immediately, hoping she might see it and feel calmer, unless she's
already here.

Hey Sis!
*Fecha and I are here. We are in the court law library waiting
for you. We love you. Susan is really preparing. I know you
likely won't get this before you arrive, but I hope you do. I'm
thinking of you. Just can't wait to see you and hopefully give
you a nine-year overdue hug if they let us!*
  Love you!

A few minutes later, Susan walks back in. "It's time. She's here. Let's get
to the courtroom."

My hands are shaking as we walk through the metal detectors. The
courtroom's air conditioning is on full blast despite it being forty degrees
outside. COVID has done a number on court proceedings. Yellow tape
yelling "Sheriff Line, Do Not Cross" is plastered over most of the chairs
for socially distanced seating and we're all required to wear masks. We find
seats directly behind Susan—where Tiffany will sit.

After a few minutes, the Honorable Sarah Wall walks in. We all rise,
but she quickly says, "Please sit down." Her smile and no-nonsense tone
reminds me of Judge Rook, the wonderful D.C. Superior Court judge who
helped us found HOPE Court.

The courtroom is almost empty save for the district attorney, Fecha,
me, Susan, her assistant, our expert witnesses, and the bailiff standing
quietly in the back. Tiffany's mom and aunt are unfortunately too sick to
join us. Within the first few minutes, the judge asks our expert witnesses
to leave the courtroom. I slink down in my seat with my journal, hoping
she won't ask Fecha and me to leave too. I can feel her staring at me, and
I clutch my pen.

Susan begins with the "miscarriage of injustice" that Tiffany has faced. She concludes her opening statement by saying that Tiffany didn't even realize that she was a victim of trafficking at the time of her sentencing.

The district attorney whose slumped shoulders match his crumpled brown suit and raspy voice, replies, "Your Honor, this is a case of buyer's remorse." He wasn't the original DA in Tiffany's case, which I think is a good thing. That DA might have seen this hearing as an attack on his own legal abilities, even though it was really about her court-appointed attorney, and how he didn't do as much for Tiffany as she deserved.

That's kind of ironic, I think in response to the district attorney's opening. Tiffany didn't "buy" a plea deal, but she was certainly bought and sold for sex over and over again.

After opening arguments, the bailiff goes to get Tiffany. My heart jumps as she walks in with a prison guard, looking down. Her tan jumpsuit reads "Dept. of Corrections" on the back, and she has chains around her waist that connect to each wrist and ankle and are secured with a metal lock at her back. She shuffles her orange clogs as her chained legs navigate the courtroom pillars to get to her seat next to Susan. I can see her knee is hurting by the way she limps. For a brief moment, she turns around to smile at me, though she still keeps her head down. Susan turns around to look at me with a "do not even think of saying anything, Andrea" face. Tiffany sits down slowly, the chains making it difficult.

Susan's questions begin. The judge allows Tiffany to remove her mask so she can hear her better. Within minutes, I can hear Tiffany's voice falter. With her back to me, I can't see her face, but I know she's crying.

They go through Tiffany's legal history on her case to set up the background for how she'd had poor representation. When Tiffany went to her first bond hearing on July 1, 2011, she didn't have an attorney. She didn't have one at her second arraignment on July 11, 2011, either. She was seventeen and alone, facing charges that included child sex trafficking. These are new facts to me.

"How did you find your attorney, Tiffany?" Susan asks.

"I was told I needed to find an attorney, so I found one on a list of court-appointed attorneys and called him." She'd never had a forensic exam or even a psychological evaluation to determine if she might be a victim of trafficking or another form of abuse. Her attorney had never asked her if she needed counseling or services. She feared for her life, as Yarnell had threatened that if she said anything to her attorney or family, he would kill her and her baby, who was born two months after her arrest.

When she met her attorney the first time, Tiffany said her fingerprints were on the money that was paid by the sex buyers who raped her and Kassie. She was too scared to tell him about the abuse and sex trafficking.

"I thought Yarnell would find out and kill me or my son."

"We all got some of the money," Tiffany answers when Susan asks how her fingerprints were on the money. She sounds numb again.

"What did you use the money for?"

"I used the money Yarnell gave me to pay for his gas, his Dodge truck, his food, and utilities. Basically, Yarnell lived off my body."

This doesn't matter. Even if you receive money, you're still a victim of trafficking. A lot of pimps will give their victims a tiny bit of money to pay for food or for them to get their nails done. The traffickers brainwash them into thinking that it's generous if they get even a little bit of the money they earn.

On December 8, four months after Ayden was born, she was standing in line filling out forms to get support for herself and her child. She'd been living with her grandmother and mother since she was arraigned in July. "I hadn't told them anything about trafficking or abuse. I was so scared of Yarnell and what he could do to me."

"Wasn't Yarnell in jail?" the district attorney asks.

"Yes, but I thought maybe he could get out, like me."

When Tiffany got the call from her attorney that she needed to be in court, she had to leave Ayden with her mom.

"I had no idea what was going on, but I got to court as fast as I could."

Sitting behind her, I feel my tears coming up. Those had been her last moments of freedom, and she hadn't even known.

"I walked in and my attorney said we were making a plea deal. I had no idea what was going on. He said I'd get ten years in jail, so I'd still get to see my son grow up. If I didn't take the deal, I'd spend my life in jail. My son would grow up without a mother."

Tiffany's voice is weak. Susan's assistant hands her tissues.

Tiffany was most concerned about Ayden. "Where would he go?" she'd asked her attorney. "Will I get to see him when I'm out? Can he come see me?"

He said yes.

"I trusted him. He was supposed to have my best interests at heart."

So, her attorney just called her to court and didn't even tell her why? I'm increasingly convinced that he didn't have her best interests at heart. It doesn't sound like he was interested in her at all.

"Did your attorney speak with you about any possible defenses? Or ask you if you were a victim of trafficking?" asks Susan.

"No. He didn't. He just said I had to take the plea."

The questions continue. Last night, Susan told us that Tiffany's first attorney said defending Tiffany was fruitless because nothing ever happened in that county. "Fruitless is not a legal standard!" Susan practically yelled. "She was seventeen. She didn't need to prove she was a victim of trafficking if he knew she was involved in commercial sex. That was the law in Georgia in 2011. It's the law now."

This attorney never planned to defend Tiffany. Why? I don't understand it.

"Why didn't you speak up about the trafficking?" Susan asks again.

Tiffany sighs. "I was scared of him," she says, referring to Yarnell. Susan had told us that the judge might not have a lot of background on human trafficking. She's trying to be sure the judge understands the fear that trafficking victims have and the control that their traffickers have over them. Those are the reasons they commit the crimes that land them in jail.

"Did Yarnell ever do anything to make you scared of trying to leave him?" As Tiffany was legally a child, it doesn't matter if he forced or threatened her. But Susan wants to make sure there aren't any angles for the district attorney to attack.

"One time, he was drunk and I tried to run away. He found me walking on the road. I ran into the ditch and he tried to run me over. He said he didn't care if he killed me or my baby. He wanted me to go make him money. He dragged me by my hair back into the car." Tiffany also explains how Yarnell would beat her if she refused to meet the men he'd sold her to.

"One time, he beat me in the face and slammed my head into the wall. I have scars from the thermostat on that wall."

It's not hard to understand why Tiffany would be terrified of Yarnell.

Susan keeps going. "Did you know that Yarnell had confessed to selling you and Kassie for sex?"

Tiffany didn't know.

"Did you know that one of the men who raped you also said he had paid a Black man to bring girls to him? He said the man had a pregnant girl with him," continues Susan.

Tiffany starts to cry. She didn't know. Her attorney didn't tell her. She'd often been the one who the men texted. She didn't want to go sometimes. He would beat her until she couldn't say no.

"If you had known Yarnell had confessed to selling you for sex and one of the men had confessed to buying you, would it have made a difference?"

"Yes. I would have spoken up."

"Why would that have made a difference?"

"Because if Yarnell already confessed, I could speak up about what was going on."

Her first attorney is still not in the courtroom. I desperately wish he was here to hear Tiffany crying.

The questioning turns to why she didn't tell anyone what was going on. "I didn't want my mom and grandmother to know. I was ashamed. They already thought I was dirty."

Tiffany's mother lost custody of her when she was thirteen. At sixteen, Tiffany ran away from her grandmother's house and started doing cocaine. No missing person's report was filed.

Now Susan asks if she can share any examples of when she tried to leave Yarnell.

"Yes, we were driving to his cousin's house, and we got a call. He said he would take me to the guys, but I said no. He pulled up to his cousin Junior's house and got out and came back and got in the car. He stabbed me in the left knee and then came out and dragged me out by the hair. I was screaming in pain."

I'd read this story many times in our emails. It was one of so many times she tried to leave. But as she tells the story in court, I start to think about how Tiffany's knee has been bothering her for months. I thought maybe it was because she was locked in her room for twenty-two or twenty-three hours a day, rarely seeing the sun or getting exercise. But it hit me then: her knee has been hurting for ten years since Yarnell stabbed her and kept her from escaping with her unborn baby. *Why didn't you figure this out before, Andrea?* I ask myself. This time, my silent tears are from shame.

"Did your attorney inform you that Yarnell Donald was convicted of having sex with a minor? Or that he was an unregistered sex offender?"

"No."

"Would that have made a difference in your telling him about the trafficking?"

"Yes. I would have felt like I wasn't alone. I would have thought maybe my attorney would believe me. Yarnell said no one would ever believe me. Like, as if I was suddenly not alone anymore."

A few months ago, Tiffany wrote a blog post about community: "It will take a community to bring me home." There was no community for her the day she was sentenced.

"I got to the courthouse and the judge started to ask me questions. My mom and grandmother couldn't come," Tiffany continues. "I didn't know what to do. I just said, 'Yes, sir' to my attorney because what else could I do? He's a professional. He knew the law."

Tiffany is shifting back and forth in the green leather court chair, her chained legs swaying a little.

"When the judge asked if you had anything else to say, why didn't you say you were a victim of trafficking?" Susan asks.

"I was scared," she answers.

"Did your attorney review any possible legal defenses for you? Or why he concluded that a plea was all you could get?"

He hadn't. Susan wants to make it clear that he hadn't prepared Tiffany for her case at all. Tiffany had witnesses to her trafficking: The men who bought her. Yarnell's cousin. A former girlfriend of Yarnell's who he abused too. Maybe the hospital staff who treated her stab wound. Yet her attorney never asked her if she had any witnesses. He simply filled out the thirty-one-page plea agreement document and Tiffany signed it.

At this point, the hearing has been going on for around four hours. I look over to see the district attorney yawning and looking at his phone as if he's bored. He's been doing that a lot, and my blood boils. Susan continues to unravel the day Tiffany was sentenced.

"'I'm done. I'm sentencing you to thirty years to serve,'" Tiffany says, quoting Judge Cato's words from her court sentencing document.

"Why didn't you say something when the judge asked you if your attorney had done everything that you wanted him to?"

"I just felt like, what was the point? It was over." Tiffany sounds flat. Defeated.

At the end of the sentencing, Tiffany had been given twenty years—double the number of years her attorney said she would serve. After Judge Cato read through her conditions of release, including how she'd be on the sex offender registry, according to court transcripts, Tiffany and her attorney had stepped outside.

"What did you discuss?" asks Susan.

"I wanted to know if I could see my son. That's all I cared about anymore."

"Tiffany, how did the judge treat you?"

"Like I was a monster," she says. She looks down at the floor. Her shoulders are shaking, and I know she's crying.

Tiffany was then transferred immediately to jail. On January 23, 2012, Tiffany was told she had court again. She didn't know why. When she arrived, she was told it was another sentencing hearing.

"When I got in the transfer van, Yarnell was there in the van too."

"Did he say anything to you?" asks Susan.

"No, but he thrust his pelvis out and made a sexual face at me." Tiffany sounds terrified, even now.

Riding to another courthouse with her trafficker next to her must have been torture. *No wonder she didn't speak out*, I think.

When Tiffany got to court, she didn't fight the plea deal.

"Yarnell had threatened me if I talked, and seeing him there was too much. I just gave up. I had my son to think about."

Tiffany was sentenced again to the same charges for the same amount of time. She was transferred to Pulaski State Prison. A few months later, Tiffany started to file motions to have her plea withdrawn. "I started to see things differently. I wanted to defend myself," she says. She sent a letter to her attorney and to the judge to ask for her court documents. The court denied her motion for documents and her attorney ignored her requests.

Another inmate helped her draft her next motion to withdraw her plea because she could not reach her attorney. The court denied her request. "I felt trapped all over again," she says.

"That is when my dad sent me that *USA Today* article. I decided to write to Andrea to ask her if she could help me," says Tiffany.

Finally, Susan is done questioning Tiffany. The courtroom is cold. It's 12:30 p.m. when the judge calls for a lunch recess, letting us know that Tiffany's first attorney will be in court after all.

"Thank goodness," I whisper to Fecha. "I can't handle another continuance. We've waited too long for this."

I get up to speak to Tiffany face to face for the first time. My heart is racing as we grin at each other.

"Am I allowed to hug her?" I ask Susan as Tiffany giggles. Susan says no.

"Tiff, are you hungry? I am!"

She giggles more. "Where are my vegan tacos, Sis?" Her sense of humor never fails.

"Pretty sure you get a hamburger and fries today," I answer.

"Well, baby steps."

She's cracking me up.

Tiffany makes an air hug before the guard takes her back to the holding room for lunch. She testified for over two hours.

I stay behind in the courthouse for a bit and find a spot to email Alana. A month earlier, she'd accepted a plea deal for thirty-two years in prison. I was angry and sad. Her mother seemed calmer though. "Alana's attorney said if they went to court, they would go after capital murder. She would do life without parole. This way, she could do twelve of the thirty-two and be out right after her son graduates from high school," she'd told me.

I haven't heard from Alana since she sent me a Christmas card.

I know I'm still a part of Karana Rising. I'm in a lot of pain right now and kind of in shock. But it's over. No more fearing doing life in prison. Thank you for everything. Love, Alana

She'd been moved to a new prison, which was a small comfort after her rapist had visited her in jail. I encourage Alana to complete college while in prison and prepare for the rest of her life. "I'm not going to give up on you, Alana," I write. I add that I'll call her when I get back from Georgia.

I close my computer and run across the street to a diner with the sign "We serve meat" on the door. Susan, our witnesses, and Fecha are waiting to be seated, along with what look like locals and other court employees. Ketchup and mustard containers are everywhere.

"How do you think we're doing?" I ask Susan as we sit down in a booth. Susan is never one to share what she thinks, but her smile says it all.

Chapter 15

I THINK THEY FINALLY BELIEVE ME

"Do you think we can hug?" I ask again.

After lunch, Tiffany is there with the retired FBI agent, Barbara Brown, waiting for court to begin again. Susan isn't in the room.

"You better be fast," Barbara says, smiling.

I run around the banisters that separate Tiffany and me and throw my arms around her.

"Love you, Sis," Tiffany whispers, though she isn't able to wrap her arms around me because of the chains.

Barbara grabs my phone, saying, "I'll take your photo." Fecha jumps over too, and we pose for a few quick shots before running back to our chairs.

As the judge returns to the bench, I can still feel that hug. I look down at my phone, to the photos of us smiling with our arms around Tiffany, my pink knitted gloves over her tan shirt. *She is glowing*, I think.

The district attorney first calls Tiffany, who remains seated as he begins his questions.

"Did Yarnell know Kassie before you both picked her up and drove to the trailer park?" he asks.

"Yes, he met her because my mom was friends with Kassie's grandmother. I was already living with Yarnell, so he took me to see them."

I wonder what Tiffany's mom thought of Yarnell being thirty-four while Tiffany was seventeen. Did she wonder if something was going on?

"So, basically, you were the connection between Kassie and Yarnell?" he presses.

Tiffany sighs. "Yes, I knew Kassie and I knew Yarnell."

Susan had told me that this point was all they really had on Tiffany. We just had to make the case that if Yarnell wanted to do something, he did it. Tiffany couldn't say no.

"Why didn't you tell your mom that Yarnell was trafficking you?" Susan asks.

"I thought they would be ashamed of me." Most victims are, and as children, many also don't know how to describe what's happening to them.

"Who arranged to meet with the four men who had sex with you and Kassie?" the DA asks.

He says it so casually. This was not "having sex"; it was rape. It's as if he's actively refusing to believe Tiffany is a victim of sex trafficking.

"Yarnell did."

Tiffany had already said Yarnell arranged it. Susan also had said that one of the four men had confessed he was arranging to buy Tiffany and Kassie for sex from Yarnell. *It all sounds so cut and dried*, I think. Words like "arrange," "buy," and "sell" make it sound transactional. Maybe to the district attorney, the rapists, and Yarnell, that's all it was.

"He always controlled where we went. I couldn't leave. I couldn't say no to anything he wanted," Tiffany continues.

"When Kassie was interviewed, did you know that she said she didn't want to have sex with these men, but she said you looked at her like you would be disappointed if she didn't do it? Would that have made a difference? Would you have told the court about the trafficking if you had known?" he continued.

A lot of court cases are rehashing the same information over and over. Tiffany had also already been asked if knowing Yarnell had spoken out about selling her would have made her speak up. She was asked the same thing about two of the men who said they bought her from Yarnell. Every time, she says yes.

"I would have felt like people would have believed me. I would have thought Yarnell already told them everything."

It's important to impress upon the judge the suffocating effect of Tiffany's fear, but I'm feeling a burning frustration in my chest. Judge Cato and her original attorney both knew Tiffany was seventeen and being sold by a thirty-four-year-old man for sex. Her attorney had knowledge of the statements by Kassie, the rapists, and Yarnell. Tiffany shouldn't have had to speak up at all! Or at the very least, she should have had all the same knowledge so she could have felt safe to do so. I wish I could jump the guardrails and scream this to the courtroom. Instead, I keep saying to myself, *Trust Susan, Andrea.*

"Did you ever try to leave?" he asks. More repeated questions from earlier in the day.

"Yes, one time he grabbed me and threw my face into the wall. The air vent scarred my face before I fell to the ground. Then, another time I tried to run when he was drinking with friends. I got out and was running down the street. He got in the car and came after me. I ran into the ditch so he wouldn't hit me with the car. He grabbed me and threw me in the car and threw my phone out the window."

The judge is staring intently at Tiffany, who's crying again. Her voice falters and fades to a whisper.

The judge calls another recess after the district attorney ends his questioning of Tiffany. This time, I don't even try to be sly. Fecha and I run right over to talk to Tiffany. It's 2:30 p.m.

When we return, Susan calls Barbara, who's so petite that when she sits in the witness box, she sinks below sight. The laughter is a welcome relief. The bailiff tries to raise the chair, but even still, all we can see is her forehead and eyes. Still, as a former FBI agent, she paints a vivid picture of what an actual investigation could have done to help Tiffany avoid the last ten years in jail.

"You don't really need to prove force or coercion in Tiffany's case because she's a minor, but there was force and control. If I were investigating the case, I would have had a psychological evaluation done for Tiffany and watched the interviews to learn about the past abuse. I would have found more about Yarnell's history of abusing and sexually assaulting children."

I wonder if Tiffany was thinking what I was thinking: *I wish Barbara had been here in 2011.*

Then, Tiffany's first attorney arrives. I watch as he walks to the witness box, his suit annoying me for no reason other than he's wearing it. Susan gets another one of her binders out. I've already made eight pages of notes and my hand feels like it's on fire.

No one is smiling as he takes the stand.

After a few odd minutes asking him about his mailing address, Susan asks, "What was your relationship like with the then assistant district attorney?"

"He was kind of a jerk."

I look at Fecha. Even the female prison guard's eyes grow big.

"He said if I didn't get Tiffany to take the plea, I would never get another plea deal out of him."

I wasn't sure if Tiffany's first attorney was already planning to run for district attorney, or if he was just trying to keep the assistant district attorney happy for future cases, but I was sure that he'd sold Tiffany out.

"Did you tell him that Tiffany was a victim of sex trafficking?"

"I don't recall if she told me she was a victim of trafficking or not. I knew Yarnell was turning her out, though."

"Turning her out"? What lawyer speaks like that about his then seventeen-year-old client?

"He would not have cared," he adds, also saying that the judge didn't like Tiffany either. This feels like a feeble attempt to diffuse the blame.

"How did you build rapport with Tiffany?"

He rubs his forehead and swivels in his seat. He says he was in contact with her and had several meetings. Earlier that morning, Tiffany testified she only met with him once before the sentencing hearing in December. I believe Tiffany.

"Did you show Tiffany the videos of Yarnell's interviews?"

"Did you show Tiffany the video of Kassie's interview?"

"Did you share with Tiffany that Yarnell had failed to register as a sex offender after raping another child?"

"Did you conduct an investigation?"

"It would be my practice to do so," he responds to all these questions.

That is not an answer, I think. Yet, like a parrot, it's his common refrain. He testifies he had lost his case files years earlier. He didn't have anything to prove what he did, when he met with Tiffany, or what happened in their meetings. So, he had no evidence of what he actually did, making it his word against Tiffany's. I'm wondering what Tiffany, sitting quietly beside Susan, is thinking.

"Did you ever attempt to interview Kassie or Yarnell?"

"It would be my practice to do so."

Fecha and I are talking with our eyes, trying to hide our contempt.

"In court, how did you feel about Judge Cato's attitude toward Tiffany?"

"He was harsh. He felt she hung around with certain people. He was not sympathetic."

About Judge Cato, Susan asks, "He used the term 'shacking up,' referencing Tiffany's trafficking. How was his tone when he used that term?"

"Sarcastic."

So, if the judge was heckling Tiffany, his teenage client who was a victim of sex trafficking, why didn't he speak up in court to make clear she was a victim? I was writing furiously in my journal, my hand cramping up.

"You referred to Tiffany as 'damaged goods' in the sentencing documents I have before me. What did you mean by this?"

He swivels more in his chair, clearly uncomfortable as he continues to rub his forehead. "I mean that she had suffered like Kassie."

Okay, so now he's saying she suffered like Kassie, but he also doesn't know if he knew she was a victim of trafficking. *Which is it?* I write in my notes, tipping it toward Fecha so she can see. She nods.

"Did you receive the letters from Tiffany requesting assistance in filing motions to receive her court documents or to withdraw her plea?"

He says no. But how can he know for sure if he lost his files? Plus, Tiffany testified she got a letter from her attorney's assistant in response to one of her letters stating that they could no longer assist her. It's pretty convenient that there's no paper trail to verify his claims.

He is still. His head in his hand.

"Do you believe Tiffany Simpson received justice in her case?" asks Susan.

"No," is all he says.

"I have no more questions for this witness," Susan concludes.

It's 5 p.m., but there's one last witness to be questioned, an expert in trauma.

"When I say we can stay after 5 p.m., I mean we'll go all the way until the end," says the judge.

Dr. Whitmore, a clinical psychologist from Atlanta, is going to speak about what sex trafficking is, how the trauma might make it hard for a victim to recognize the trafficking or speak up, and why they might do what their trafficker says, no matter what it is. This is key because the district attorney had referred to Tiffany multiple times as the "connector" between Yarnell and Kassie, and if the judge believes that she instigated Kassie's rapes of her own free will, the case is over.

Dr. Whitmore, in her four-inch stilettos, impresses even the prison guard. "Okay, girl," she mumbles from behind her mask. Tiffany looks over and smiles.

"Sex trafficking doesn't just happen," Dr. Whitmore says, in total command of the courtroom. "There is a host of things like prior sexual abuse, abandonment, or poverty that happens to lead most victims into it. Sexual abuse is like an open wound that, if not healed, can easily be reinjured."

Tiffany had experienced abuse well before meeting Yarnell. Dr. Whitmore hadn't been allowed to watch Tiffany's testimony earlier in the day; she was only here to speak about victims of sex trafficking generally, not to unpack the specifics of Tiffany's case. She probably didn't know how bad it had been for Tiffany while she was being trafficked. The wound was more than reinjured. It was blown open.

"The repeated sexual abuse a victim of sex trafficking experiences sometimes has a numbing effect," she continues, looking up at the judge.

This explained why Tiffany would sound numb while talking to her attorney or anyone else. She often sounded that way when we first began writing letters.

"Traffickers create a sort of cult culture. There is an allegiance that a young person seeking community or love will give their trafficker to please them."

Tiffany said something similar in the film we made. "I thought it was love, but it was an ocean of fear drowning me." It's a fear they learn to hide, one that people often don't see unless the victim is crying.

"Traffickers will say they will take care of you, show you a better life. They sell the dream you most want," Dr. Whitmore continues.

Yarnell offered Tiffany that weird blend of a father and a lover. Yarnell's abuse clearly showed he was the opposite, but the mixed messages kept Tiffany hoping it could get better. Tiffany hadn't had an example of fatherly love since she was six years old.

"Of the thousands of survivors of sex trafficking I've met, many are forced to commit crimes by their traffickers. Sometimes it's trespassing or skipping school. Other times, it's more violent, like sex trafficking."

That's been my experience too. I could fill my journal with the names of survivors who were forced into robbing buyers, like Jessica and Jordan, or stealing, like Alyssa. Forced criminality is hardly ever discussed, even by advocates. It goes back to believing that a victim has to be perfect. They can't have prior records. They can't act angry. They have to be totally innocent. I think that was what angered Judge Cato. Tiffany hadn't acted "perfect enough" for him to believe her. Again, he could have just followed the law. Instead, he let his prejudice against Tiffany's past take away nine years of her life, and counting.

"Traffickers make you feel like you are not human anymore. You are just theirs to make money off of. They get their victims to feel worthless in addition to being afraid. Many won't see their own victimization or speak up," Dr. Whitmore adds.

"Society wanted to put me in a cement box, so they didn't have to look at their mistakes," Tiffany once said to me.

"Trauma lives in the brain. It stunts your growth. It will make a survivor trust people in authority and not question what they are being told. Trauma mutes your brain," Dr. Whitmore explains.

This could explain why Tiffany said she trusted her attorney had her best interests at heart.

"Had I known that there were other girls he sold and beat, I would have felt less alone. I would have felt like I could say to others what was happening to me," Tiffany had testified earlier.

It's called community. Looking around the courtroom as the judge explains what will happen after court ends, I see the community of women there for Tiffany. Me, Fecha, Susan, Dr. Whitmore, and Barbara.

The court will have the transcripts of today's hearing in two months, followed by Susan's one month to file a brief, and then one month for the district attorney to reply. Then, the judge will make her ruling. So, four to six months before resolution.

Tiffany gets up and I hug her again quickly before she's taken back to the holding room. From there, she'll returned to prison. Fecha and I make heart hands at her. She holds up her chained hands and returns the gesture.

"See you Saturday," I whisper. It'll be the first day I'll be allowed to visit Tiffany in prison and have a face-to-face conversation with her.

That night, on the drive to Atlanta to the hotel we'd booked for the night, Susan is so excited about the hearing that she calls her parents. I'd trusted her before, but now I adore her.

* * *

I stay with Fecha in Atlanta over the next few days, and on Saturday morning I'm up before dawn to meet Susan's friend. I'm paying her to drive me the two hours to the jail in Pulaski, which is far from any public transportation.

At the prison, the parking lot is mostly empty. I take my ID and debit card, leaving everything else with Susan's friend, who will wait in the car. This will help expedite me getting in to see Tiffany. Under my black sweater, I have my "Free Tiffany" shirt on. *A tiny rebellious act*, I think.

I walk through a maze of metal doors and down a long hall. Finally, I encounter a sign: "Visitation Room." I open the door and there she is, sitting at the end of a line of inmates and their visitors, each set separated by tiny tables and chairs. It almost looks like a cafe where everyone has decided to wear the same tan suit.

The buzzing of the lights and banging of the vending machines is almost deafening, and it feels like maybe it's on purpose so we can't hear each other. The fluorescent lights glare over us. She gets up to greet me, her lilac eyeshadow standing out against all the brown around us. We aren't really supposed to touch or hug, so we just look at each other, really drinking each other in with our eyes. I can feel I'm hugely grinning, and my excitement is reflected in Tiffany's face too. I convince her to get a Dr Pepper and pay with my debit card. Other inmates are intently talking to their guests as we sit back down at her table. I can't wait to know what she was thinking during the hearing. We get right into it.

"I can't believe he just sat there and lied like that on the stand. I mean, who is the professional?" Tiffany says, referring to her first attorney.

I laugh. She's right. "He thought he could get away with it, I guess. I mean, he got away with not doing anything ten years ago," I reply.

She nods.

"Susan totally nailed him to the wall," I say. "I was cheering you on. I'm sorry it was hard, though."

"I was really nervous," Tiffany admits, saying she'd been shaking the whole time.

"Of course you were. You'd not had good experiences in court before."

We move on to talk about her mom being sick, my trip back home, and all the things she wanted to do when the habeas hearing was granted.

"I really think the judge will grant it," she says, and I can hear the hope shining in her voice.

"I do too, Tiffany. You did so well, and the judge was really watching you and listening."

"I noticed. She was really paying attention. It felt so good to have you and everyone there with me in my corner. This is already a win for me."

While I agree, I want her to finally walk out these doors, run to the ocean, and be free.

"I can't believe we're sitting face to face after nine years! Hey, how is Jessica?" Tiffany wants to know. "I got a letter from her the other day. I worry about her."

"I worry about her too. Well, her and Jordan both. Jordan has some kind of jury trial on January 21. His attorney is filing a motion to have the charges dropped because he's been there nineteen months without trial and he's a child. Jessica's trial is set to begin in February."

Tiffany frowns a bit. "I wish we could find her another attorney. She's scared of having to take a plea like Alana or me."

I feel the same. We had so many leads that didn't pan out. For a while, I was hoping her court-appointed attorney would step up. He hasn't, and she's a month out from trial. We'd also lined up a donor who was going to pay for an attorney for Jessica, but then they dropped out, saying they wanted to support child survivors instead. *That's exactly what Jessica is!* I had thought. She could spend life in jail if the trial doesn't go well. Tiffany didn't need to think about this today, but I couldn't deter her.

"I'm going to write to her today," she says. "I just want her to be safe. She doesn't deserve to spend life in jail. She didn't even do it."

"I could be wrong, but I think the judge might be more open to her being a survivor than the prosecutor. We'll keep fighting, Tiffany. You could write an affidavit to support Jessica. I can show you how I do it."

Tiffany starts smiling again. "I'm on it!"

The timer goes off. It's already time to go. "That went so fast," Tiffany says.

We stand up. "I don't care if we get in trouble," I say, hugging her tightly and letting go fast before we get caught.

She turns to walk to the line of female inmates waiting to leave the room, but then turns back, looking me intently in the eyes. "Andrea, I think they finally believe me now."

"Me too, Tiffany. I really do," I say.

We make heart hands and then I walk out the door, through the maze of gates and halls, and out of the prison, the prison guard checking my ID at the gate. I look back at the metal barbed wire circling over the locks. It gleams cruelly in the cold Georgia sunshine. The rows and rows of buildings locked inside hold over 200 women—all of whom are loved by someone on the outside. Tiffany should never have had to walk through those doors. As I walk to the car, she stays inside, shuffling back to her cell.

Now, we can only wait to see if they really do believe us.

Chapter 16

THE WAITING GAME

ack in San Diego, life continues. A month passes and I'm sure the court transcripts will arrive by the sixty-day deadline. Tiffany and I play out the deadlines in our almost daily calls.

"Court was January 4, so that means transcripts should be here by March 4. We need those before anything else can happen. Susan will have a month to respond with her brief, so April 4. The district attorney will have a month to file a response, so May 4. The wild card is when the judge will make her decision."

Susan continues to say she feels good about Tiffany's case, but the judge could still rule against the habeas hearing. The more I read, the more I worry. When I type into Google "What percentage of habeas hearings are granted," the first thing that comes up is a Bureau of Justice statement: "3.2 percent of the petitions were granted in whole or in part, and only 1.8 percent resulted in any type of release of the petitioner. Successful habeas corpus claims in most cases do not produce a prisoner's release, but rather a requirement for further judicial review." Law reviews, studies, and articles confirm that it's rare that even a successful habeas hearing results in a prisoner's release.

On the second to last page of Tiffany's sentencing document, after Judge Cato sentenced her to thirty years with twenty to serve, he said, "I advise you pursuant to O.C.G.A. 9-14-42 that the period of limitation for the filing of habeas corpus actions in felony convictions such as this is four years. If you are unhappy or dissatisfied with the sentence, I will let you withdraw your plea and you can have a jury trial. Do you wish to withdraw your plea?" Tiffany said no. She agreed to everything her attorney and the judge said that day.

If Tiffany were released, she could still face the restrictions of the sex offender registry. She could be trapped in the very county where she was abused and sold and no one helped her. She could have to take drug tests and be prohibited from being around children, even her son. That's a virtual jail. It even stated she should avoid "places and persons of disreputable or harmful character."

Or she could simply be set free. The possibilities are the stuff that wakes me up in the night. Veronika asks me every day when Aunt Tiffany is going to come live with us. I wonder if I've done the right thing by telling her about what we're doing to free Tiffany.

"Mommy, if the law says Tiffany didn't do it because she was being hurt by that bad man, why can't they let her go? It's like time-out for no reason. It's not fair."

I agree. A time-out where you're threatened with abuse and denied your human rights. Every day.

Tiffany keeps saying I need to be more patient, a virtue she appears to possess more than me. Fecha, Ashley, and I make a list of the basic things Tiffany will need: clothes, shoes, and things like a phone and computer. Over the past few months, I've been speaking with universities in California, New Jersey, Massachusetts, and Texas who might be open to offering Tiffany a scholarship to study. First, though, she needs a place to live and to learn about the world a decade after she was shut out from society.

In mid-January, a former colleague at the Office of Attorney General in D.C. reaches out to learn more about our work with survivors of trafficking who are experiencing arrest and incarceration like Tiffany. She's part of a huge multi-national corporation that wants to fund efforts to end the arrest and incarceration of African Americans and aid those who are seeking employment after being released. She's been following our work with Tiffany and others, and thinks we might be a match for a grant of up to $700,000 they're working on.

I think about the course I taught last October at Pepperdine Carurso School of Law. I can still hear the "Oh my gods" and the sniffles after the law students watched Tiffany's film.

"What if," I asked Fecha at the time, "we could train defense attorneys how to use affirmative defense, how to identify if their clients are victims of trafficking, and how to help them get services? This could be transformational. We could train and pay more survivors like Ashley. We could train students to support cases, and we could get stronger laws passed to prevent these arrests."

We could also finally pay Fecha, Ashley, and me a full-time salary. Piecing together enough income for my daughter and I to survive over the last few years has been a constant stress. Every month, I watch my bank account fall while rent and electricity goes up. Plus, I often send Tiffany money to make sure she has what she needs to get by and can call me. I count my blessings, like my mom buying my daughter clothes and all the consulting jobs sourced from my years of working with survivors around the world. Still, there are end-of-the-month moments where I skip dinner so I can buy Veronika bananas and snacks for school.

Though Tiffany's mother hadn't been able to attend her hearing, I know from Tiffany's calls that she wants to see her mother after all these years. Last year, her mother was diagnosed with stage-4 lung cancer. When I first reached out to her in spring of 2020, she said she was happy we were helping her daughter. I could barely understand her because of her accent and perhaps her illness.

After court, I try to call her to give an update on her daughter's case, but she never answers. Tiffany worries she's given up on life. She's stopped going to her chemotherapy appointments and rarely talks to Tiffany.

In 2008, my mom was diagnosed with colon cancer. At first, she made it sound like it was no big deal. I fell for that until I was in Russia and tried to call her, like I did almost every day, and she couldn't answer. My dad said she was too sick. I felt the wind stop, my arms suddenly cold in the eighty-five-degree Moscow air. It was the first time I wondered if my mom would survive. I was in a foreign country, alone, terrified of losing my mom, and knowing there wasn't anything I could do about it.

Tiffany is feeling this now, and so am I. She's not in a foreign country, but prison is an island where sadness is a weakness that can drown you. In there, other inmates and guards will exploit you in every way possible. Tiffany taught me this through all her stories about so many other inmates, many of whom themselves had histories of abuse, being yelled at, having their things destroyed, being denied medications, and enduring physical violence like rapes and beatings.

I promise her I will try to reach her mom. Then, I have an idea. I dial up my own mother.

"Mom, could you try to call Tiffany's mom? You know what it's like to be where she is. Get her to see that she has to hold on so Tiffany can see her. We only have a few months and she'll be free."

Surely, Tiffany's mom can hold on just a little longer. My mom isn't sure about us intervening. She thinks choosing to have chemotherapy or not is personal.

"Yes, it is, but Tiffany needs her mom to stay alive, so she can at least finally say goodbye in person. Mom, please."

My mom calls her, and they talk for two hours. My mom promises to keep in touch with her until Tiffany is out of prison. The next day, Tiffany writes me.

> *Tell your mom I said thank you for her support for my mom and taking the time out to talk with her. She enjoys it. She was so happy to tell me that she heard from your mom, you could hear the excitement in her voice! I talked to my sister last night too and she thinks the same thing—that mom isn't going to be around much longer. She can tell she's given up on life just with the cancer, and now Grandma's death is going to take its toll on her eventually and when it does, I think it's going to kill her.*

I get a text from Tiffany's Aunt Brenda one afternoon while working on our grant. Tiffany's mom has died. I have to talk to Tiffany. I cry the whole way while I walk to pick up Veronika from school. I make myself stop before my daughter sees my eyes are red and puffy.

I'd felt like something was going on before I got the message. Something had shifted that day. I rarely thought about things like karma. That morning, when I checked to see Tiffany's petition signatures, they had suddenly jumped up by 20,000 signatures overnight. All day, Fecha and I were asking ourselves what was going on. Mira Sorvino hadn't posted anything. Neither had other well-known friends. I wondered if the night Tiffany's mom died, the universe left Tiffany the gift of 20,000 signatures as a way to show her she's loved.

> *Tiffany, hey Sister, when you get this, will you call me?*
> *Love, Andrea*

She'll know what's happened when she sees my email. I never write her just a one-liner like that, but I can't act like things are fine. I wait. The next day, she doesn't call. That night, I see a message on my phone that I have an email from Tiffany.

> *I just am speechless. I can't even find the words to express how I feel. I just talked to her finally last Wednesday and she sounded so much better. I just should have called her Tuesday because she was on my mind real heavy and I wanted to call her but I kept thinking of her telling me to go easy on the phone calls because my uncle couldn't keep putting money on her phone. I was not expecting this to happen. I haven't been sleeping. I am just in school today. I'm so angry. I'm so angry I'm in here and I never got to say goodbye or hug her or anything. I know it's just a few more months but this is just so unfair, sister. It's just so unfair.*

I write her back about the signatures, hoping that might ease her mind a bit, and promise to help her find a way to honor her mom when she's out. I tell my mom, Fecha, Ashley, and my boyfriend. I'm grieving for Tiffany. I'm angry too. It's unfair she couldn't even say goodbye to her own mother.

Two days later, Tiffany writes again.

> *I'm just trying to take it one day at a time right now. . . . It's been a little easier as far as not crying all day but I'm still not normal, I still can't eat, I try and every time I get sick. All I've ate in three days is 2 small packs of grits, a cup of soup, an orange, and a few crackers.*

I wish I could be there to hold her while she cried, or make her good food. Not jail grits.

* * *

Karana Rising has almost no funding. I cannot pay Fecha or Ashley. We're almost completely driven on volunteer hours. I finally have to start looking for other income too. It feels like defeat, but the thought of not making rent is relentless, and it takes up so much of my energy.

My former colleague, Brad, shares with me about a role to be the director of a new initiative at a nonprofit called Panorama Global to help build services and advocacy for survivors of online image-based sexual violence. I need a stable income as a single mom living in one of America's most expensive cities, and I'm passionate about the cause, but I'm scared this new job will make it harder for me to help survivors like Tiffany. When I take the role, it's with excitement and terror.

So, now I'm deep into finding survivors of what's often called revenge porn, deepfakes, or sextortion. I have twenty survivors from eight countries who meet with me in a private three-day summit in Los Angeles. At least five of the women aged twenty to forty-one are victims of sex trafficking. In one case, the FBI didn't understand that when her abuser posted her images on Pornhub, a known site for amateur and often abusive nonconsensual pornography, he'd actually made money. So did Pornhub. It reminded me of Backpage all over again. And just like Backpage, they were facing lawsuits and advocates trying to shut them down.

After those three days, I'm exhausted from taking in all the survivors' stories and trauma. I lay on my hotel bed with my Eponine and cry. How can this world be so cruel? In the virtual world, it's not just the original abuser but all the thousands of people who see the abuse, shame the victim, and share the video.

There are over thirty young people aged eleven to twenty-four whose cases I'd found by public record who'd taken their own lives. In one case, a fifteen-year-old Canadian girl, Amanda Todd, was tricked by an abuser when she was twelve. He pretended to be a young boy her age who liked her and coerced her into sending intimate photos. When she stopped sending them, he sent the photos to her classmates. She moved schools three times because of the bullying and threats from classmates. At each new school, her abuser would find her and share the photos. Eventually, she took her own life.

The utter unkindness makes me sick. The fire to support the survivors I'm now working with is stronger, though. As part of an initiative with Panorama Global, we visit the White House, sharing what survivors need to have justice. We're advocating for a federal law to criminalize all image-based sexual violence called the Shield Act. It reminds me of the way we had to fight for sex trafficking laws back in D.C. In June 2023, we officially name our initiative The Reclaim Coalition.

In all of our cases at FAIR Girls and most of our cases at Karana Rising, the women and girls we serve have been sold online by their traffickers. Explicit photos or videos—often coerced—are used to advertise them. Their images often stay up or are used by other traffickers to sell other victims. More and more of life is online, and women and girls are being exploited, abused, and digitally raped. Having images like that on the internet haunts victims and can come back to ruin their lives. Sometimes it's a former lover who takes out their abuse as a revenge for their girlfriend breaking up with them. Sometimes it's a total stranger who hacks into a woman's phone or creates altered images using a woman or girl's face on a pornographic video. The possibilities are endless and growing, and there are no federal laws to stop it.

"It's the new frontier of sex trafficking," I say to anyone who will listen. How will I do this *and* keep our cases going *and* find a way to fund Karana Rising?

"You can't do all this, Andrea," my therapist tells me. Only, I have to. I can't let these survivors down. I can't let Veronika down. My heart feels like it's constantly racing. *At least I get to help people and do what I love,* I write in my journal. I don't tell Tiffany about the new job. Though I know she'd understand, I don't want her to think I won't be there for her even for a second.

I make a schedule for myself:

5:30 a.m.: wake up, journal, yoga

6 a.m.: Karana Rising time

7–8:30 a.m.: Get Veronika up and to school

8:30 a.m.–5:30 p.m.: Reclaim Coalition

5:30–8 p.m.: Veronika time, bed, story, pack for school the next day, guitar and singing classes for Veronika

8–10:30 p.m.: Karana Rising time

Of course, life isn't a bento box where each different item fits neatly into a different little compartment. Still, I'm determined to keep it all going.

The weeks pass. "Transcript Due Day," as we call it, is right around the corner. I ignore what I read about habeas hearings having a 98.2 percent failure rate and keep looking into colleges for Tiffany. Point Lomo Nazarene University in San Diego offers a full scholarship to survivors after they've had about two years of college. I find a woman online at the Department of Corrections in Georgia who works on college and educational chances for inmates, but she hasn't written me back in days.

Tiffany wants to get her bachelor's in criminal justice or social work in addition to her master's cosmetology degree that she was close to finishing. When Tiffany entered prison at eighteen, she hadn't even completed eighth grade. She's since obtained her GED and has been working toward her dream. She dreams of starting her own full-service salon where survivors like her can work, heal, and be in community. She wants it to be a safe place for women leaving prison to work and survivors to get help. She writes to me about her business plans, and I love reading her dreams.

> *Hey Sis, I think you can call the lady again and see about getting info on what we could do to see about getting the college credits if that's where I'd go, but also in the meantime, get info on the other schools as well. I want choices lol. I'm really interested in what the colleges offer, especially since I'm already doing cosmetology here. It's something I want to continue going to school for but I also wanna have something else along w/ it. . . . I wanna have more than one thing under my belt, ya know. That way, I will really get it with that salon.*

Things are also getting really bad in the prison. Tiffany introduces me to another woman who's been brutally beaten and raped with a bottle by other inmates. She says more and more women are being attacked, and the guards don't do anything. Tiffany wants to speak out, but I'm scared that she'll be targeted next or the guards will set her up to be attacked.

> *Tiffany, let me see how I can help. I'll find that reporter. You don't have much longer in there, just please be careful.*

I find a journalist, Danny Robbins, and write him on Twitter. When he calls, I tell him everything Tiffany has told me about the rapes and the elderly woman who she thought was dead. I tell him how the guards ignored my client's cries for help. I share the details of the woman who was raped with a bottle. It's a touchy and dangerous subject though, and I impress upon him how these women's lives could be at risk.

"Please do not quote me or use Tiffany's name. They could go after her too. I'm only talking to you to help my other clients and to make sure Tiffany can share what she knows." He promises. I write Tiffany that there are articles coming out, hoping that no one is reading our messages. She writes back the next day.

Can you actually send me the articles?? Yea it's crazy over there w/ what they got going on in this war. I just don't understand why we have to have all this stuff going on anyway . . . . Why we just can't have peace??? Life is so short and there are other issues going on to be arguing and killing ppl. Things in the world have really gotten out of control.

Soon, the *Atlanta Journal-Constitution* reports, "Pulaski State Prison: Gang threats of violence and extortion." Perhaps as a result of that article, Senator Jon Ossoff of Georgia urges the FBI to investigate the gang violence in Pulaski State Prison in June 2022. A day after I read the news of the FBI investigation Tiffany tells me investigators are interviewing women inmates. Two young women who are survivors of trafficking and were assaulted and raped by inmates while guards did nothing reach out to me for help. A week later, one is moved to a smaller, safer prison. Still, I worry because Tiffany is still there, and I beg her not to do anything to show that she's telling me what's going on. My heart hurts when I think of her being assaulted in there.

Suddenly, it's March 4. It's sunny outside and the beach air is warm. It's another perfect day in San Diego. I keep refreshing my email and restrain myself from texting Susan the fifty times I think about doing it. That night, Tiffany calls.

"Andrea, have you heard anything? Did the court send my transcripts?"

"I'm sorry. I don't think so. I'll keep checking, though. I promise."

"I guess it's just a few more days, Andrea. We got this."

We say our "I love you, Sis" and move on.

We waited the two months, and we're still waiting. Susan emails me that night that the court doesn't have to be on time, as they are backlogged with cases. *What could be more important than a child victim of sex trafficking who's been in jail for over ten years?* I wonder.

Tiffany's freedom still feels like a mountain looming above us. There's nothing we can do but wait.

* * *

While we wait on the transcripts, more and more survivors are reaching out from behind bars for help. In addition, our other clients still need help. Jessica's attorney doesn't respond to my emails. Alana has disappeared into a different prison where I cannot reach her. Jordan and Jessica's trials are coming up, with both facing possible life in prison. Jordan's capital murder trial is set for mid-April, before Jessica's and their trafficker's. My emails to his attorney are usually unanswered and our offers of testimony or other experts aren't replied to either.

Jordan is now sixteen years old and legally an adult as far as the court is concerned. He has been in jail for eighteen months. Amy texts me daily. She can't handle the thought of never hugging him again. In the year and five months since I've become Jordan's advocate, I've not found other advocacy groups to join us in supporting him. I often wonder if there are things I don't know or if these other groups just believe Jordan is a lost cause.

I've no way to reach Jordan or let him know that I'm trying to support him, that Ashley has written a letter to the judge, or that Fecha is posting daily to support his release through our petitions on social media. In April, Amy's fiancé attends the trial every day from start to finish. Amy updates me each evening.

The jury includes former military and law enforcement, which could taint their view of Jordan because the man who was shot was former military. Breez testifies in trial, and so does an eighteen-year-old woman who was sixteen at the time of the shooting—another victim. By testifying against Jordan, she becomes a state's witness and can avoid her own prosecution. Jordan still doesn't see Breez as a trafficker or understand the sexual abuse. Amy says he looked crushed as Breez testified that she didn't know who the shooter was.

A week after the jury delivers a hung verdict, two female jurors on Jordan's trial reach out directly to Amy to share what was going on behind the jury deliberation door. Evidence of Jordan's trafficking was never presented. Killeen media reports on Jordan's hung jury. The truth, that a fifteen-year-old boy was being sexually abused by a twenty-four-year-old woman, is never mentioned.

Amy continues to post about her son on a Facebook group that focuses on incarcerated youth in Killeen. Identifying who actually killed the man whose murder Jessica and Jordan are being charged with would be a major help. Amy learns about a man named Lucky, who was likely at the shooting according to people who know Breez. Two sisters who were abused by Lucky reach out; he broke one of their jaws and almost killed the other. Currently, Lucky is in jail for the murder of someone else. Could this be the killer? A new trial for Jordan is set for September 2022, and Jessica's trial is moved to the week before.

"I think they want Jessica and Jordan to testify against each other," Amy texts me.

I agree. I have a suspicion that Jessica's attorney wants to get rid of her case. Just like Tiffany's attorney, he's paid by the case, not by the hour. It pays to plea, not go to court.

Jessica and Jordan could end up with life sentences and we're still waiting on Tiffany's transcripts. We could lose every case. I'm struggling to keep up with our cases while working a new job that never takes less than ten hours of my day. I don't know if Fecha and Ashley are ready to run Karana Rising, and I don't want to slow down despite my new job being emotionally draining. Doubt fills my mind each night, waking me with panic dreams. Our grant is in limbo, and everyone is working for free except when I can use my personal money to pay for Ashley and Fecha's time.

Over four months after Tiffany's habeas hearing, Susan sends an email to say Tiffany's transcripts are ready—all 256 pages.

> *Tiffany, the transcripts are here. So, if Susan files in a month and the DA files thirty days after, well, maybe you can be here by end of summer.*

> *Andrea, I can't wait. I'm just trying to focus on school and keep my head focused on the future.*

I pay the fees for the transcripts and stay up for nights reading them, even though I'd been there in court. In mid-June, Susan writes that she has a new strategy. All spring, Susan and advocates around Georgia were working to expand the Georgia law to vacate the records of human trafficking survivors to include any crime and to allow for any survivor, even if they were still incarcerated like Tiffany, to appeal for vacatur. In May, the Georgia legislator passed a full vacatur bill. Already, trafficking survivors and their attorneys were using the law to vacate their records. The catch? So far, none of the cases were for violent crimes. They were for prostitution or small crimes. Tiffany was convicted of a violent crime because Kassie was only fourteen at the time.

Fecha and I have been careful about how much media or posting online we've done since Tiffany's court hearing—we don't want the judge to think we're trying to pressure her. Susan now wants us to lay low while she prepares to file the vacatur motion for Tiffany. If this works, Tiffany will be completely free of her past. No criminal record. No sex offender registry. She will be free to go to college, get any job she wants, and live with Ayden someday. I agree with Susan—this approach could get Tiffany out sooner, and without the virtual chains that would follow her.

"What happens if we lose the vacatur motion?" I ask.

"Then we just go back to the habeas hearing," Susan responds.

Two months later, I file an expert witness affidavit to go along with Susan's filing for Tiffany. I have to prove that I'm qualified. My history includes advocating for the federal vacatur law that still hasn't passed, advocating for the D.C. vacatur law that did pass in 2018, helping create the D.C. HOPE Court, and building sex trafficking trainings for law enforcement. Still, I worry I'm not going to impress the judge.

"I'm not a lawyer. I'm not a therapist. I'm an advocate. But what does that mean?" I text Fecha.

Fecha texts back, "You are her community. Her sister. You know her better than anyone else after all these years." Fecha always knows what to say to help me calm down. I just don't want to fail Tiffany after waiting so long to advocate for her in court. I include the following statement in my affidavit:

I met Miss Simpson in October of 2012 following the receipt of her handwritten letter to me in my then role as co-executive director of FAIR Girls. Miss Simpson learned of FAIR Girls when we were featured on the front page of USA Today's *September 26, 2012, publication, "Sex trafficking in the USA hits close to home." This article featured FAIR Girls' work to prevent child sex trafficking through educational programs inside schools. In her first letter, Miss Simpson asked me if she was a victim of sex trafficking or a prostitute.*

Miss Simpson has risen far in her education, life goals, and personal growth. I am fully committed as her advocate to support her healing, continued education, personal growth, and other life goals. I have had the privilege to act as Miss Simpson's advocate and personal friend initially at FAIR Girls and now at Karana Rising. Miss Simpson is an inspiration to so many survivors across the country and I am proud to share this affidavit with you on her behalf.

I close my six-page affidavit with hope. I know Tiffany could thrive, if only they'd give her the chance. "This is your time," I say to Tiffany on a call that week. Susan files her motion with my affidavit and others, including one from Barbara Brown.

That Friday, I walk along the beach and think about Tiffany's dream of being here. I also think back to three and a half years earlier, when the news broke that Tennessee trafficking survivor Cyntoia Brown would be granted clemency by their governor. I wistfully remember thinking that was the blueprint for Tiffany's freedom. Later, I learned we couldn't get clemency for Tiffany because the state of Georgia didn't allow for a governor's pardon.

Instead, we had to change the criminal punishment system from the inside. We needed legal grace and to make the law define trafficking survivors as victims, not criminals. Every time Tiffany's former pro bono attorney failed to show up in court or refused to speak with

Tiffany, he caused Tiffany's case to disappear. With the petition, the film, a newly expanded vacatur law, and supporters around the world, the time felt right.

Susan plans to call District Attorney Joe Mulholland and gauge his support. He could fully object, he could agree with conditions, or he could grant the motion. Or he could do nothing and, after thirty days, Tiffany would be free.

"It would be best if he just did nothing. He doesn't have to bruise his ego or even say anything," I tell Susan.

"Right, and we've proven that we're never giving up," Susan replies.

The weekend passes. Kid parties, swimming, and mom life keep me busy, but all the while, Tiffany's fate plays in my mind. At night, I pray, "Please, open your heart, Mr. Mulholland. Please open your heart."

Susan texts me early Monday morning. "DA Mulholland has already filed his objection to Tiffany's vacatur plea."

I don't think he's even read any of Susan's motions or our affidavits. He never planned to, it seems.

"So, what do we do?" I text back.

"We have to have a hearing. Sometime this fall."

Sometime this fall. The timeline feels weak and faded. I have to tell Tiffany. For the moment, though, I need to cry. I walk to a meditation garden two miles from Veronika's school after dropping her off. All my fight is gone for the moment. He objected. We would have to convince the judge. Tiffany would have to testify again, sharing all of her pain and abuse to yet another judge.

A few hours later, I send Tiffany a JPay message and ask her to call me. That evening, I see her number on my phone and draw in my breath. I know she'll be hurt and disappointed. I have to do this right.

"Tiffany, Susan called me this morning. DA Mulholland objected, and that sucks, but Susan is already on it. We will have a new day in court soon. She told me the judge is a woman, and I think she'll be more understanding." Once again, we'll have a female judge and I'm hoping she's as sympathetic as Judge Sarah Wall seemed from our habeas hearing.

Tiffany is quiet for a moment. My heart is racing.

"I'm disappointed, Sis," she finally says. "I'm hurt. But maybe this is God's way to help me finish my master's degree and get ready. I'm not going to get down."

Tiffany's grace is always there. I promise to send her money for clothes and commissary, and to talk to her the next day.

Time moves forward.

During the day, I work toward a global summit for survivors of online sexual violence. I research cases of survivors, talk to global advocates, and listen to stories from victims around the world. At night, after Veronika is in bed, I text and write to Amy, write Tiffany, and work with Ashley to advocate for our growing Karana Rising client list.

I'm starting to struggle with sleep. It reminds me of when I was feeling utterly overwhelmed trying to keep FAIR Girls going toward the end of my time there, and this time I have an eight-year-old daughter who needs me to be present.

Tiffany's court date is set for November 21, the Monday before Thanksgiving. When it arrives, I'm just getting back from a global conference on online sexual violence in Lisbon with my new role. My return flight goes from Portugal through Madrid to Miami to Tallahassee, where I meet Fecha at almost 2 a.m., forty-eight hours after leaving Portugal. Flight delays, missed baggage, and broken down Ubers can't stop me from getting to Tiffany. *They can't stop us now*, I write in my journal. Fecha and I take an Uber to Albany, Georgia, and check in to our donated room in the same Holiday Inn that Susan and the other Georgia advocates are staying at. In the lobby, I see holiday decorations and the beginnings of the breakfast spread for the morning.

In the room, I lay out my court clothes but don't take anything else out of my suitcase. I tell Fecha, "We don't need to unpack. Tiffany is coming home with us tomorrow. We'll only be here one night."

I turn out the light, close my eyes, and pray again, "Mr. Mulholland, please open your heart."

Chapter 17

WE HAVE ALL THE MINUTES REMAINING

The courthouse is no bigger than my parents' house. The cinderblock walls are painted white and the "witness stand" is a red, taped X on the ground in front of the judge's bench, with the United States flag hanging to the right. Four guards are busy preparing for the day's hearings.

I recognize Mulholland right away. In 2011, he oversaw the assistant district attorney who prosecuted Tiffany in Baker and Grady Counties. It's ten years later, but I know it's him in a bright red sweater under a beige blazer sitting at a small wooden table with his files and notebooks.

Jessica Contrera from the *Washington Post* is already here taking notes. Mulholland turns around several times, nervously looking at her and her photographer, whose large camera is visible from where I am across the room.

The left side of the room is filling up with advocates and supporters for Tiffany, some of whom I've never met. Earlier that morning at the motel, I'd met Lindsey, a Georgia advocate for trafficking survivors. She has a bag of new clothes for Tiffany, so if released, she can leave her prison clothing behind.

I keep looking at the door, knowing that Tiffany is waiting behind it. Susan and Barbara come and go several times. When she takes a seat, I reach over to Barbara and slip a little black jewelry box into her hand.

"Do you think Tiffany could wear this necklace in court?"

"I don't know. I'll try." Barbara hides the black box in her hand and walks back toward the door behind which Tiffany is waiting.

Two years ago, I stayed up late one night after putting my daughter to bed and watched a documentary my therapist had recommended, *My Octopus Teacher*. It follows Craig Foster, a depressed South African documentary filmmaker. For nearly a year, he filmed a small female octopus he would see during his dives off the shores of his South African home. In the beginning, she hid and didn't trust him, but over time she slowly began to follow him. After she was attacked by a shark, he broke the rules of journalism, going beyond mere observation to give his small octopus friend some food.

I could relate to Foster and his story because the rules of social work say not to become overly attached to your client. I'd long ago broken this rule with Tiffany. I loved her. It was clear to me that if we were to get her out of prison, it would be because our advocacy was fueled by love as much as it was legal strategy.

In one scene of the documentary, the little octopus played with the fish around her, then swam over to the filmmaker and began to gently stroke his arms and hug his torso. At the end of the documentary, Foster looked into the camera and said she'd brought him back to life and taught him how to truly live fully.

As I reflected on all the setbacks, worries about Tiffany's safety, disbelief from other advocates and everyone who said her release wasn't possible, I knew Tiffany was my octopus. Love can be fierce, and it means not ever giving up or losing yourself.

I found a Turkish artist on Etsy who created small, golden octopus necklaces, and I bought one for Tiffany and one for me. I was wearing mine and had just handed Tiffany's to Barbara. They weren't expensive, but they encapsulated our ten-year story.

As I'm texting Tiffany's Aunt Brenda to see if she's still coming, I see the door open out of the corner of my right eye. There Tiffany is, wearing black slacks and a loose, camel-colored, turtleneck sweater. The gold from her octopus necklace glitters on her neck, just like mine does against my black dress. She smiles discreetly, so as not to attract attention. This is the first time she has been allowed to wear jewelry in eleven years. She sits in the small wooden chair by the door, behind DA Mulholland and the *Washington Post* reporter. A few minutes later, the guard comes to take her back. *That's weird*, I think, my heart rising to my throat.

Susan's yellow highlighter is moving fast over the pages of discovery and evidence. I'm nervously holding my black briefcase full of the petition signatures and Tiffany's blogs. Susan told me that morning that I shouldn't even mention California or the petition. She wanted to stay as local and Georgia as possible.

I keep staring at DA Mulholland, whose white coffee cup is dripping onto the dark brown desk where his files are spread out. *Open you heart*, I whisper in the back of my mind. Suddenly, an older woman sits next to me, smiling as if she knows me.

"Aunt Brenda?" I ask. She smiles bigger, and I hug her as if she's my own aunt. I always called her Aunt Brenda when we spoke. She's Tiffany's father's sister and Tiffany loves her.

"I saved up my money so I'd have $18 to drive over here." I feel a little bad that I didn't think to ask her if she needed me to send her money.

"I'm so glad you made it, Aunt Brenda."

Susan pulls her suitcase of case law over to DA Mulholland's desk and they quietly speak, pointing to various highlighted pages. I lean in, trying to shut out the noise of Susan's colleagues, who are talking right in front of me. Susan takes a piece of paper with a lot of text out of the room, to where I think Tiffany is waiting. I look at Barbara, but she shakes her head to indicate she doesn't know what's going on.

A few minutes later, Susan returns and sits down in front of us. The same door opens again and Tiffany walks out, her hands chained, and she sits down in between Susan and Barbara. Fecha, Aunt Brenda, and I are directly behind her. Judge Heather Lanier comes in and we all stand up. Her dark brown hair is tied back in a ponytail and her makeup is perfect. She doesn't look a day over forty.

All the work we've done is rushing through my head. It's been years of advocating for a federal vacatur law, introduced by Senators Kirsten Gillibrand and Rob Portman in 2016. Republican senators opposed the bill, saying that it would allow for violent offenders to walk free after their crimes. Like most state-level laws, they were only interested in vacating crimes like prostitution or loitering.

Before I met Tiffany, I might have given in to this logic, thinking that at least we would get many records vacated. But after working with thousands of survivors, I now know that trafficking happens in the spaces between the cracks where society lets vulnerable people fall—or more accurately, society pushes them down those cracks. Victims are already vulnerable from neglect, abuse, and poverty. I don't know how I would have fought back if I was being violently trafficked and then forced by my trafficker to contact another young victim. I don't know if I would have seen myself as a victim or a prostitute either.

Mulholland stands up, smoothing his red sweater.

"I was not the one who prosecuted Tiffany. My colleague, the former assistant district attorney, did."

I write in my notes that he's protecting himself from blame, even after all these years. Susan is reading a document quietly to Tiffany as she looks down at her hands with a serious expression. While she reads, Mulholland continues.

"I think we have come to a conclusion that this can be settled with an extraordinary motion to vacate her charges in Grady County and Baker County," he says while shuffling the papers on his desk.

My heart jumps in my chest and I almost gasp out loud. Would Tiffany walk out of court with us?

The federal vacatur bill was still stalled in Congress, but now—in the small Georgia town of Camilla, with a population of about 5,000, and a courthouse that wasn't even a courthouse but a justice center adjacent to the county jail—Tiffany has her chance at freedom. If so, it'll be the first case vacating a survivor with a violent charge like child sex trafficking. If Tiffany walks free, we have proof that this expanded vacatur law could work despite years of other advocates saying it would never happen, much less in a traditionally conservative state.

Habeas, with its less than 3 percent chance of working, and clemency, which was not an option for Tiffany anyway, were not about changing the system from within. The vacatur law was about changing the law to believe a victim of sex trafficking was, in fact, a victim. Tiffany, by sharing her story, has helped us get this far.

Things are looking up, but we still have to present evidence. Susan calls an expert witness, Dr. Whitmore, who testified in Tiffany's habeas hearing ten months earlier. This time, she's spent time talking to Tiffany before testifying.

"Tiffany was seventeen when she was trafficked. While seventeen is considered an adult in Georgia, she was still considered a victim of child sex trafficking. At seventeen, your mind is still being molded. Her trafficker used her past instability, sexual abuse, and desire for stability to lure her. He also got her pregnant and fostered a situation where Tiffany initially felt loyal to him. Then, after he finished grooming her, he exerted abuse over her."

I'm looking at Tiffany's back, so I can't see if she's crying as the doctor details the beatings, the stabbing, and the threats to burn down her grandmother's house.

"So, at any age under Georgia law, would Tiffany be considered a victim of human trafficking?" asks Susan.

"Yes, she would, because there were elements of force, fraud, and coercion."

Then Susan brings up Kassie, explaining that traffickers commonly use victims to recruit and control other victims. I suck in my breath as she says that the traffickers call this type of victim a "bottom bitch."

"Did Tiffany understand that Yarnell intended to traffic Kassie for money?" asks Susan.

"No, she didn't. She thought he was just using her phone and that they would simply be going to pick her up," Dr. Whitmore replies.

I can hear Tiffany now. She's crying.

Then, Susan asks the expert witness what she would recommend to help Tiffany after she is released from prison. I already knew from the conversations with Susan over the last few months that she would recommend Tiffany stay in Georgia in a transitional program. As much as I dreamed of her coming immediately to California, I understand that she needs a transitional program. Susan found programs in Georgia to recommend because she thought the judge would not agree to placement in a different state. Susan thought even suggesting it would hurt Tiffany's chances of release. I still hold on to a hope that Tiffany could be fully released, free to go where she wants.

Mulholland doesn't have any questions and Susan doesn't call any other witnesses. All along, Susan has asserted that vacatur would assume the crimes Tiffany was convicted of were a direct result of her trafficking. Still, Mulholland is unwilling to relent.

"We can vacate her original sentences in Grady County case 22CR131," he continues.

I'm writing down the case file numbers as fast as I can, hoping to keep track of what's happening. Then, Mulholland presents the new charge Tiffany would plea to: "Keeping a house of prostitution for the purpose of victimizing herself."

So, Tiffany will be asked to sign that she prostituted herself? That she victimized herself? I looked at Fecha.

"This is crazy," I whisper. Pleading to these charges meant no vacatur. However, it would ensure that Tiffany wouldn't be charged with anything related to Kassie. She wouldn't be placed on the sex offender registry either.

The judge asks why the attorneys couldn't just agree to vacate her record. For a moment, it seems she'll rule for full vacatur. Then, just as quickly, the judge says she'll grant the motion with the condition that Tiffany agrees to the new crime. Mulholland brings the paperwork to the judge.

"Do you agree to the charge of keeping a house of prosecution?" asks the judge.

Everyone laughs.

"I mean, prostitution. The form has been filled out incorrectly."

"I'll fix that right now," says Mulholland, his face turning almost as red as his sweater.

Tiffany agrees. She agrees to 500 hours of community service. She agrees to the status of "first offender," meaning she must follow the rules and recommendations of the court or risk being sent back to prison for the duration of her original term. She cannot commit any crime or get into any trouble at all. She could lose her rights to vote, hold public office, certain benefits for housing, or some forms of employment.

My hands are clammy. This is really happening.

Susan is whispering in Tiffany's ear.

"Is this your signature in two places?" asks the judge.

Tiffany answers yes.

Her new charge carries a ten-to-fifteen-year sentence and could include time served. The court orders her to a thirty-day treatment program and, after that, to live in a transitional home with other women who've experienced trafficking. Once Tiffany completes the programs and probation, she'll be free. Her case will be dismissed with no fines.

"I highly advise you to have limited contact to Mr. Donald's mother, who has custody of your son," the judge adds. It sounds cruel to me, but I think the judge is worried that Yarnell's mother might attempt to get Tiffany into trouble. Still, Tiffany is Ayden's mother. She's already lost so many years with him.

"Your honor, do you believe that Miss Simpson could leave court today to join her program?" asks Susan.

"No, I cannot determine her release. She must be transported back to Pulaski and wait for the Department of Corrections to determine her sentence." She concludes that once released, for some period of time, Tiffany will have to stay in Georgia and any travel would require an agreement between the state of Georgia and the state she wished to move to or visit.

I can feel the tears well up. *No, Andrea. Not now. Don't cry. She's getting out.* The ocean will wait.

When everyone stands up, the security guard starts to take Tiffany out of the room. *Will I even get to say goodbye before she goes back to Pulaski prior to her release?*

"Would it be possible for a few of us to go back to spend a little time with Tiffany before she's transported?" Susan asks the guard, and she nods.

"Andrea, would you like to go first?" Susan asks me, already knowing the answer.

"Yes," I say. I jump up and almost trip over Aunt Brenda as I make my way to the front of the courtroom to walk past the attorneys' desks and toward the door.

Tiffany is sitting quietly while the female guard fumbles to unlock the chains binding her ankles together. The small room looks like a kitchen pantry and is filled with brown bags, labeled with the faces and names of inmates, mostly men. Their belongings must be inside. I'm sad to think of their worlds stuffed into paper bags, but I'm simultaneously overcome with relief. It's like a wave washing over me at the sight of Tiffany sitting there.

"Are you okay, Tiffany? Is the plea okay with you?"

She smiles, and looks down, like she often does.

"Yes, I am. Sister, I really am. This is the best way out of here."

She's right. She could have gone for the hearing and the judge might have ruled against her. Then, another four years before even a chance at parole. Who knows what could have happened in those years?

"You know I'm going to support you no matter what," I whisper. "We did it."

Tiffany rests her hands on the table, still bound by chains, and I reach for her. She squeezes my hand.

"Are we allowed to hug?" I ask. The guard smiles at us, then unlocks Tiffany's hands.

She's literally being unbound before my eyes, I think, and then we're hugging, for real, without any worry that we're breaking rules.

The guard then says Tiffany can go back to the courtroom to say hi to her other people. Tiffany runs out. Before I even get into the courtroom, she's hugging Aunt Brenda, who's crying. Another guard, carrying a box of tissues, asks me if it's Tiffany's mom.

"No, Tiffany's mom died last year." He takes a tissue, puts the box down, and walks away with a sniffle.

"You all need to stay strong; I'll see you for Thanksgiving," Tiffany says, looking around at all the tear-streaked faces. She's the only one not crying, it seems. Calm was a survival mechanism that she learned all those years in prison. Too soon, she has to go back to the small room where she'll be re-chained and sent back to Pulaski Prison.

Mulholland has already left to file Tiffany's paperwork, but Susan warns us that Tiffany could easily be there another week. Another week of her sitting there with chains, the terrible "jail breakfast" my daughter often worries about, and the constant threat of abuse. It also means another week of hotels and meals and endless expenses I can't afford and Karana Rising doesn't have funding for anymore. I also need to find $5,000 to pay the expert witness. I feel my body tensing up. Then, I think of Tiffany's hand squeezing mine. *It's all okay, Andrea. She's going to be here soon*, I tell myself.

Susan, Fecha, and I drive to a local Tex-Mex place to eat and celebrate. Although I'm tired, I don't know if I'll be able to sleep until I know Tiffany is out.

On the two-and-a-half-hour drive from Camilla to Atlanta, Susan and I both call our mothers to tell them how court went. Fecha curates our travel playlist and we stop for tea and snacks. Finally, we arrive at the small hotel in midtown Atlanta where Fecha and I will stay while waiting for news of Tiffany's release.

That night, I go up to the roof deck of the hotel to see the view of the city. Hotel guests are already celebrating Thanksgiving down below. I become lost in responding to messages from those who are waiting to know if Tiffany is free. Fecha is already sleeping when I return to the room. I wash my face and fall into bed too, but I can't sleep.

I'm thinking about Jessica, who will soon be sentenced after agreeing to an open plea of up to forty years in prison. She's twenty years old. Jordan is looking at an eighteen-year sentence. Amy said she didn't know how she could live if she lost both of her children for so long. I write in my journal as I lay half-awake in bed.

> *Now, we can go back to Texas to push with advocates to expand a vacatur law like Georgia's. This isn't New York, California, or New Hampshire. It's another Southern state and that might work with Texas.*
>
> *This is proof that what Tiffany once wrote in her blog for Karana Rising's Survivor Justice Initiative was true: "Ending sex trafficking means building community for those who never had true community."*

I fall asleep with my journal next to me, the uncapped pen on top.

On Tuesday, I wake up an hour earlier than my alarm is set. My list of to-dos is full of things like finding Tiffany a purse and a suitcase for all the donated clothing.

At 5 p.m., I text Susan, but there isn't any word yet. Susan's law firm and advocates have been driving all over Georgia filing paperwork in person in an effort to advance Tiffany's release before Thanksgiving, which is now just a day away. If it doesn't happen tomorrow, Tiffany will have to wait until Monday, after the holiday. All I can do is wait.

Tiffany calls as I sit alone at a local cafe.

"Any word?" I ask her. "I think it's going to happen tomorrow."

"I don't know, Sister. I have all my stuff packed, all my letters, our photos, everything."

"I'm ready too!" I tell her. "I have a suitcase full of clothes for you. I even took a bear from the toy box, so you'd have something soft to sleep with when you get out."

"Andrea, you're too much!"

"I just hope you can get out tomorrow. We're so ready!"

The usual "You have one minute remaining" notice comes on. I growl and Tiffany laughs at me. We say our usual "I love yous" before the phone goes dead.

Maybe it's for the last time, I think.

It's the day before Thanksgiving. I've made a reservation for three at a rooftop vegan restaurant with skyline views, just in case Tiffany is released. I'm choosing to believe she will be, even though I know it's not likely. I spend the day in our hotel, writing email after email to friends, family, and anyone I know who cares for Tiffany. I've posted so many updates on her Change.org petition, and now, finally, we can say it worked. I write an online update to the 75,000 signers and the comments start rolling in.

> *Tiffany DID NOT victimize herself!! She was a VICTIM of human trafficking and forced to do things she would NEVER do of her own volition! This is ridiculous, these charges should be dismissed, and allow her to rebuild her life without shadows hanging around her!!*

I understand why DA Mulholland added "for the purposes of victimizing herself" to the charge. It will keep her off the sex offender registry. But he didn't have to object to her vacatur. Maybe he thought that if she were released without any restrictions, she would just fall back into crime. Whatever the case, he was just continuing the pattern of men in Tiffany's life who thought they could control her.

> *I am glad you are free, but don't stop fighting for your rights! Live your best life!!*

> *I'm beyond happy for Tiffany. She and I did time together in Pulaski and she is such a sweetheart. It warms my heart she is gaining her freedom.*

This wasn't the only former inmate at Pulaski who'd commented on Tiffany's petition over the years.

"*Tiffany, the possibilities are endless,*" read my favorite comment.

We wait all day for the call. My phone never leaves my hand.

At 4 p.m., I finally say to Fecha, "I guess it's not going to happen. We better plan to stick around until Tuesday in case she's released on Monday. There's no way we're leaving until we see her!"

Fecha is still positive. "No, I'm not giving up yet. We got this. I'm calling on my Kenyan ancestors to manifest her release today."

I want to believe. I want to think it could still happen, but the darkening sky is increasing my doubt. "Okay, I'm going to keep believing," I say, even though I've already extended our hotel booking through Tuesday.

An hour later, my phone rings with the familiar Pulaski State Prison number. *It must be Tiffany calling to check in*, I think. When I answer though, I hear a woman's voice, not a machine recording.

"Hello, this is Andrea."

"This is Ms. Griffith at Pulaski State Prison. I have Miss Simpson here. You need to come get her immediately."

Oh, I didn't expect it would be me they called. Tiffany must have told them to call me, not Susan.

"I think I should call Tiffany's attorney, Susan. I don't have a car and I'm in Atlanta."

"You need to come get her because she's being released now."

I tell her that Susan will call her right back. I don't even know if Tiffany will be allowed to stay with Fecha and me in the hotel or if she'll have to go to the transitional program directly. I don't even know where the program is located. I get Susan on the line, but there's a problem.

"My car won't start. I can't get there."

What?

Fecha is next to me and whispers, "This is just a hurdle. We can get to her. Don't worry."

So, Susan is stuck like me, but she quickly arranges for a victim advocate named Amy, who's only an hour away from the prison, to pick Tiffany up. Amy had been in court and was an expert from Georgia who worked to support survivors of crime. I'd liked her a lot when we met. Only, selfishly, I really want to be there to see Tiffany walk out of prison. I want to hug her first. My heart is racing.

"Can she come here? Where will she go?" I press. I know I'm being pushy.

"I don't know. Hopefully, we can arrange to have her spend time with you for Thanksgiving or before you leave Georgia. I'll tell her to call you."

Tiffany will be in a car in just a few hours. Not in jail clothes. Just driving to Atlanta like we did two nights ago after court.

Two hours later, Amy calls. "I'm with her. There are some issues with paperwork, but we should be out soon."

The voices of the other people around me fade as I focus on what Amy is saying.

"What kind of issues?"

"They were trying to get Tiffany to sign up for the sex offender registry."

"What?! Why? Don't they have the paperwork from the district attorney?"

"Don't worry about it," Amy replies calmly. "She'll be out of here soon. I'll call you from the road."

At 8 p.m., my phone buzzes with a text. There's a picture of Tiffany holding a slushy and hot fries. Her "Strong as a Mother" sweatshirt and jeans look so normal on her, as if the eleven years in jail have evaporated. In their place is a smiling young woman standing outside a fancy gas station, posing for the camera. I just sit there, staring at the photo with Fecha.

"She's our sister," Fecha says.

"Amy, where are you headed now?" I text.

"I'm taking her to the program. They will call you or Susan tomorrow to make plans to see Tiffany."

I want to see her immediately, but the program feels it's better for her to adjust to the house and other women there. Thanksgiving is the next day. Fecha and I stay in the hotel all day, waiting to hear from Susan or Amy. At 4 p.m., I text Susan but don't hear back. I wonder if Tiffany is doing okay. Does she have her own room? Was she able to get some rest?

I know all about running a safe home, and this program was stricter than ours had been. Tiffany's not allowed to have a phone or computer. She can't leave by herself; she has to be with a program staff person if she goes anywhere. It didn't sound as free as I'd thought she would be. But it's transitional for a reason. After eleven years of being totally controlled—down to when and what you ate or when you could step out into the sun for fresh air—maybe just jumping on a flight to San Diego was a crazy idea after all.

The next morning, Susan texts. "I can pick you up at noon and we can head to see Tiffany at a park near the program." Tiffany often said she wanted to be in nature again. A park in the Atlanta suburbs is as close as we can get for now.

Fecha and I sit with the large suitcase full of Tiffany's clothes, journals, books, makeup, toothpaste, and vitamins. Susan arrives and we stuff it all into the trunk of her dark blue SUV, which is already filled with the cardboard boxes of discovery files, court documents, and previous sentencing documents. All eleven years of Tiffany's life in prison were in those boxes, next to a suitcase full of things for her new life.

The rain that was falling earlier in the day has finally stopped by the time we pull up to the park. A white van pulls in beside us, looking like so many of the vans I've seen at homeless shelters, youth drops, and city outreach programs.

"Fecha, that's her. I know it." I jump out.

I'd thought of this moment for over ten years. The moment Tiffany and I could hug without chains, without getting in trouble from watchful guards, the day we could talk without rushing to say "I love you" before the call was cut off. I thought about our first video call and all the times I ran with my phone to the beach to show Tiffany the world that was waiting for her. Would I have been so dedicated if I'd known the years it would take, the financial debt, and the nights of worry that lay ahead?

I know for sure I would.

Tiffany gets out, smiling, and walks toward me. I thought maybe we'd be nervous. Or not know what to say. But suddenly, we're walking through the empty park, the fall leaves all around us in bright shades of purple, gold, amber, and cinnamon. Tiffany picks up one of the amber leaves.

"I haven't seen fall leaves in so long. I love this one."

"Me too. I think they're throwing you a welcome home party, Tiff."

We talk and take photos together. I hand her back the tiny gold octopus necklace that she wore in court but couldn't wear back to Pulaski State Prison. She smiles and I help her with the clasp.

"It feels weird to have jewelry on." She tugs gently at the chain.

I hadn't thought of that. She hasn't felt a gold chain around her neck for years, only the chains around her wrists that didn't belong there.

"Tiffany, do you need anything for the next few weeks?"

"I need a book for my master's exams in cosmetology."

"I'll do it! And as soon as you can have one, there will be a computer and phone waiting for you."

"Sister, you don't have to do all that."

"You know I want to. You're family, Tiffany."

She's happy. I can see it. She's truly happy with us all here, and that's what's important. The sky is darkening. More rain is coming and Susan motions that it's time to go. Tiffany loads her suitcase into the van and hugs Fecha and Susan goodbye while her case manager starts the van.

I can feel tears welling up as Tiffany walks toward me.

"I guess, after this program, you'll go to another program. We have to figure out how you'll do that 500 hours of community service while you take classes."

"It's like, I'm grateful. I am. But how long does Georgia get to own a part of me?"

After eleven years, you would think freedom would mean freedom. It's like this journey is never over. Still, the sun is setting around us. The fall leaves smell dewy. A woman is walking her dog. It's a normal day, and no one passing by us would know that Tiffany just came out of a cement box.

"I have dreams," she continues. "I want to open my own salon. I want to be with my son. I want to go to California and start over."

I want to give her a date, a time. I want to tell her that we have a plan. We do. And we don't. The plan is all of those dreams, but for now, we have to play it safe. One false move, one mistake that violates the court order, and Tiffany will go back to that cement box for the rest of her term. Nine more years. I look her in the eyes.

"I know this isn't the dream of you jumping on a flight to San Diego with me. The ocean. The surfers and the sunshine. But we'll get there in a few months, Tiffany. I promise. We have all the time in the world now."

I know we're both thinking of the automated voice that interrupted every one of our calls, telling us we only had one minute remaining.

Tiffany leans in as we hug, and whispers, "Andrea, we have all the minutes remaining now."

Afterword

This isn't just a story about sex trafficking in America. It's about creating a community of survivors and then learning how to take our collective pain and turn it into our power. It's also a love story between two women who believe no girl should disappear. Through Tiffany, I've come to understand my own past abuse in a new way. Through me, Tiffany says she's found hope and a fire to help other survivors as her life purpose.

Together, we created an advocacy film, co-hosted national walks with thousands of allies, led live panels with attorney Susan Coppedge, and spoke to law schools around the country to educate new attorneys on how they can help survivors like Tiffany. We were featured in *Washington Post* articles and did Instagram Live events with actors like Mira Sorvino, Elsa Hosk, and Justin Baldoni. But what Tiffany and I most loved was when other survivors across the country heard her story and began speaking up for themselves, realizing that they weren't criminals, and asking for help to prevent their own incarceration or get free.

More and more, survivors are the ones facing their own injustice head-on, while their attorneys rarely understand their clients as victims, not criminals. It wasn't until 2020 that Susan, an attorney who was truly Tiffany's advocate, took on her case. While nine years is a terribly long time to wait for proper representation, many survivors don't have that long to wait. Some imminently face the death penalty for killing their traffickers. Others are at risk from violence inflicted by other inmates or guards.

What I have learned in these eleven years of advocacy is that kindness and love are more than just good things. They are vital to helping free survivors like Tiffany. With the kindness of so many who believed in Tiffany and even in me, Tiffany would still be in prison, and the ripple effect of her journey to freedom would not reach others—like defense attorneys and judgess—who can ensure that survivors of sex trafficking are treated as victims. That is the power of community, and Tiffany and I are determined to help other survivors with the community of support we have created together.

Where Are They Now?

If there's one thing I hope you take away from this book, it's that believing survivors isn't just the right thing to do. Your belief in a survivor could change their lives. It changed mine. It's an act of stepping outside yourself and seeing a whole person, not a story. This is more than a story about sex trafficking and injustice, it's about kindness in its more fierce form. It's about not listening when others say it's impossible. And, as I've personally learned, it's about this one truth: believing in your own power to do good in the world will result in a better life for you and everyone you touch.

It's been close to a year since Tiffany's release from prison. She's working in a cafe and continuing to study while completing her community service. I hope by the time you're reading this that Tiffany is in California to visit and is finally able to feel the ocean around her, as she's dreamed. One of my favorite parts of the day is texting with Tiffany and no one ever saying we have no more minutes. I'm watching her develop friendships, find love, meet family like her sister Heather for the first time. Our friendship continues to deepen now that there are no walls between us.

Tiffany's dad remains in prison and Tiffany writes to him. I wish she could spend time with him for a day. That day won't come because of prison rules, but at least now they can call and talk. They're on the "You have one minute remaining" plan now. I'm forever grateful that I met him regardless of his past, both dark from his own childhood abuse and the darkness he put in the world. He is, above all, Tiffany's dad. He's how Tiffany found me when he sent her that *USA Today* article in 2012. So much has changed, and yet he still remains in the very place where he first sent her that letter with the article that started it all.

Susan continues to support survivors of all forms of gender-based violence. She's a tireless advocate and one of the women I admire most on Earth. Susan put trafficker after trafficker behind bars, and now she helps survivors avoid the injustice that Tiffany experienced. I'm not saying Susan should run for President of the United States. However, if she were to do so, I'm going to happily help her win! The world simply would be a better place with many more Susans.

Jessica and Jordan are now both incarcerated in Texas prisons. Jordan took a plea deal for eighteen years but likely will serve seven. He'll be in his mid-twenties and still have a chance for a full life outside of prison. A few months later, Jessica also a took a plea deal and, in December 2022, she was sentenced to thirty-six years in prison. She'll be in her late fifties when she's released. Amy, their mom, has moved with their siblings to try to start a new life. This has been an incredibly painful time for her. We're planning to push for the kind of vacatur law that now exists in Georgia thanks to Susan Coppedge, Tiffany, and advocates there. This could be a way to free Jessica and Jordan. It'll take time, but we won't stop advocating.

Alana has been in prison for over a year with twenty-nine years to serve. I rarely find ways to reach her and often worry for her safety. Her children, including her son, live with her aging mom. Alana could be in her seventies before she sees freedom. We hope to prove that she's a victim of trafficking and free her with the same vacatur laws we hope will free Jessica and Jordan in Texas.

The last that I heard from Alyssa, she was living on the East Coast and continues to work in the anti-trafficking movement. I sadly don't know where Asia is, though I hope someday to hear from her. She's struggled deeply after COVID and trying to make ends meet for her and her little girl.

Phoebe lives on the West Coast with her young son and continues to work and study. She and I stay in touch, and I consider Phoebe to be one of the smartest individuals I know. I tell her all the time that she should go to law school to become the next Susan Coppedge. I think someday she might.

Lisa and Anita still live in D.C. with their sisters and extended family. Lisa will always hold a deeply special place in my heart. I'm proud of her for surviving such tremendous pain inflicted on her as a young child. I'm proud of her every time I see her smiling face on social media. She's happy and that's the best form of survival I know.

Fecha lives in Denver and is in graduate school for business. In April 2022, her life partner of four years passed away from a stroke at the age of thirty-five. We've both grieved and continue to feel the pain of his loss. Every day, I'm in awe of her strength and know that our friendship is a place where she can rest when being strong isn't possible.

Ashley is now married and lives with her and her husband's five children in North Carolina, where she's in school. I sometimes recall the first time we met when she was seventeen and inside a juvenile jail in D.C. I know she'll reach her dream of running her own youth program for girls like her who deserve more than spending their adolescence behind bars.

FAIR Girls and the Vida Home are still open despite serious challenges. I'm sometimes in touch with their board of directors and hope that they continue to serve survivors like Lisa, Anita, and Phoebe. The Vida Home is still my first "baby" and I'm committed to their success.

Karana Rising remains small but as active as we can be with a fully pro bono team, including me. We aim to create the full Survivor Justice Initiative but still struggle with funding while Fecha and I work full-time. In September 2023, we stood with a young woman client named Minnesota whose trafficker, like Tiffany's, physically and emotionally abused her and forced her to recruit other young girls. She faces three years in prison and being placed on the sex offender registry. We have a long way to go with ensuring survivors of sex trafficking do not pay for their trafficker's crimes. Our film, *Lack of Love*, has reached 3,500 views on YouTube, but more importantly, it continues to be used in law enforcement trainings and our programs. Tiffany finally watched it for the first time a few months after her release from prison. She says it felt almost unreal to imagine being there now that she's free. We continue to look for the support we need to help keep other survivors from her fate.

On August 8, 2023, the federal trial against the executives of Backpage began just one month after one of the co-defendants and Backpage founder, Jim Larkin, died by suicide. Each of the defendants faced 100 counts that focused on facilitating or promoting prostitution or money laundering. None of the charges were related to running a business that's profit model was based in some way on sex trafficking. On November 16, Michael Lacey and other conspirators were convicted in a federal jury trial in Phoenix, Arizona, of multiple counts of promoting prostitution business enterprises and, additionally, multiple counts of money laundering that included conspiracy offenses. They each face a maximum penalty of twenty years on each money laundering count, but at the time of writing, we await a federal district county judge's determination on sentencing. There are and were many survivors—children and adults—whose lives were forever damaged by the callousness of these men's actions, including those I love.

While I don't care about consenting prostitution and even support those in the sex trade who wish to engage in commercial sex, the truth is that Backpage's owners knew that their business was based in part on profiting off pimps selling victims. I know they knew. I and many advocates and survivors told them over and over again. What strikes me is that it took so very long to free Tiffany from the injustice of her incarceration due to her own trafficking. She was sentenced ten years over the US sentencing guidelines. Meanwhile, Backpage's owners made over $500 million in profits and will never face justice for the sex trafficking they enabled on their website.

The investigation into Pulaski State Prison is ongoing. Since Tiffany left, I've watched Senator Ossoff advocate to ensure the investigation continues. Across the country, alarms about violence inside women's prisons continues to rise. For me, it's more than data or statistics. It's personal. I'm thankful every day for Susan and every single person, most of all Tiffany, who ensured Tiffany is free.

The HOPE Court program and many court programs across the country designed to identify and support system-involved youth who may be at risk of human trafficking continues to thrive. It remains one of my most proud professional achievements to take part in the shaping of this program under the leadership of Judge Mary Rook and with my dear friend, Megan Aniton, who's now left the Office of the Attorney General in Washington, D.C.

I've learned that supporting survivors comes in many ways, and I'm now taking my years helping build survivor-designed programs for human trafficking survivors and applying this knowledge to a new and emerging form of gender-based violence: image-based sexual abuse. In the time since Tiffany's release, I've joined a group of survivors of image-based sexual violence—often called "revenge porn," "deepfakes," or "sextortion." They too deserve justice and rarely get it. Laws and support are lagging behind the crime, just as it has done for survivors of human trafficking. My days are filled with conversations with survivors like Katie, Leah, Matthew, Noelle, Adriane, Megan, Norma, Indi, Breeze, Christina, and so many more. Once again, it's survivors who are creating the changes against the tides of those who exploit them, including online bad actors. I hope to bring my experiences to this new form of exploitation and sexual violence online.

My daughter and I live in a small beach apartment outside of San Diego with our little bunny. I still hope someday for Tiffany to come stay with us for a time, but for now, she's happy in Georgia working, studying, and finally being able to realize her dreams as the chains around her past fade. I used to say that even if all that ever happened was that I helped one person, it would be worth it. Seeing Tiffany free was worth it, and in all honestly, freeing her helped free me too. Tiffany, thank you for trusting me on this uncharted journey with Susan, Fecha, Mira, Ashley, Christabelle, Liz, Noel, and one generous man whom I love who wishes to remain anonymous.

To everyone who signed Tiffany's petition, believed in us, helped Karana Rising with all of the survivors we care about and know, thank you.

How to Help

While financial help is truly needed, there are also other ways to support survivors and their advocates. It starts with community.

Those who helped Tiffany to freedom acted from a place of kindness and a deep sense of wanting to right a terrible wrong. Over time, more and more people believed Tiffany, like I did and still do. We used donated airline miles, worked nights on top of other full-time jobs, and paid out of pocket. Susan, with support of her law firm, Kremlin and Horst LLP, donated hundreds of hours of her time. My family and friends often sent money to ensure I could send Tiffany money, clothes, and things she needed. So, in the end, money isn't everything.

Community is the key to stopping the cycle of exploitation and abuse so many survivors face, even after trafficking. Community can also help stop human trafficking, especially child trafficking, in its tracks by creating safe spaces for children to find support.

Karana Rising: Support survivors' paths to freedom and healing after incarceration. www.karanarising.org

WellSpring: A safe house program in Georgia that I can personally say does amazing work! www.wellspringliving.org

FAIR Girls: The Vida Home serves young women and girls with a holistic housing program that truly is survivor-centered. www.fairgirls.org

Free to Thrive: If you want to give to an organization that's changing how survivors are treated in court and ensuring freedom is possible, this is a great organization. www.freetothrive.org

Human Trafficking Legal Center: This is an incredible nonprofit that helps survivors access civil redress after trafficking. www.htlegalcenter.org

So, what if you want to give of your time and energy? The wonderful news is that we can all help make the world a better place for survivors. I'm going to share some ideas, based on actual experiences with kind and giving people who used their talents, passions, and minds to help survivors.

Here are examples of ways you could give

Students: You have access to an incredible network of young, vibrant people. You can start student awareness groups, or create advocacy efforts in your local community or state to advocate for laws—like the vacatur law that helped free Tiffany. You can host sustainable fashion educational efforts to educate your fellow students on the links between ethical fashion and ending labor trafficking.

Dentists: Contact a nonprofit serving vulnerable youth or trafficking survivors and offer free pro bono aid. Traffickers don't let their victims go to the dentist (surprise), so this is critical.

Doctors and nurses: Human trafficking has a devastating effect on victims, including physical and mental illnesses. If you're a medical professional, learn the signs of human trafficking because many victims do visit a medical professional while they're being trafficked. Here's one my favorite sources: www.safehouseproject.org/healthcare

Teachers: If you're an educator of any kind, familiarize yourself with human trafficking and signs to support a student or young person in crisis. Two excellent resources are: www.unitas.ngo for teachers in the United States and Europe, and 3 Strands Global, founded by my friend, Ashlie Brynat, at www.3strandsglobalfoundation.org

Lawyers: Family lawyers, juvenile court lawyers, criminal and civil law attorneys, and legal professionals, you play a critical role in the life of a survivor if they're your client. You can learn the signs and how to educate your staff and provide the best legal support by going to these resources, which includes learning about US-based vacatur and affirmative defense claims and policy.

Human Trafficking Legal Center: www.htlegalcenter.org

Free to Thrive: www.3strandsglobalfoundation.org

The Freedom Network: www.freedomnetworkusa.org/training

If you're a judge or prosecutor:

Woman Judges: www.nawj.org/catalog/community-outreach-programs/human-trafficking

The Office of Victims of Crime has an incredible wealth of resources: www.ovc.ojp.gov/program/human-trafficking/training-and-technical-assistance and www.htcbc.ovc.ojp.gov

Law enforcement: There are a number of trainings where you can learn more about the different aspects of human trafficking. To learn more, visit: www.dhs.gov/blue-campaign/blue-campaign-training

Yoga teachers and educators: Go to Exale to learn how to better support and provide trauma-informed yoga for survivors: www.exhaleproject.org/about-us

Therapists and social workers: Go to the Sanar Institute to engage, learn, and join a community of professional care providers: www.sanar-institute.org/our-services/wellness-center

People with lots of airline miles or hotel points: You can call the National Human Trafficking Hotline to learn about the local nonprofit in your area who may need airline points or hotel points for survivors. 1-888-3737-888, or donate to Karana Rising and we'll provide airline and hotel points to survivors who are in need!

About the Author

After growing up in a small Texas town, Andrea left Texas to travel to Germany on a foreign exchange program where she met a young woman who was a domestic labor trafficking victim enslaved by her husband. Andrea searched for her friend after she disappeared. In 2001, after graduating with a Master's in European Union Law and Economics, Andrea moved to Boston where she founded FAIR Girls to support young women and girls who have survived human trafficking. During the next fourteen years, and after relocating to Washington, D.C., Andrea led FAIR Girls in creating the Vida Home, a safe home for young women survivors of human trafficking. She worked with survivors and advocates to create outreach programs and to advocate for justice for survivors. In 2019, Andrea founded Karana Rising to advocate for systemic change to ensure survivors of sex trafficking are not wrongfully arrested and incarcerated as a result of their own trafficking. In 2022, Andrea became the Director of The Reclaim Coalition, a global survivor-centered movement to end image-based sexual violence and gender-based violence online. Andrea is a poet, author, multimedia artist, and mom to one human girl and one rabbit girl. You can find Andrea writing in cafes and on the beaches in Encinitas, California. Andrea believes in a life where doing good in the world is about placing kindness at the center of everything we do.

About the Publisher

Founded in 2021 by Bryna Haynes, WorldChangers Media is a boutique publishing company focused on "Ideas for Impact." We know that great books change lives, topple outdated paradigms, and build movements. Our commitment is to deliver superior-quality transformational nonfiction by, and for, the next generation of thought leaders.

Ready to write and publish your thought leadership book with us? Learn more at www.WorldChangers.Media